Religion and Law in Estonia

Religion and Law in Estonia

Third Edition

Merilin Kiviorg

This book was originally published as a monograph in the International Encyclopaedia of Laws/Religion Law

Founding Editor: Roger Blanpain
General Editor: Frank Hendrickx
Volume Editor: Wouter Druwé

Wolters Kluwer

Published by:
Kluwer Law International B.V.
PO Box 316
2400 AH Alphen aan den Rijn
The Netherlands
E-mail: international-sales@wolterskluwer.com
Website: lrus.wolterskluwer.com

Sold and distributed by:
Wolters Kluwer Legal & Regulatory U.S.
7201 McKinney Circle
Frederick, MD 21704
United States of America
E-mail: customer.service@wolterskluwer.com

ISBN 978-94-035-4122-8

e-Book: ISBN 978-94-035-4123-5
web-PDF: ISBN 978-94-035-4124-2

The Author

Merilin Kiviorg (DPhil, University of Oxford, mag iur University of Tartu) is Associate Professor in international law at the University of Tartu School of Law, Estonia and an author of many articles published on law and religion, and on European human rights law and practice regarding freedom of religion or belief. She has also written extensively on various themes of law and religion in Estonia. She has been affiliated with various academic institutions. She has taught Public International Law at Balliol College (University of Oxford) as well as being a Max Weber Fellow at the European University Institute, Florence, Italy. She has been a visiting scholar at the University of Helsinki and Oxford and a lecturer in International Law and EU Law at the University of Tartu, Estonia, teaching various courses on international law, human rights and law and religion.

Her research interests are in the field of theory and practice of human rights, comparative human rights and international law. A specific focus of her research is the interplay between human rights law and religion. Specific topics of her research have included: the concept and scope of religious autonomy (individual and collective), the role of the European Court of Human Rights in protecting this autonomy (*de lege lata* and *de lege ferenda*) and topics such as human rights and security, and impact of international human rights treaties at the domestic level. She is a principal investigator in the 2020–2024 project 'Russia and Consolidation of Regional International Law in Eurasia'.

She has advised non-governmental and governmental bodies (the Estonian Ministry of Internal Affairs, the Legal Chancellor, and the Estonian President). Since 2016 she has been a member of the Panel of Experts on Freedom of Religion or Belief of the OSCE/ODIHR and since 2019 a member of the Chancellor of Justice's Human Rights Advisory Board in Estonia. In 2018 she was the president of the European Consortium for Church and State Research. In 2002 she was involved in drafting the current Religious Communities Act (Churches and Congregations Act) in the Estonian Ministry of Internal Affairs. She was also a member of an expert group advising the Law Commission of the Estonian Parliament on the validity of international treaties concluded between the Estonian Republic and the Soviet

Union. As a fellow at the Estonian Law Centre (NGO), she was responsible for leading a constitutional law project aimed at the improvement of the quality of research and the application of constitutional law by the Estonian legal community.

She is a member of major academic organizations and networks in the field of law and religion (e.g., European Consortium for Church and State Research, International Consortium for Law and Religion Studies).

Table of Contents

Table of Contents

List of Abbreviations

CCA	Churches and Congregations Act
EAOC	Estonian Apostolic Orthodox Church
ECHR	European Convention on Human Rights and Fundamental Freedoms
ECtHR	European Court of Human Rights
EEA	European Economic Area
EELC	Estonian Evangelical Lutheran Church
EKD	Estonian Christian Democrats Party
ESSR	Estonian Soviet Socialist Republic
ICCPR	International Covenant on Civil and Political Rights
ICESCR	International Covenant on Economic, Social and Cultural Rights
NPOA	Non-profit Organizations Act
NRM	New Religious Movement
OECD	Organization for Economic Cooperation and Development
OSCE	Organization for Security and Co-operation in Europe
RT	Riigi Teataja (State Gazette)
UNDHR	United Nations Universal Declaration of Human Rights
USSR	Union of Soviet Socialist Republics

List of Abbreviations

General Introduction

1. When the Estonian Constitutional Assembly held heated discussions over each provision and meaning of the draft Constitution of the Republic of Estonia at the beginning of 1990, there was no real discussion about the provisions relating to freedom of religion or belief and State and Church relationships. In the process of re-building the Estonian Republic immediately after the collapse of the Soviet Union, there were more urgent issues to be dealt with. The Estonian Constitution was adopted by the referendum of 28 June 1992.[1] Although many aspects of the relationship between State and religious communities are still under discussion, the relationship between religious communities and the State is generally amicable and cooperative.

2. Estonia does not consider itself a country of immigration. Currently, religion seems to play a minor role in questions relating to integration, immigration or asylum. Estonia is not yet facing any of the challenges related to the growing Muslim communities experienced in other European countries. Religion does not play a major role in public debates or in politics. However, this does not mean that there is currently no national debate relating to law and religion. There is an ongoing debate on the preferential treatment of traditional religious communities and on the possible influx of culturally and religiously diverse communities to Estonia, where immigration rules to be relaxed. Recently, the draft law on co-habitation has caused reaction from religious communities as being far too liberal. For years, one of the hotly disputed issues was religious education in public schools. There has been some sort of compromise achieved on this topic. However, the debate has been recently revived again mostly by religious communities. Additionally, not long ago wording of the draft provisions on hate crimes made religious associations concerned about the future of religious expression. These present and previous debates seem to be related to wider questions about identity or the re-building of Estonian identity after the collapse of the Soviet Union, and more recently in the context of membership in the European Union (EU).

§1. General Background of the Country

3. The independent Republic of Estonia was born in the aftermath of World War I (1914–1918), when it broke away from the Russian empire. The Proclamation of

1. Estonian Constitution, RT 1992, 26, 349. The Constitution entered into force on 3 Jul. 1992.

Independence was followed by the War of Independence in 1918–1920. The date of Estonian independence is 24 February 1918.

4. The first Estonian Constitution (ratified in June 1920)[2] was influenced by the liberal thinking prevalent in Europe after World War I. The 1920 Constitution emphasized the principle of a state based on the rule of law. One of its essential components was the acknowledgement of the fundamental rights of the person. As a result, it was one of the most democratic constitutions in Europe at that time. The 1930s saw significant political changes in Estonia, characterized by the centralization of the state administration, the concentration of power, a decline of democracy and the expansion of state control. The second Estonian Constitution (1938)[3] introduced a number of amendments on fundamental rights. It laid down a new philosophy, according to which the legal rights and duties of an individual emanated from his or her status as a member of a commonwealth. This reflected the more collectivist (communitarian) orientation of the era.

5. The outbreak of World War II disturbed the peaceful development of the country, which was subsequently occupied by the Soviet Union (1940–1941, 1944–1991) and Nazi Germany (1941–1944). A resurgence of Estonian national identity began in the late 1980s, leading to break up of the Soviet Union and Estonian independence in 1991.

6. The current population of Estonia is approximately 1.3 million, with about 69% Estonians, 26% Russians, 2% Ukrainians, 0.9% Byelorussians, 0.6% Finns and 1.5% of other nationalities.[4] Estonia is situated on ca. 17,462 sq. mi (45,339 sq. km).

7. Estonia is a politically unitary state. The Estonian system of government is a parliamentary democracy. There is a strong division of the executive, legislative and judicial powers based on checks and balances. The predominant bodies provided for in the Constitution are the Parliament, called *Riigikogu*, the President of the Republic, the administration, the Chancellor of Justice and the courts. The division of the territory into administrative units is established by law – there are currently fifteen units (*maakond*) administered by the State. There are also seventy-nine municipalities.[5] All local issues are resolved and regulated by local governments, which operate independently and in accordance with national law. Obligations may be imposed

2. Estonian Constitution, RT 1920, 113/114, 243. The Constitution entered into force on 21 Dec. 1920. In 1933 the Constitution was substantially changed to the extent that it started to be called 1933 Constitution. Legally speaking, the 1920 Constitution was just amended, and the amendments entered into force on 24 Jan. 1934. R. Narits et al., 'Sissejuhatus' in Ü Madise jt (toim), *Eesti Vabariigi põhiseadus. Kommenteeritud väljaanne* (Tallinn: Juura, 2017); M Luts-Sootak H Siimets-Gross, Eesti õiguse 100 aastat (Post Factum, 2019) 19.
3. Estonian Constitution, RT 1937, 71, 590. The Constitution entered into force on 1 Jan. 1938.
4. According to the Estonian Statistics Office the Estonian population on 1 Jan. 2021 was 1,329,460 inhabitants. Estonian Statistics Office, www.stat.ee, 08 Apr. 2021.
5. Eesti Vabariik, Üldandmed, https://www.eesti.ee/et/eesti-vabariik/eesti-vabariik/ueldandmed/, 8 Feb. 2021.

upon local governments only in accordance with the national law or with the agreement of the local government. All permanent residents, regardless of citizenship, are eligible to vote in local elections. The Constitution makes a specific provision for ethnic minorities, granting a large degree of autonomy and cultural self-government.[6]

8. The Constitution of Estonia that came into force in 1992 is, in a number of ways, a compilation of aspects of Estonia's previous constitutions. It has continued the democratic spirit of the 1920 Constitution, with some added mechanisms to maintain the balance of power of the state. In drafting the document, great attention was paid to fundamental rights. International treaties, the European Convention on Human Rights (ECHR) and constitutions of other democratic states were taken as models. The Constitution of the Federal Republic of Germany has had the greatest influence on the Estonian Constitution. The Republic of Estonia shapes and develops its statehood on the basis of the principles of social justice, democracy and the rule of law. Fundamental rights and freedoms form an inherent and central part of the Estonian national legal order.

9. At the beginning of the 1990s, the Estonian state clearly expressed its desire to join the EU. On 14 September 2003, 66.83% of voters decided in favour of joining the EU.[7] Estonia joined the EU on 1 May 2004.[8] Estonia is also a member of many international organizations, including the United Nations, Council of Europe, Organization for Security and Co-operation in Europe (OSCE), North Atlantic Treaty Organization (NATO) and Organization for Economic Co-operation and Development (OECD), and has ratified key conventions protecting freedom of religion or belief. A half-century of communism did not diminish the desire for religious freedom and Estonia's core constitutional and legislative provisions provide the basic level of protection for freedom of religion. The Estonian Constitution expressly protects freedom of religion for individuals and religious communities. There is no State Church, but cooperation between state and religious communities has been accepted within the limits of law.

10. Estonia does not consider itself a country of immigration. There are two main reasons for this. First, since the end of the Soviet occupation (1991), Estonia has not been a country of extensive immigration. On the contrary, it has experienced a quite troubling net outward-migration. This means the loss of an educated and skilled labour force and a decrease in its native population. Second, due to the extensive in-migration administered by the Government of the Soviet Union after World War II, Estonia is left with a considerably large Russian-speaking minority. Of the total population, approximately 26% is from an immigrant background. However, the exact numbers are debatable and depend on what is taken as the basis

6. *See also* Part II below.
7. There were 867,714 eligible voters in Estonia, of which 555,835 citizens or 64.06% (approximately one-third of the total population) took part in the referendum. Estonian Ministry of Foreign Affairs, 'EU Referendum', www.vvk.ee/varasemad/rh03/tulemus/enght.html, 25 Apr. 2010.
8. Treaty of Accession, RT II 2004, 3, 8.

for determining immigrant background. Nevertheless, this large minority has had and does have an effect on demographics and politics in Estonia. Three characteristics of this minority need to be mentioned: a higher fertility rate compared to the native population; a higher rate of marriages; and very few mixed marriages with ethnic Estonians. Population growth since 1945 is entirely attributable to immigration, with a profound influence on the age and ethnic structure of the population. The children of immigrants are highly segregated. It also needs to be noted that there is an uneven regional distribution of the immigrant population, with up to 90% concentrated in urban areas. In some North-Eastern towns of Estonia, the proportion of the Russian-speaking population is almost 80%. These factors make the integration of this minority into Estonian society more complicated.[9] However, as Rannut has pointed out, the main dividing factor has not been ethnicity as such, but rather the mother tongue, representing the main source of information and opinion and value creation (both communally and through the media). Language has been the main barrier to various societal goods and values, societal mobility and economic well-being.[10]

11. Currently, immigration to Estonia is discouraged, although all forms of immigration are possible; such as family reunification, immigration for work and study purposes, asylum and protection from inhuman treatment. According to research carried out by the Estonian Migration Foundation, the prevailing political view seems to be that as Estonia already has a significant number of immigrants (as a result of the administered migration during the Soviet occupation), it needs to deal with the integration problems of this group before liberalizing its immigration rules.

12. Thus, Estonia steers, although somewhat reluctantly, towards integration of the existing community into Estonian society. The reluctance is evident in rather strict language policies and requirements set up for acquiring citizenship. There is very slow access to citizenship for people of an immigrant background. This policy seems to be directly related to preservation of the Estonian language and to controversial concerns about loyalty of the immigrant population to the State.

13. There have been debates about liberalizing immigration rules and reducing exam requirements for citizenship, because of the ageing population and a shortage of skilled labour.[11] As noted above, there is a rather troubling net outward-migration. As to the existing migrant community, events in Ukraine may have given a push to take more effective steps to integrate the community into Estonian society. Thus, not so much the concern about the rights of the immigrant population but the fear of Russia has accelerated the process.

---

9. M. Kiviorg & L. Roots, 'Immigration, Asylum and Religion Estonia', in *Immigration, Asylum and Religion in Europe*, ed. A. Motilla (Leuven: Peeters, 2012).
10. M. Rannut, 'Estonian Language Strategy in Progress', Paper given at the World Congress on Language Policies (Barcelona, 2002), www.linguapax.org/congres/taller/taller3/article22_ang. html, 8 Jan. 2010.
11. M. Kiviorg & L. Roots, 'Immigration, Asylum and Religion Estonia', in *Immigration, Asylum and Religion in Europe*, ed. A. Motilla (Leuven: Peeters, 2012).

§2. Social Facts about Religion

14. The Lutheran Church has historically been the largest religious institution in Estonia since the sixteenth century. During the first independence period 1918–1940 (before the Soviet occupation), Estonia was more or less religiously homogenous. Most of the population (ca 78%) belonged to the Estonian Evangelical Lutheran Church (EELC).[12] The second-largest Church was the Estonian Apostolic Orthodox Church (EAOC). According to the 1934 census, approximately 19% belonged to the latter church.[13] When Estonia was occupied by the Soviet Union (1940–1941 and 1944–1991), the religious life of the country was oppressed and religious freedom was almost non-existent. After regaining independence at the beginning of the 1990s Estonia experienced what can be called a 'return to religion'; which was quite common in all Eastern European post-communist societies. This was partly an expression of national identity and partly a reaction to the suppression of individual freedom by the Soviet regime. However, the religious enthusiasm caused by independence ended quickly and the rapid growth of religious organization membership stopped. Estonia can be considered as quite a secularized country today.

15. Most Estonians do not belong formally to any religious organization. It has been often argued that this is due to Soviet occupation and atheistic education. This is only partially true. It might be interesting to mention that the Evangelical Lutheran Church experienced confrontation between German and national clergy in the 1920s and 1930s, when Estonia was an independent state for the first time in its history. The membership numbers presented above may appear to suggest that the Lutheran Church could have been regarded as the national Church of Estonia. However, it would be more accurate to say that the Lutheran Church of Estonia may have been on the verge of becoming a truly national Church when World War II and Soviet occupation following the war put a definite stop to that development.[14] Professor Saard has pointed out that until the early twentieth century Lutheranism had a colonial nature in Estonia: 'the mentality showed its first signs of retreating only in the 1920s'.[15] The church was controlled by German gentry up to the twentieth century and played little role in the nation-building process of the nineteenth century. Moreover, the analysis provided by the Statistical Office of Estonia reveals that although the census carried out in 1934 showed high numbers of Lutheran believers, the numbers refer to both active and passive members of the church. The data indicates that the number of those who actually paid their membership fees was considerably lower. According to the Statistical Office this was a definite sign of the

12. According to the national census 1934, there were 874,026 Evangelical Lutherans in Estonia of a total population of 1,126,413. Estonian Institute, www.einst.ee/society/Soreligion.htm, 2 Feb. 2000; *See also* Statistical Office of Estonia, '2000 Population and Housing Census: Education. Religion' (Tallinn: Statistical Office, 2002), 17.

13. Riigi Statistika Keskbüroo, 'Rahvastiku Koostis Ja Korteriolud: 1 III 1934 Rahvaloenduse Andmed' (Tallinn: Riigi trükikoda, 1935), Vihik II.

14. *See*, e.g., M. Ketola, 'Some Aspects of the Nationality Question in the Lutheran Church of Estonia, 1918–39', *Religion, State and Society* 27, no. 2 (1999): 239.

15. R. Saard, 'The Church at Decisive Periods of National Identity in the 19th and 20th Centuries', *Estonian Culture* IX (2007). Historical context is described in §3 Historical Background below.

secularization of Estonian (urban) society already at that time.[16] Today, low religiosity in Estonia has also been attributed to the relative success in its economic transition among post-communist societies. For example, Norris and Inglehart have come to this conclusion by comparing Estonia and the Czech Republic with Albania and Romania.[17] Additionally, Kilp points out that religious traditions and national identity have been weakly connected both for Czechs and for Estonians compared to Lithuanians and Poles.[18] Estonian identity has been more strongly connected to language than to religion.

16. According to the last population census from 2011, 54% of the adult population (those aged 15 and above, or 1,094,564 from a total population of 1,294,455) declared that they do not adhere to any particular creed. Only 29% considered themselves to adhere to any creed. This percentage has not changed since the last census (2000). Of this figure, about 10% (13.6% in 2000) declared themselves to be Lutheran, the majority of whom are ethnic Estonians. The largest religious tradition in Estonia currently is the Orthodox Church, with 16% of the population considering themselves as Orthodox (12.8% in 2000).[19] Since the census in 2000 the Orthodox community has grown in numbers and has become bigger than the historically dominant Lutheran Church. According to information provided by the Ministry of Internal Affairs, the EELC has 180,000 members and Orthodox churches (Estonian Apostolic Orthodox Church and Estonian Orthodox Church of Moscow Patriarchate) have approximately 197,000 members.[20]

17. The Department of Religious Affairs within the Estonian Ministry of Internal Affairs collects statistical data about religious communities and their membership. It has to be emphasized that religious organizations are not obligated to provide the Ministry of Internal Affairs with statistical information of their membership. Religious organizations have voluntarily informed state officials about the number of their adherents. Although the figures presented leave considerable room for various interpretations, they hopefully reflect to some extent the objective reality of religious life in Estonia.

18. The Statistical Office has pointed out that according to the data, Estonians are generally less religious than non-Estonians. It has been confirmed by various surveys that, compared to Russians, Estonians are less religious.[21] This has been

---

16. Statistical Office of Estonia, '2000 Population and Housing Census: Education. Religion' (Tallinn: Statistical Office, 2002), 40.
17. R. Inglehart & P. Norris, *Rising Tide: Gender Equality and Cultural Change around the World* (Cambridge: Cambridge University Press, 2003), 127. *See also* Part V below.
18. A. Kilp, 'Secularisation of Society after Communism: Ten Catholic-Protestant Societies', in *Religion and Politics in Multicultural Europe*, ed. A. Saumets & A. Kilp (Tartu: Tartu University Press, 2009), 226.
19. Population and Housing Census 2011, http://www.stat.ee/phc2011, 1 Aug. 2013.
20. Information about current membership of religious organizations is based on data from the Ministry of Internal Affairs. The data in the Ministry of Internal Affairs is updated to January 2013, https://www.siseministeerium.ee/36748/, 1 May 2014.
21. *See*, e.g., R. Liiman, *Usklikkus muutuvas Eesti Ühiskonnas* [Religiosity in Changing Estonian Society] (Tartu: Tartu Ülikooli Kirjastus, 2001).

explained by the fact that for Russians and other non-Estonians religion is a uniting factor which strengthens their identity. 'The bond between religion and national identity becomes especially important for people who live outside their historical homeland.'[22]

19. The Orthodox community in Estonia is divided between the EAOC and the Estonian Orthodox Church of Moscow Patriarchate. Most orthodox believers belong to the latter church. It also needs to be mentioned that most members of this church are Russian speaking, which indicates that the majority has an immigrant background. The relations between the two Orthodox Churches, one under the canonical jurisdiction of the Ecumenical Patriarchate and the other under the canonical jurisdiction of the Moscow Patriarchate are somewhat complicated due to historical, legal/canonical and ethnic reasons. The only major conflict relating to law and religion in Estonia since 1990 was the conflict between these two Orthodox Churches over legal continuity and property as both of them claimed to be descendants *in jure* of the Estonian Orthodox Church, subordinated to the Ecumenical Patriarchate, and existing in Estonia before the Soviet occupation (1940). The Estonian Orthodox Church was canonically subordinated to the Moscow Patriarchate until 1920 when it was granted autonomy. In 1923, it came under the canonical jurisdiction of the Ecumenical Patriarchate. The courts recognized that the EAOC continued its activities in exile because of the Soviet occupation. The Estonian Orthodox Church of Moscow Patriarchate, however, was established with the help of Soviet occupation in 1945, eliminating the EAOC Synod in Estonia. The elimination was in conflict with the by-laws of the church.[23] The property conflict was triggered by the land and property reform which started at the beginning of the 1990s allowing restitution and compensation of illegally expropriated property to legal entities (including churches) who owned the property before 1940.

20. A spin-off of the property conflict was a somewhat political decision of the government not to register the Estonian Orthodox Church of Moscow Patriarchate. The official reason was that the name of the Church proposed was too similar to the EAOC which was already registered. In the 1990s, there were heated debates concerning registration of the 'Russian' Orthodox Church. There were controversial accusations about this church being a 'fifth column' with the potential to undermine Estonian territorial integrity. Both the registration and property conflict were eventually solved. It needs to be mentioned that these past conflicts do not seem to have had a detrimental effect on the religious life of Orthodox believers today.

22. Statistical Office of Estonia, '2000 Population and Housing Census: Education. Religion' (Tallinn: Statistical Office, 2002), 31.
23. M. Kiviorg, 'Eesti Apostlik Õigeusu Kirik ja objektiivne kirikuõigus' (*Estonian Apostolic Orthodox Church and Objective Ecclesiastical Law*), *Juridica* 10 (1997): 518–523.

21. All other Christian and non-Christian religious communities have adherents of approximately 3% of the adult population (aged 15 and above).[24] The largest religious communities among those are Roman Catholics, Old Believers,[25] the Baptists, Pentecostals and Jehovah's Witnesses.

22. Muslims have lived on Estonian territory since approximately the eighteenth century. The majority of Muslims are ethnic Tatars who arrived in Estonia during the late nineteenth and early twentieth century. During the first independence period (1918–1940), there were two registered Muslim communities in Estonia. The Tatar community established two mosques and also graveyards and followed their particular Islamic cultural and religious life.[26] In 1940, the Soviet regime prohibited the activities of the communities. During the occupation the Muslim community carried on its activities unofficially. The ethnic composition of the Muslim community changed during the Soviet period due to new arrivals from other republics of the former Soviet Union, such as Azerbaijan, Uzbekistan, Kazakhstan and other traditionally Muslim nations of the Caucasus and Central Asia. However, Tatars maintained their leading role in cultural and religious activity.[27]

23. In the late 1980s with a more liberal political atmosphere and the independence movement in Estonia, ethnic minorities started to organize (re-establish) cultural societies. In 1989, the Tatar cultural society re-established the Estonian Islamic Congregation. The community was registered in 1994. Currently there are two registered Muslim religious associations. The Estonian Islam Congregation has approximately 1,400 members and has quite a unique nature. In the same congregation there are both Sunnites and Shiites. In 1995, thirteen believers left the congregation and formed the Estonian Muslim Sunni Congregation. All thirteen left the Estonian Islam Congregation, not for religious reasons, but rather because of personal misunderstandings.[28] The majority of the Estonian Muslim community is still made up of individuals who came from the territory of the former Soviet Union: Tatars, Chechens, Azers, etc. They have integrated well into Estonian society and there is no reason to associate them with radical Islam. Linnas has pointed out that Islam in Estonia is liberal and lost many of its specific features. She also notes that

---

24. Population and Housing Census 2011, http://www.stat.ee/phc2011, 1 Aug. 2013.
25. The Old Believers are Russians who fled to Estonia because of religious persecution. 'In 1652, Patriarch Nikon of the Russian Orthodox Church introduced a number of reforms aimed at centralising his power and bringing the rituals and doctrines of Russian Orthodoxy in line with those of the Greek Orthodox Church. Old Believers rejected Nikon's reforms. Consequently, the Old Believers were cruelly persecuted, exiled, tortured and executed all over Russia. Their churches, icons and homes were burnt. As a result they took refuge abroad.' Estonia. Official Gateway to Estonia, http://estonia.eu/about-estonia/society/russian-old-believers-in-estonia.html, 2 Feb. 2010.
26. R. Ringvee, 'Islam in Estonia', in *Islam v. Európe* (Bratislava: Centrom pre európsku politiku, 2005), 242–243.
27. *Ibid.*
28. *Islam Eestis*, www.islam.pri.ee/ieestis.php, 26 Apr. 2010; I. Au & R. Ringvee, *Usulised ühendused Eestis* [Religious Associations in Estonia], (Tallinn: Allika, 2007).

Estonian society is tolerant of Muslims which she attributes to the traditionally indifferent attitude of Estonians to religious matters in general.[29]

24. The two mosques (architecturally it meant one regular house and one apartment turned into a prayer hall) established during the first independence period were destroyed in 1944. The building of a new mosque, after the collapse of Soviet Union, has encountered financial difficulties and relatively mild political opposition from some political parties (this will be elaborated in Part V of this monograph). However, since 2009 there has been a prayer hall in the Islamic Cultural Centre 'Turath', which serves as a mosque for the Islamic community in Tallinn. Across Estonia there are also several other converted premises for serving the religious needs of Muslims.

25. According to public information provided by the Estonian Internal Security Service (KAPO), the number of Muslim immigrants arriving from the so-called risky countries (from the standpoint of counter-terrorism: North Africa, the Middle East and Islamic Asian countries) is on the increase. In the past three years, the number of people arriving from these countries has increased to 112%.[30] Applications for visas from the aforementioned states have increased approximately 187%. Interest by such persons in coming to Estonia has increased due to Estonia's joining the Schengen zone at the end of 2007. There have been more cases of persons applying for an Estonian visa with the aim of entering the Schengen area and continuing from here to some other EU Member State. However, according to the Estonian Internal Security Service there has been an increase also among numbers staying in Estonia. The increase in the Muslim community is also attributable to new migration mostly for purposes of studying or doing business in Estonia. 'Formerly a transit country, Estonia has seen a significant change in migration patterns in recent years.'[31] Migration to Estonia has been affected by the global changes since 2014, involving countries in North Africa, the Middle East and Central Asia. Some foreign Islamic groups have also expressed interest in contacts with the local community (e.g. Jamaat Tabligh and Al-Waqf Al-Islami). According to the Estonian Internal Security Service the increase in the Muslim population has contributed to the interest of radical or conservative Islamic organizations in Estonia. In its 2019/2020 report the Service has added that the increase in the population may contribute to the segregation and closeness of the community that would inhibit integration and contribute to radicalization.[32] No unlawful activities or preaching radical Islam have been identified. Al-Waqf Al-Islami has helped to finance the Estonian Islamic community.[33] The Estonian Internal Security Service similar to previous years has identified nearly fifty individuals linked to Islamic extremism or terrorist organizations

29. R. Linnas, 'Islam Eestis' (Islam in Estonia), in *Mitut usku Eesti*, ed. L. Altnurme (Tartu: Tartu Ülikooli Kirjastus, 2004), 65.
30. KAPO Aastaraamat 2019-2020 (Annual Review of the Estonian Internal Security Service), https://www.kapo.ee/en/content/annual-reviews.html, 8 Feb. 2021, 43.
31. *Ibid.*
32. *Ibid.*
33. Estonian Internal Security Service, Ministry of Internal Affairs, www.kapo.ee/eng/areas-of-activity/terrorism/situation-in-estonia, 1 May 2014.

who either arrived in or transited Estonia. 'Representatives of organisations promoting Islamic fundamentalism regularly visit Estonia, but their activities here have not achieved the desired effect. These are not internationally wanted criminals.'[34] However, there have been incidents of local individuals joining or wanting to join as fighters in conflict zones such as Syria. In comparison with some other European states the number of wannabe ISIS fighters has been small.[35]

26. Before Estonia joined the EU in 2004, there were discussions on the possible influx of migrants from traditionally Muslim countries, or Muslims from other EU countries[36] (these debates will be reflected in Part V of this monograph). So far, despite the increase, there are still only a limited number of new arrivals, especially of those who actually stay in Estonia. They are from different regions globally and do not form any significant ethnic religious communities. There is an interesting, relatively recent trend among ethnic Estonians and Russians to convert to Islam. According to Chief Mufti Ildar Muhhamedshin in 2012 each month there were approximately two to three persons who would convert to Islam.[37] According to some unofficial and unproven estimates there are approximately 10,000 Muslims all together in Estonia. According the last census (2011) there are 1,508 Muslims (those aged 15 and above) in Estonia.[38] The number of people who go to regular prayers is, however, significantly smaller.[39]

27. The Estonian indigenous religious tradition is represented by the House of Taara and Native Religions. There is not much known about the pre-Christian beliefs of Estonians. Reconstruction of such beliefs has been largely based on oral tradition, the collection of which began in the second half of the nineteenth century by the Lutheran priest Jakob Hurt. An attempt at restoring this faith was made during the 1920s and 1930s under the name 'Taara-belief'. The main goal of Taara believers was to raise national self-awareness.[40] The name 'Taara' comes from the Heinrici Chronicon Livoniae (The Chronicle of Henry of Livonia), which described the Roman Catholic crusade against Estonians in the thirteenth century. The

---

34. KAPO Aastaraamat 2019-2020 (Annual Review of the Estonian Internal Security Service), https://www.kapo.ee/en/content/annual-reviews.html, 8 Feb. 2021, 42.
35. *Ibid.*, 41.
36. R. Khair Al-Din, 'Eesti Euroopa Liiduga ühinemise protsess: Moslemi vähemuse õiguste kaitse islami õiguse seisukohast', Akadeemia 12 (2000): 2616–2628.
37. 'Eestlannadele õpetati hidžaabi sidumist' (Estonian Women were Taught How to Wrap Hijab), Eesti Ekspress, 15 Nov. 2012, www.ekspress.ee/archive/article.php?id=65265616, 20 Sep. 2014.
38. Population and Housing Census 2011, https://www.stat.ee/en/statistics-estonia/population-census-2021/2011-population-and-housing-census, 27 Jan. 2021.
39. R. Ringvee, 'Estonia', in *Yearbook of Muslims in Europe Vol. 5*, ed. J.S. Nielsen et al. (Leiden: Koninklijke Brill NV, 2013), 229.
40. Encyclopaedia Estonica, 'Religion', www.estonica.org/eng/lugu.html?kateg=41&menyy_id=101&alam=56&leht=9, 1 Apr. 2010; Embassy of Estonia in Tel Aviv, 'Jews in Estonia', https://telaviv.mfa.ee/jews-in-estonia/, 27 Jan. 2021; S. Tambur, 'Remembering the once vibrant Jewish community of Estonia', Estonian World, 27 Jan. 2021, https://estonianworld.com/life/remembering-the-once-vibrant-jewish-community-of-estonia/, 27 Jan. 2021.

Chronicle of Henry mentions 'Tarapita' – whom, according to Henry, the inhabitants of Saaremaa (the largest island in Estonia) invoked in battles.[41] This has been interpreted to mean 'O Taara, help!' and it has been conjectured that one (or even the main god) of ancient Estonians was called Taara. There have been attempts to connect Taara both with the Scandinavian thunder-god Thor as well as with Northern Siberian Finno-Ugric Khantys' and Mans' Torum.[42] One way or the other some practices of indigenous religious tradition are popular and important for many in Estonia.

28. Jewish religion has been represented in Estonia for centuries. However, a more permanent congregation emerged in the nineteenth century. The first Jewish settlers were the Cantonists, who also opened the first synagogue. By 1883, the Jewish community (700 families strong) commenced the construction of a synagogue building in the centre of Tallinn. During the Nazi occupation in World War II many Jews lost their lives. In fact, Estonia was declared 'Judenfrei' by the Nazis. The old synagogue was destroyed in the bombardment of Tallinn. After the war, some native Jews returned to Tallinn, joined by many Russian Jews. Attempts were made to organize prayers, but the Soviet regime outlawed any open observance of Judaism. Today there are several Jewish organizations in Estonia and a new synagogue was opened in 2007. There is also a Jewish secondary school (gymnasium) in Tallinn. In January 2019 the European Commission published a Special Eurobarometer report that dealt with antisemitism in the European Union up to December 2018.[43] According to the research 86% of Estonian citizens did not think that antisemitism is a problem in Estonia, and 60% believed that it has not been a problem for at least five years. People who believed that antisemitism is a problem divided the evidence of the problem into nine categories: denial of holocaust (9%), antisemitism in internet (12%), antisemitic graffiti or vandalism (8%), public threats or public animosity (7%), vandalism of cemeteries (9%), physical attacks (5%), antisemitism in schools, universities (7%), politics (6%) and media (7%).[44]

29. The registered religious communities do not give a full picture of religious life in Estonia, because some of the groups have not deemed it necessary to register in order to obtain a legal personality (registration of religious communities is not required by law), and some of the religious communities have chosen to register as ordinary non-profit organizations rather than religious associations.[45] The associations that have chosen to register as ordinary non-profit associations are, for

41. Henriku Liivimaa kroonika (Heinrici Chronicon Livoniae), ed. E. Tarvel (Tallinn: Eesti Raamat, 1982), 216.
42. Encyclopaedia Estonica, 'Religion', http://www.estonica.org/en/Culture/Religion/Pre-Christian_native_religion_and_attempts_of_restoration/, 27 Jan. 2021.
43. Special Eurobarometer 484 Report: Perceptions of Antisemitism (European Union, 2019).
44. *Ibid.*
45. M. Kiviorg, 'Religious Entities as Legal Persons', in *Churches and Other Religious Organisations as Legal Persons*, ed. L. Friedner (Leuven: Peeters, 2007), 79–100.

example, the Friends of the Western Buddhist Order in Estonia, the Family Federation for World Peace and Unification and the Collegiate Association for the Research of the Principle.[46]

30. Besides the official statistics there have been several surveys conducted by different Estonian researchers. One of the surveys conducted in 1999 suggests that about 41.7% of Estonians at that time considered themselves as religious persons (total questioned 1005). According to this particular survey it was a fraction larger than in Great Britain (41.6%).[47] Kilp concludes from this that Estonian society is not far from the category of 'believing without belonging'. Based on these statistics he suggests that although numbers of affiliation to religious organizations are low, Estonian society cannot be considered as the most secularized society in Europe. Kilp also concludes on the basis of the survey that Estonians are more positive than, for example, East Germans regarding religious ceremonies at birth (63.7% and 25.6% respectively), marriage (65% and 34%) and death (75.6% and 39%). He suggests that it is not the attitude regarding religion or church per se that is extremely low among the Estonian population, but the willingness to be formally affiliated to the church.[48] Some other and more recent surveys suggest the low importance of traditional (Christian) religious communities. According to the Euro barometer survey ('Social Values Science and Technology') carried out in 2005, Estonia was shown to be the most sceptical country in Europe in regard to belief in the existence of God. Less than one out of five declared any belief in God (approximately 16%). This probably shows a relative coolness towards traditional religions. However, more than 54% believed in a non-traditional concept of 'some sort of spirit or life force'.[49] One of the most recent surveys in a way confirms this earlier finding. The survey carried out by Lea Altnurme at the Theology Faculty of the University of Tartu in 2014 indicates that there is a high degree of individualization of religion. More than half of the people questioned said they have their individual beliefs, which are not dependent on a specific religion or church (58%), and little less than a half (48%) said that although they do not consider themselves believers they have great interest in religions and spiritual practices (New Age). Most believed in new spiritual practices like meditation, yoga, self-help/improvement. Interestingly about 55% of Estonians and 77% of other nationalities considered Christian teachings as grounds for becoming a moral person and about the same percentage said they like Christian principles. However, 28% said that religion inhibits free development of persons and 35% considered churches as tools for manipulating the masses in order to keep them under control.[50] A survey carried out in 2015 indicates that about 11% of Estonians and 38% of non-Estonians consider themselves to be believers. According to the same survey 38% of the population believes there is a god (1,002

46. R. Ringvee, 'State, Religion and the Legal Framework in Estonia', *Religion, State and Society* 32, no. 2 (2008): 192–193.
47. World Values Survey, 'Estonia 1999', www.worldvaluessurvey.org, 1 May 2010.
48. A Kilp, 'Secularisation of Society after Communism: Ten Catholic-Protestant Societies', in *Religion and Politics in Multicultural Europe*, ed. A. Saumets & A. Kilp (Tartu: Tartu University Press, 2009), 210–211.
49. European Commission, 'Special Eurobarometer: Social values, Science and Technology' (2005), 11.
50. 'Uuring: eestlastel on oma usk' ('Estonians have Their own Belief'), *Äripäev*, 22. Apr. 2014.

questioned).[51] Although there are discrepancies between different surveys, they seem to suggest that religion is both an individual and private matter in Estonia. These surveys also give one confidence in saying that the majority of the Estonian population is at least spiritual and not hostile to religion. According to the last-mentioned survey only 10% of people questioned identified themselves as atheists.

§3. Historical Background

31. The key factors which have shaped Estonian history are its geopolitical location and small population. Raun points out that the Eastern-Baltic region with important ports (e.g., Riga, Tallinn, Narva and Pärnu) has been highly coveted by all Northern European powers, especially since the thirteenth century.[52] From a national security point of view the limited number of Estonians has been a major factor in their inability to ward off foreign invaders.[53] Estonian history since the thirteenth century is a history of numerous conquests by Germans, Danes, Swedes and Russians who fought against Estonians and among themselves for the control over this territory, each one having a turn in ruling and consequently in influencing the development of Estonians. In fact when Estonia declared its independence from the Soviet Union in August 1991 (marking the end of fifty years of Soviet occupation), for only the second time[54] since the beginning of the thirteenth century, Estonian soil was free of foreign conquerors and its local inhabitants were able to determine their own fate.[55]

32. Compared to other Baltic Sea countries, Christianity arrived in Estonia relatively late. There were missionaries in Estonia before the thirteenth century. However, the Christian religion failed to assert itself without military force.[56] Several different and often competing religious and lay powers participated in a determined effort to conquer the Eastern coast of the Baltic Sea: The papal curia, the archbishops of Hamburg-Bremen (to whom the Pope had granted the right to conduct missionary work in North Estonia as early as mid-ninth century), the Teutonic Order (which relocated from the Holy Land to Poland and Prussia) and the Danish and Swedish crowns.[57] The most interesting and most valuable surviving description and insight into the events of the time is *Henrici Cronicon Lyvoniae* (Chronicle of Henry of Livonia). Henry of Livonia was a Catholic priest. The chronicles describe events from 1180–1227 and may have originated as a report to the papal legate William of Modena, to whom Henry was assigned as an interpreter in 1225–1227.

---

51. K. Maasoo, 'Elust, usust ja usuelust' (Saar Poll, 2015), http://www.saarpoll.ee/UserFiles/File/Elus,%20usust%20ja%20usuelust_2015_ESITLUS_FINAL.pdf, 1 Mar. 2021.
52. T. Raun, *Estonia and Estonians*, 2nd edn (Stanford: Hoover Institution Press, 2001), xviii.
53. *Ibid.*
54. The first independence period was from 1918 to 1940.
55. K. Sillaste, 'Conquest and Survival: An Outline of Estonian History', *World Affairs* 157, no. 3 (1995): 119. For detailed account on Estonian history *see*, e.g., T. Raun, *Estonia and Estonians*, 2nd edn (Stanford: Hoover Institution Press, 2001).
56. *Encyclopaedia Estonica*, 'History', www.estonica.org, 1 Apr. 2008.
57. *Ibid.*

33. Crusaders conducted a war of attrition with the local people from 1208 until 1227 when the struggle finally ended with their victory and the division of Estonia. The crusaders (who were mostly of German origin) occupied the southern part of Estonia, then named Livonia (which also comprised the approximate territory of present-day Latvia), while control over Northern Estonia (*Estland*) was held by the Danes. In the middle of the fourteenth century, however, following a series of fierce peasant uprisings, the Danes were forced to relinquish their control over Northern Estonia and sell their lands to the Order of the Teutonic Knights, who thus gained control over all of Estonia.[58]

34. Cultural life from the thirteenth century onwards was divided along national and social lines. Raun observes that although the Baltic Germans were *Kulturträger* in one sense, their culture remained foreign to Estonians.[59] 'The Catholic Church – the one local institution that might have formed the bridge between the two worlds – was not very successful in this regard.'[60] The monastic orders (such as Dominicans, Cistercians, Franciscans and the Order of St. Brigitta) were only a fraction closer to the local people. As a result pagan beliefs remained strong. For example, Christian marriage and baptism were slow to take root. Pagan burial customs continued more strongly than among neighbouring people. 'Although the reforms were discussed and even recommended by the Livonian Church (e.g., the Riga Synod 1437), no significant results were achieved before the upheaval occasioned by Martin Luther.'[61] The translation of religious texts into Estonian also played a significant role at the beginning of the sixteenth century (more on this in Part IX, Education). However, it should be mentioned that ideas of reformation were slow to come to Estonia. Cities adopted the ideas in the 1520s, but rural nobility showed little interest in change. In the 1530s, the first religious services in Estonian were conducted in urban areas. The major change, however, came with the collapse of medieval Livonia.[62]

35. Medieval Livonia came to an end in 1561, during the Livonian wars (1558–1583). The war started with the invasion of Old Livonia by Ivan the Terrible. As a consequence, Russia gained control over some Northern Estonian territory. In 1559, the bishop of Saare-Lääne sold his territories (the Western territories of Estonia including the main islands) to the Danish king. In June 1561, the city of Tallinn and nobility of Northern Estonia swore loyalty to the Swedish king Erik XIV, who had become increasingly interested in the Baltic region. In November 1561 the southern regions of Livonia capitulated to the Polish king.

36. After two more decades of fighting between different sovereigns, by 1581–1583 an unofficial border had emerged between the Swedish and Polish possessions in Estonia. The Peace of Altmark in 1629 eventually established Swedish

58. K. Sillaste, 'Conquest and Survival: An Outline of Estonian History', *World Affairs* 157, no. 3 (1995): 119.
59. T. Raun, *Estonia and Estonians,* 2nd edn (Stanford: Hoover Institution Press, 2001), 23.
60. *Ibid.*
61. *Ibid.*, 24.
62. *Ibid.*

control over the entire continental Baltic area north of the Daugava River.[63] A valuable account of the history of Livonia is a chronicle (*Chronica der Prouinz Lyfflandt)* written by a Lutheran priest Balthazar Russow, which describes the history of Livonia up to 1583.[64]

37. In the seventeenth century, when Estonia came under the sovereignty of Sweden, a systematic reorganization of social and religious life under the Lutheran Church began, and the Catholic Church was practically expelled from Estonia.[65] The Catholic Church in Estonia was not re-established until the nineteenth century.

38. The end of Swedish rule came with the Great Northern War at the beginning of the eighteenth century waged by Russian Tsar Peter I and his Danish, Polish and Saxon allies against Sweden. In the beginning Peter I was not successful in his conquest of Estonian territory. His much larger forces were defeated in Narva (North-East Estonia) by Charles XII (King of Sweden) in 1700. After that, however, the Swedish king had to turn his attention to fighting in Poland which wasted his resources and ended without success. In 1710 Estonian territory came under Russian rule.

39. From 1710–1860 Estonia remained a traditional and hierarchical agrarian society. 'The Baltic German nobility, clergy and merchants continued to form the elites in both rural and urban areas.'[66] The Estonian population (peasants or members of the lower orders in the cities) found little opportunity for upward social mobility.[67] As Raun points out, it is not coincidental that the first intellectuals who identified themselves as Estonians appeared immediately after liberation from serfdom (1816–1819).[68] The development of Estonia in the second half of the nineteenth century is characterized by general modernization: the reorganizing of a static agrarian society into a modern European society, industrialization, urbanization and the success of the newly emerged nationalist awareness.[69] This proceeded along the same lines as in other small East and Central European nations (Czechs, Finns, Latvians, etc.), who lacked the experience of independent statehood in their recent past. The leading force in the Estonian national movement was the new elite – primarily emerging intellectuals aspiring to better their social position, the middle layer consisting of civil servants, merchants and artisans, and, increasingly, the ethnic Estonian clergy. Low social status, and the lack of any right to make decisions, as a result of Russian centralization of power, and the Baltic-German-dominated

63. T. Raun, *Estonia and Estonians*, 2nd edn (Stanford: Hoover Institution Press, 2001), 28.
64. Balthasar Russow, *Liivimaa Kroonika*, trans. Dagmar Stock & Hermann Stock (Tallinn: Hotger, 1993).
65. For a more detailed history of religions in Estonia *see Encyclopaedia Estonica,* 'Culture', 'Religion', www.estonica.org, 1 Apr. 2008.
66. T. Raun, *Estonia and Estonians*, 2nd edn (Stanford: Hoover Institution Press, 2001), 37.
67. *Ibid.*
68. *Ibid.*
69. *Encyclopaedia Estonica*, 'History', 'National Awakening', www.estonica.org, 1. Apr. 2010.

cultural situation, then motivated the elite of 'awakened peasants' to build up their own independent nation and national society. This was to be separate from the existing German and Russian ones.[70]

40. As to religious freedom, some liberties were guaranteed in the nineteenth century: for example, the Grace of Tsar Alexander I in 1817 permitted all the activities of the Herrnhut Movement (Moravian Church).[71] This movement arrived in Estonia in the 1730s and spread extensively in the nineteenth century. Some of the activities of the Herrnhut Movement were prohibited from 1743, as a potential threat to social order. It is believed that the movement contributed to peasant uprisings, but also its reactionary part conflicted with the official Lutheran Church. It has been recognized that the Estonian national cultural awakening in the nineteenth century owes a lot to this movement. The Moravian Brethren contributed to the development of written Estonian and therefore the modernization of the culture. It has also been pointed out that these contributions undoubtedly brought Christianity closer to the people and intertwined the religion more tightly with Estonian culture. The movement had the result of contributing to the neglect and demise of semi-pagan folk poetry and ancient traditional music. It should be kept in mind, however, that the Herrnhut Movement never involved more than a fraction of the Estonian peasantry, and its regional penetration varied greatly. Despite this movement, Christianity as an institution remained dominated by Baltic Germans until the time of Estonian independence, during which efforts at the 'Estonianization' of the Lutheran Church were being made.[72] Today the movement has about 100 members and continues its activities in close connection with the Lutheran Church.

41. In the 1840s it was possible to convert from the Land Church (Lutheran Church) to the Tsar's Church (i.e., the Russian Orthodox Church), but not vice versa. The Orthodox Church and the Roman Catholic Church are the oldest forms of Christianity in Estonia, but Estonians did not join the Orthodoxy in great numbers until the middle of the nineteenth century. The prime reason for peasants to convert was the tsarist policy of Russification and the hope that along with the 'tsar's faith' one would be given land.[73] In the 1880s, the first Free Church (Baptist) congregations were established. Freedom of religion was formally guaranteed to all the subjects of the Tsar by the Tolerance Act of 17 April 1905.

42. The national awakening in Estonia turned more political in the last two decades of the Russian empire, which was struggling with ferment and revolution. After the 1905 revolution Estonians worked out programmes for political autonomy in a federalized Russia. Although the reaction to 1905 somewhat suppressed the

70. *Ibid.*
71. *Eesti Entsüklopeedia*, II kd. (Tartu, 1934).
72. *See, e.g.*, I. Jürjo, 'Influences of Pietism and the Moravian Brethren', in *Estonica: Encyclopaedia about Estonia*, www.estonica.org/en/History/1710-1850_The_Baltic_Landesstaat/ Influences_of_Pietism_and_the_Moravian_Brethren/, 1 Jun. 2010.
73. *See Encyclopaedia Estonica*, 'Culture', www.estonica.org, 1 Apr. 2008.

hopes for political change, 'the growing socioeconomic power of the Estonian population as well as cultural flourishing in this era could not be halted'.[74]

43. As pointed out in paragraph 3 of this monograph the independent Republic of Estonia was born in the aftermath of World War I (1914–1918).[75] The Estonian state emerged from the simultaneous collapse of the Russian and German empires. However, Estonian self-determination had to be asserted by force of arms (War of Liberation). This war was waged both against the Baltische Landeswehr (the Baltic-German forces, which were formed from local Baltic-Germans led by General Rüdiger von der Goltz) and Bolshevik Russia. Peace was finally secured by the 1920 Tartu treaty between Soviet Russia and the Estonian Republic.[76]

44. The history of law on religions in the Republic of Estonia may be divided into four main periods. The first started with the formation of the independent State in 1918 and with the adoption of the 1920 Constitution, which set forth the principle of a strict separation of State and Church. It stated that 'there is no State religion').[77] The main examples used for drafting the 1920 Constitution were the 1874 Constitution of Switzerland and the 1919 Constitution of Germany. But the religious freedom clause contained ideas adopted from the USA.[78] The Constitution was followed by the 1925 Religious Societies and their Associations Act, which reaffirmed the principle of equal treatment of all religious organizations, and the separation of state and religion.[79]

45. The second period (the 1930s) saw significant political changes in Estonian society, which were characterized by the centralization of State administration, the concentration of power, a decline of democracy and the expansion of State control. This period is commonly called 'the era of silence' which lasted from 1934–1939. In 1934 the Churches and Religious Societies Act was enacted, not by Parliament but by decree of the State Elder (President).[80] This Act established different legal treatment for churches and for other religious societies, and it set out special provisions for churches. Churches were given not only additional rights but also restrictions; the government of all churches was subjected to control by the state. The 1934 Act also appeared to impose the idea of 'one creed, one religious association'. For example, several protestant congregations that had become independent under the 1925 Act had to join the Estonian Evangelical Lutheran Church (EELC). However,

74. T. Raun, *Estonia and Estonians*, 2nd edn (Stanford: Hoover Institution Press, 2001), 81.
75. For more detailed account on these turbulent times and about Estonian Independence War *see*, *e.g.*, T. Raun, *Estonia and Estonians*, 2nd edn (Stanford: Hoover Institution Press, 2001); D.J. Smith, *Estonian Independence and European Integration* (London: Routledge, 2001); R.J. Misiunas & R. Taagepera, *The Baltic States: Years of Dependence, 1940–1990*, expanded and updated edn (California: University of California Press, 1993).
76. *See*, *e.g.*, R.J. Misiunas & R. Taagepera, *The Baltic States: Years of Dependence, 1940–1990*, expanded and updated edn (Berkeley: University of California Press, 1993), 8–14.
77. RT 1920, 113/114, 243.
78. E. Maddison, 'Usuühingute ja nende liitude õiguslik iseloom' [Legal Character of Religious Societies and their Associations], *Eesti Politseileht*, no. 11 (221) 13. märts 1926, 161–162.
79. RT 1925, 183/184, 96.
80. RT 1934, 107, 840.

there is no recorded evidence of serious religious persecution or discrimination in the 1920s. In 1934, mirroring attitudes in some other European countries at the time, the Estonian government prohibited the activities of Jehovah's Witnesses as being a threat to Estonia's internal and foreign policy/security. They continued their activities 'underground' and were only able to register their organization as a legal entity after the end of the Soviet occupation in 1991. There is no evidence of equivalent discrimination against other religious communities during the first independence period. Besides a multitude of Christian communities, Jewish and Muslim communities had established their organizations between 1918 and 1940. The status of some churches, especially large ones (with membership over 100,000), was to a certain extent similar to the status of a State Church.[81] According to section 84(1)(b) of the 1938 Constitution, the leaders of the two largest churches (the EELC and the EAOC) gained ex officio membership in the *Riiginõukogu* (Upper House of Parliament).[82] The 1934 Act set out special provisions for churches.

46. The third period began with the Soviet occupation of Estonia. Estonia was annexed by the USSR in 1940 (apart from a three-year interruption during the German occupation from 1941 to 1944) and had little legislative independence during the occupation. The USSR law dictated Estonian laws on freedom of religion for the entire occupation period. The law on religions in the Soviet Union was based on the 1918 Leninist decree on the separation of church from state, and school from church. The bizarre fact is that the separation of state and church (religious organizations) was actually a non-separation, because the state controlled all aspects of religious organizations, including their leaders and sometimes even their members. In 1977 a new decree on the General Statute of the Religious Collectives was adopted, but the basic principles remained the same. During the Soviet period several institutions were established in the USSR to monitor and supervise religious life. In 1965 the position of the Commissioner of Religious Affairs was established by the authorities to manage religious activities in Estonia.

47. The fourth period began with the regaining of independence at the beginning of the 1990s and with the adoption of the 1992 Constitution.[83] Estonia started to re-build its legal order on the principle of restitution, while at the same time acknowledging the changes over time in the European legal order and thinking. In fact some of the laws liberating the activities of religious communities were adopted already at the end of the Soviet rule. In 1990, the Supreme Council annulled the 1977 General Statute of the Religious Collectives[84] and applied the Civic Societies

81. M. Kiviorg, 'Religion and Discrimination Law in Estonia' in *Religion and Discrimination Law in the European Union*, ed. M. Hill QC (Trier: University of Trier, 2012), 112.
82. RT 1937, 71, 590.
83. Estonian Constitution, RT 1992, 26, 349, https://www.riigiteataja.ee/en/eli/ee/530122020003/consolide/current, 27 Jan. 2021; Ü Madise et al. (eds), *Eesti Vabariigi põhiseadus. Kommenteeritud väljaanne* [*Commentaries of the Constitution*] (Tallinn: Juura, 2020), https://pohiseadus.ee, 30 Jan. 2021.
84. ENSVÜVT 1990, 1, 14.

Act of 1989 to religious communities.[85] In 1990 the institution of the Commissioner of Religious Affairs was abolished in Estonia.[86]

85. ENSVÜVT 1989, 18, 255.
86. R. Ringvee, 'State, Religion and the Legal Framework in Estonia', *Religion, State and Society* 32, no. 2 (2008): 183; *see also* M. Kiviorg, 'Kirikuõigus Eesti Vabariigis avaliku õiguse osana (aastate 1918–1940 ja 1991–1996 võrdlev analüüs)' ['Law on Religions in Estonia: Comparative Analysis of the Periods 1918–1940 and 1991–1996'], *Juridica* 9 (1997): 465–471.

Part I. Legal Framework and Sources

Chapter 1. Constitutional Position of Religion

48. The current legal and political framework of religion in Estonia was designed by the Constitution adopted by the referendum of 28 June 1992.[87] This Constitution meets the standards of freedom characteristic of Western democracies, European and international law entirely and was a clear indication of how Estonia wanted to identify itself after years of Soviet occupation. In drafting the document, great attention was paid to fundamental rights. International treaties, the European Convention on Human Rights (ECHR) and constitutions of other democratic states were taken as models. However, as noted above, when the Estonian Constitutional Assembly held heated discussions over each provision and meaning of the draft Constitution of the Republic of Estonia at the beginning of 1990, there was no real discussion about the provisions relating to freedom of religion or belief and State and Church relationships. In the process of re-building the Estonian Republic immediately after the collapse of the Soviet Union, there were more urgent issues to be dealt with. The absence of this discussion has to some degree determined that aspects of the relationship between religion and state still need to be clarified. The following will first give a description of sources of law on religion and then address the main constitutional provisions and principles regarding religion.

The legal sources of the law on religions in Estonia are as follows:

(1) Provisions set forth in the Constitution.
(2) Provisions set forth in international law and law of the European Union.
(3) National law (the Non-profit Organizations Act, the Churches and Congregations Act and the other acts directly or indirectly regulating the individual and collective freedom of religion).
(4) The interpretation of fundamental freedoms and rights in the administration of justice (including decisions of the European Court of Human Rights and the European Court of Justice).[88]

87. Estonian legal acts can be found at the web page of the State Gazette (*Riigi Teataja*), Riigi Teataja https://www.riigiteataja.ee/en/ accessed 30 Jan. 2020. This is an official webpage of the State Gazette where all the laws and other legislative acts and court decisions of Estonia are electronically available. It also includes unofficial translations into English and Russian of selected legal acts. The translations do not have legal force and cannot be relied on in judicial or any other official proceedings. In Estonia, legislation has legal force only in Estonian.

88. *See also* K. Merusk & R. Narits, *Eesti Konstitutsiooniõigusest* [About Estonian Constitutional Law] (Tallinn: Juura, 1998), 169.

49. The Estonian Constitution expressly provides protection to freedom of religion. Article 40 sets out that:

- Everyone has freedom of conscience, religion and thought. Everyone may freely belong to churches and religious associations. There is no state church.
- Everyone has the freedom to practise his or her religion, both alone and in a community with others, in public or in private, unless this is detrimental to public order, health or morals.

50. Article 40 is deemed to protect a wide variety of beliefs. Even during a state of emergency or a state of war, rights and liberties in Article 40 of the Constitution may not be restricted (Article 130 of the Estonian Constitution). The religious freedom guarantee of Article 40 of the Constitution has to be interpreted in conjunction with the other articles of the Constitution as one reflects on freedom of religion or belief. Article 41 on the freedom of belief and Article 42 on the privacy of one's religion and belief add strength to the commitment to freedom of religion. In addition, other constitutional provisions complement basic freedom of religion. For example, Article 45 concerning the right to freedom of expression, Article 47 concerning the right to assembly, and Article 48 concerning the right to association: each provides specific protection for different aspects of religious freedom.

51. The right to freedom of religion in Estonia is also protected by international law. Article 3 of the Estonian Constitution stipulates that universally recognized principles and standards of international law shall be an inseparable part of the Estonian legal system. Under Article 3 of the Estonian Constitution the universally recognized principles and standards of international law have been incorporated into the Estonian legal system and do not need further transformation. They are superior in force to national legislation and binding for legislative, administrative and judicial powers. It should be noted that Article 3 incorporates both international customary norms and general principles of law into the Estonian legal system. The international treaties (ratified by Parliament) are incorporated into the Estonian legal system by Article 123(2) of the Constitution. Article 123 states that if Estonian legal acts or other legal instruments contradict foreign treaties ratified by the *Riigikogu* (Parliament), the provisions of the foreign treaty shall be applied. Estonia is a party to most European and universal human rights documents.[89] Estonia is also a member of many international organizations, including the United Nations, Council of Europe and Organization for Security and Co-operation in Europe (OSCE), and has ratified key conventions protecting freedom of religion or belief.

52. Some general theoretical observations can be made about the Constitution. The Estonian Constitution is perceived to be a liberal constitution based on natural

89. *Inter alia*, the European Convention for the Protection of Human Rights and Fundamental Freedoms (1950), and the International Covenant on Civil and Political Rights (1966). European Convention on Human Rights and Fundamental Freedoms (adopted 4 Nov. 1950, entered into force 3 Sep. 1953) 213 UNTS 221 (ECHR); International Covenant on Civil and Political Rights (adopted 16 Dec. 1966, entered into force 23 Mar. 1976) 999 UNTS 171 (ICCPR).

and inalienable individual rights.[90] At the same time, the preamble of the Constitution states that the idea behind strengthening and developing the state is to guarantee the preservation of the Estonian nation, language and culture through the ages.[91] The latter is a reflection of the classical German constitutional model, which presupposes the prior existence of a people, united by culture, language and ethnicities.[92] However, it seems that in (legal) scholarly interpretation of the Constitution the emphasis is on individual rights. Moreover, the Estonian Constitution recognizes collective religious freedom (e.g., Articles 40, 9, 19 and 48) and provides protection for cultural/religious minorities and for their autonomy (Article 50).

53. The Estonian Constitution encompasses several important principles determining freedom of religion and the relationship between State and religious communities. These principles are neutrality, equality and self-determination/autonomy.

§1. Neutrality

54. Article 40 of the Constitution stipulates the principle of institutional separation of the State and religious associations ('There is no State Church'). However, this has not been interpreted as a rigorous policy of non-identification with religion. The cooperation between the State and religious associations in areas of common interest is an established practice today. Thus, the principle 'there is no State church' is not interpreted similarly to disestablishment in the United States or the principle of *laïcité* in France. The Estonian Constitution does not make any reference to secularism as a constitutional principle. The stipulation 'There is no state church' has been interpreted as a stipulation of the principle of neutrality. The principle of neutrality in the Estonian Constitution is a reflection of the neutrality and impartiality principle adopted by the European Court of Human Rights, which should be understood as an obligation of the state to be a neutral and impartial organizer of various beliefs. There have been heated debates over preferential treatment of Christian churches in Estonia. Maruste has rightly observed that under the Estonian Constitution the state needs to be careful when giving preference to one religious community over another – it has to have objective and reasonable justification, especially when financial subsidies or public services are in question.[93] In this regard he makes special reference to the equality principle. However, it is probably fair to say that the meaning of the principle of neutrality in Estonian constitutional

---

90. R. Narits, 'About the Principles of the Constitution of the Republic of Estonia from the Perspective of Independent Statehood in Estonia', *Juridica International* XVI (2009): 56.
91. *Ibid.*, 58; *See also* the Preamble of the Estonian Constitution.
92. *See also* J. Reingelheim, 'Minority Protection and Constitutional Recognition of Difference', in *The framework Convention for the Protection of national Minorities: A Useful Pan-European Instrument*, ed. A. Verstichel (Antwerp: Intersentia, 2008), 33–49.
93. R. Maruste, *Konstitutsionalism ning põhiõiguste ja –vabaduste kaitse* [*Constitutionalism and Protection of Fundamental Rights and Freedoms*] (Tallinn: Juura, 2004), 522. *See also* M. Kiviorg, 'Religion and Secular State in Estonia' in Religion and the Secular State: National Reports (Madrid: Servicio de Publicaciones de la Facultad de Derecho de la Universidad Complutense, 2015).

theory and practice regarding religion is under development. The issues relating to the meaning of neutrality will be discussed throughout this monograph.

§2. Equality

55. The general right to equality is one of the general principles of Estonian law. These general principles stem from the preamble and Article 10 of the 1992 Constitution (enshrining principles of human dignity, a state based on social justice, and democracy). The preamble of the Constitution proclaims that the state is founded on liberty, justice and law. The principle of equality is explicitly set forth in the first sentence of the first paragraph of Article 12 of the Constitution, which states that all persons shall be equal before the law. The second paragraph of Article 12 lays out the principle of non-discrimination, prohibiting discrimination, inter alia, on the basis of religion or belief. As the Constitution protects both individual and collective freedom of religion, these principles have to be applied to religious communities as well. The rationale of the law dealing with religious discrimination is based both on the principle of equality and on freedom of religion or belief (Article 40 of the Constitution). This is reflected in the understanding that the article has to be interpreted in conjunction with the other articles of the Constitution. It is also reflected in the understanding that the equality principle should provide not just formal but also substantive equality. The concept of substantive equality has been in principle endorsed by the Estonian Supreme Court.[94] Additionally, the understanding of direct and indirect discrimination in Estonia has been influenced by and has evolved alongside its development in European Union law[95] and in the case law of the ECHR.[96] The exact application of the equality principle in relation to religion has not been tested in Estonian courts.

Although freedom of religion or religious discrimination was not debated during the writing of the 1992 Constitution, subsequently, the role of the major churches (especially the EELC) in Estonia, equal treatment of religions and religious education have all been topics for political and public debate. There have been visible tensions in the triangle of Christian communities, non-Christian communities and the state, but also within the triangle of Christian churches (primarily the EELC), state and the secular community (especially regarding religious education in public schools). Non-Christian religious communities have several times voiced their concern about equal treatment and discrimination.[97]

---

94. *Eesti Vabariigi Põhiseadus. Kommenteeritud väljaanne* [Commentaries on the Estonian Constitution] (Tallinn: Juura, 2002), 121.
95. For example, Council Directive 2000/78/EC on Employment Equality [2000] OJ L 195/16; Council Directive 2000/43/EC on Racial Equality [2000] OJ L 180/22.
96. *Thlimmenos v. Greece* (App. No. 34369/97) (2001) 31 EHRR 411; *DH and Others v. the Czech Republic* (App. No. 57325/00) (2008) 47 EHRR 16. The concept of indirect discrimination is related to the substantive equality approach.
97. M. Kiviorg, 'Religion and Discrimination Law in Estonia' in *Religion and Discrimination Law in the European Union*, ed. M. Hill QC (Trier: University of Trier, 2012).

§3. Self-Determination/Autonomy

56. The general right to self-determination of persons (both individuals and groups) stems from Article 19 of the Estonian Constitution. Article 19(1) of the Constitution states that: 'all persons shall have the right to free self-realization'. The right to religious (church) autonomy is also considered to be an essential part of collective freedom of religion which is protected by Article 40 of the Constitution and by Articles 48, 19(1) and 9(2).[98] Autonomy of religious associations also means the right to self-administration in accordance with religious law and prescriptions.[99]

§4. Limits to Freedom of Religion or Belief

57. Article 40 itself states that freedom of religion, 'alone or in community', is assured 'unless it endangers public order, health, or morals'. In addition, the Constitution contains four general limitation clauses: the first sentence of Article 3(1),[100] Article 11, Article 13(2),[101] and Article 19(2). Article 11, however, is the most important limitations clause: 'Rights and liberties may be restricted only in accordance with the Constitution. Restrictions may be implemented only insofar as they are necessary in a democratic society, and their imposition may not distort the nature of the rights and liberties.' Thus, every case of restriction of rights and liberties has to be justified and pass the test of proportionality. Article 19(2) constitutionalizes the common sense idea that, in exercising their rights and liberties, all persons must respect and consider the rights and liberties of others ('and observe the law').[102] However, it is not entirely clear what standard or level of rigour/scrutiny the courts are prepared to apply as regards restrictions on freedom of religion or belief. The current case law leaves an impression that no rigorous scrutiny has been applied as to possible justifications provided for restricting freedom of religion or belief by State or local governments. Sometimes no proportionality test has been applied.

58. The Constitutional Review Chamber of the Supreme Court has, however, provided some important interpretative principles as to the limiting of fundamental rights and freedoms generally.[103] First, many restriction clauses in the Fundamental Rights and Freedoms Chapter of the Constitution (e.g., Articles 11, 47) permit reservations in accordance with law. The term 'law' used in the restriction clauses of

98. This was expressly stated in the Presidential veto to the 2002 Churches and Congregations Act, RTL 2001, 82, 1120.
99. *Ibid. See also* Part III, Ch. 2 below.
100. 'State power shall be exercised solely on the basis of the constitution and such laws which are in accordance with the constitution.'
101. 'The law shall protect all persons against arbitrary treatment by state authorities.'
102. *See* R. Alexy, 'Põhiõigused Eesti põhiseaduses' ['Fundamental Rights in the Estonian Constitution'] *Iuridica,* eriväljaanne [the special issue] (2001): 5–96.
103. *See* Decisions of the Constitutional Review Chamber of the Supreme Court, Case No. III-4/A- 4/93, 4 Nov. 1993 (RT III 1993, 72/73, 1052); Case No. III-4/A-1/94, 12 Jan. 1994 (RT III 1994, 8, 129); Case No. III-4/A-2/94, 12 Jan. 1994 (RT III 1994, 8, 130).

the Fundamental Rights and Freedoms Chapter of the Constitution, means an act of *Riigikogu* (Parliament). This means in effect that restrictions must appear in the Constitution or as set forth in laws enacted by the Parliament. Setting limitations to rights and liberties in lower administrative or executive acts would be unconstitutional. Second, relating to the former principle, the Supreme Court has also ruled that the Parliament cannot delegate its legislative powers regarding duties specifically vested in it by the Constitution.[104] Third, restrictions to the fundamental freedoms and rights are unconstitutional if they are not clear and detailed enough to enable the putative subjects of law to determine their conduct on the basis of informed choice.[105]

104. Case No. III-4/A-1/94, 12 Jan. 1994 (RT III 1994, 8, 129).
105. Case No. 3-4-1-5-02, 28 Oct. 2002 (RT III 2002, 28, 308); P. Roosma, 'Protection of Fundamental Rights and Freedoms in Estonian Constitutional Jurisprudence', *Juridica International* IV (1999): 35–44.

Chapter 2. Other Legislation with Regard to Religion

59. The religious freedom clauses in the 1992 Constitution were followed by the 1993 Churches and Congregations Act (*Kirikute ja koguduste seadus*).[106] When the drafting of the new law began in the early 1990s, there was pressure from the EELC for special legal status. The Church in question also proposed to make a distinction between 'old' and 'new' religions.[107] The head of the Office for Religious Affairs expressed her concerns in the official newspaper of the EELC. She pointed out that small churches have problems, not least attempts by the Lutheran Church to take hold of all key positions. 'Some representatives of the Lutheran Church support the idea of a State Church although they do not want to admit this in public.'[108] It needs to be emphasized that there was no unified approach in this regard within the EELC itself. Ringvee points out that in line with the general libertarian trend in Estonian policymaking at that time, the 1993 law did not eventually follow the tradition in many Continental European countries of a multi-tiered system of legal recognition of religious associations.[109] This tradition was followed in many other post-socialist countries. The 1993 law treated all religious associations equally, regardless of membership numbers or length of existence.[110] Ringvee observes that:

> 1993 law established the subsequent liberal policies on religion in Estonia. There were various reasons for this liberal approach. After independence in 1991, Estonia chose the road of radical liberal reform in both economic and social life, and these reforms had their effect in the field of religion. The principle of the free market was introduced to the religious sphere, and it turned out to be well suited to the generally individualist mentality of Estonians.[111]

60. However, it should be noted that although not incorporated in law, the reality of Church and State relationships indicates that Estonia may not be so different from the most common European model guaranteeing religious freedom as such at one level, but granting certain (additional) advantages and privileges to a limited number of religious groups.[112] This issue will be discussed in more detail later on in this monograph.

61. In 1996, the new Non-profit Organizations Act (*Mittetulundusühingute seadus*) was passed by the Parliament. This triggered the need to prepare a new

---

106. Churches and Congregations Act, RT I 1993, 30, 510.
107. V. Jürjo, 'Kas riigikirik?' ['A State Church?'], *Eesti Kirik,* 17 Dec. 1992.
108. A. Veidemann, 'Toimetusse helistas' ['Phone Call to the Editor'], *Eesti Kirik*, 18 Jun. 1992.
109. *See, e.g.*, R. Torfs, 'Experiences of Western Democracies in Dealing with the Legal Position of Churches and Religious Communities', *Religious studies Review* 1, no. 1 (2007): 67–73.
110. R. Ringvee, 'State, Religion and the Legal Framework in Estonia', *Religion, State and Society* 32, no. 2 (2008): 185.
111. *Ibid.*, 186.
112. *See* the analysis of this two level approach in R. Torfs, 'Experiences of Western Democracies in Dealing with the Legal Position of churches and Religious Communities', *Religious studies Review* 1, no. 1 (2007): 67–73.

Churches and Congregations Act (these two laws relate to each other as *lex generalis* and *lex specialis*). The new law was also needed because of continuous and rapid changes in other laws. The trend was characteristic of Estonian law-making at the beginning of the 1990s and can be considered normal for a country which needed to re-create its legal system after fifty years of occupation. In this state of flux it often happened that different laws contradicted each other in terminology and substance. This somewhat schizophrenic situation was challenging for both lawyers and politicians. The 1996 Non-profit Organizations Act itself did contain certain contradictions.

62. After the 1996 law was passed by Parliament, the President of the Republic refused to sign it. According to Article 107 of the Estonian Constitution the President may refuse to proclaim a law passed by Parliament and, within fourteen days after its receipt, return the law, together with his or her reasoned resolution, to Parliament for a new debate and decision. If Parliament passes the law un-amended, the President of the Republic proclaims the law or turns to the Supreme Court in order to declare the law unconstitutional. If the law is declared constitutional, the President of the Republic proclaims the law; if not, the law goes back to Parliament for amendments. The latter is precisely what happened to the 1996 law.

63. In the course of the legal and political struggle in question, the President filed a petition to the Constitutional Review Chamber of the Estonian Supreme Court with the request to declare the Non-profit Organizations Act unconstitutional.[113] The court dealt with three different issues in this case which related to freedom of religion and freedom of association. First, it addressed the legal status of non-profit associations, including religious communities, emphasizing that the right to association in Article 48 of the Constitution means the right to form associations which either have or do not have the status of a legal person. The Court found that the Non-profit Organizations Act did not fully correspond to this constitutional right as it only allowed associations with legal personality. It also determined that individuals who do not want to establish a legal person, or object to it because of religious reasons are deprived of the possibility to fully realize their constitutional rights.

64. Second, the Act did not allow persons less than 18 years of age to establish non-profit associations. Third, it allowed exclusion of a member from the association upon a discretionary decision of a State authority. The President of Estonia argued that membership of religious associations is a matter of religious belief. No state authority can oblige any person to surrender his or her religious beliefs. The Court agreed that the proposed restrictions distorted the nature of the rights and freedoms of members of non-profit associations, including religious societies, was not necessary in a democratic society, and was in conflict with Articles 11 and 40 of

113. Supreme Court of Estonia, Case No. 3-4-1-1-96, 20 Dec. 1996, www.nc.ee/?id=468, 1 May 2010.

the Constitution.[114] The Supreme Court declared the Non-profit Organizations Act unconstitutional. The unconstitutional provisions were later amended by Parliament.

65. In the process of drafting the new Churches and Congregation Act after the enactment of the Non-profit Organizations Act (1996–2002), debates about preferential treatment of some religious organizations intensified once again (as before the enactment of the 1993 Churches and Congregation Act). The representatives of the EELC proposed the idea that larger churches should have a special status as legal persons in public law or that their relations with the state should be regulated by bilateral agreements. This idea again did not get support from smaller religious communities or from the legislature. The arguments put forward for preferential treatment were not fully substantiated and explained. First it was argued that as larger churches had preferential treatment before the 1940s (i.e., before Soviet occupation), they simply needed to continue having it now. It was also not clear what such a public legal status would entail in an Estonian context. There is no legal tradition in the Estonian Republic comparable to the German experience as to the status in public law of some religious communities.[115] Lately it has been expressed that public legal personality of churches would be in contradiction with the requirement that there is no State Church.[116] Second, it was argued that traditional Churches, like the EELC and the EAOC, could not organize themselves under the law in accordance with their own understandings of their internal organization.[117] The latter concerns were sufficiently taken into account in the drafting of the 2002 Churches and Congregations Act. These concerns have re-emerged recently in a slightly different format. For example, EELC and EAOC have expressed dissatisfaction that (in their view) the law treats them as ordinary non-profit organizations. This dissatisfaction was mainly caused by the burden of annual fiscal reports to smaller congregations. The expert opinion written for the Ministry of Internal Affairs suggested that the issues of concern could easily be addressed within existing law and churches themselves can address this legal-administrative issue internally without the state infringing on their autonomy.[118]

114. Supreme Court of Estonia, Case No. 3-4-1-1-96, 20 Dec. 1996, www.nc.ee/?id=468, 1 May 2010.

115. G. Robbers, 'State and Church in Germany', in *State and Church in the European Union*, ed. G. Robbers, 2nd edn (Baden-Baden: Nomos Verlagsgesellschaft, 2005). However, some religious communities enjoyed status in public law during the Tsarist times in Estonia. *See* W. Meder, 'Ülevaade Eesti kirikuõigusest', *Õigus* 1 (1938): 10–26.

116. M. Kiviorg; P. Roosma, '§ 40, § 41' in *Eesti Vabariigi Põhiseadus: Kommenteeritud väljaanne* [*Commentaries of the Estonian Constitution*], 2 täiendatud trükk, Eerik-Juhan Truuväli et al. (eds) (Tallinn: Juura, 2008).

117. *See, e.g.*, M. Kiviorg, 'State and Church in Estonia', in *State and Church in Baltic States* (Riga: Latvian Association for Freedom of Religion, 2001).

118. M. Kiviorg, *Religiooni puudutavate õigusaktide analüüs* (*Analysis of the Laws Regulating Religion*) (Tallinn: Siseministeerium, 2012).

66. On 1 July 2002, the 1993 law was entirely replaced by the new Churches and Congregations Act (CCA).[119] The 2002 CCA expressly states that the Non-profit Organizations Act and the 2002 CCA are related as general and special legislation (§5(1)). The law gives considerable leeway for religious associations to organize themselves in accordance with their own teachings and structure. It states that: 'The statutes of a religious association may prescribe differences from the provisions of the Non-profit Organizations Act concerning membership and management if such differences arise from the historical teaching and structure of the religious association.' (§5(2)). It also provides specific legal status for religious organizations, declaring: 'A religious association is a legal person in private law. Transformation of a religious association into a legal person of a different type is prohibited' (§5(3)). This provision is a result of the debate, prior to the adoption of the law, over granting public legal personality (as a form of preferential treatment) to the two largest churches (EELC and EAOC) in Estonia.

67. The 2002 Churches and Congregations Act differed from the earlier law principally in the way in which the government registered religious organizations. Previously, under the 1993 Churches and Congregations Act, religious associations were registered by the Ministry of Internal Affairs. According to the new law, religious associations are registered by the registration departments of county and city courts (§17(3)).

68. There was another significant change introduced by the 2002 CCA. Under the 1993 CCA, legal authorities could refuse registration of a religious organization only if, upon review by the authorities, its internal statutes were not in accordance with the law. According to §14(1) of the 2002 CCA, in order to determine compliance of a religious association with the requirements provided by law, the registrar (court) may now suspend proceedings to request the opinion of the ministry with responsibility for those issues relating to religious associations or, in the alternative, the registrar may request an expert opinion from another competent agency. One possible interpretation of this provision is that the legislature has tried to expand the potential (*ex ante*) control over religious organizations. The evidence for this can be found in the explanatory note, which accompanied the law when it was sent to Parliament. According to this note the necessity for this *ex ante* control stems from the spread of fundamentalist and secularized religious organizations in the world.[120] In 2013, registration of the Satanist Congregation was suspended to ask opinion from the Ministry of Internal Affairs. The ministry suggested not to register the congregation. The refusal to register the congregation was controversial. The issue will be discussed in more detail in the Part III (Legal Status of Religious Communities) of this monograph.

---

119. Churches and Congregations Act, RT I 2002, 24, 135; RT I, 30.12.2017, 1 (last amended), https://www.riigiteataja.ee/en/eli/ee/511012018004/consolide/current, 30 Jan. 2021.

120. *Kirikute ja koduste seaduse eelnõu seletuskiri*, 16 Mar. 1999 (Kirikute ja koguduste seadus, 5 SE I), Riigikogu, www.riigikogu.ee, 1 May 2010.

69. There are various other acts which directly regulate the relationship between the State and religion. Some examples are given below. A more detailed account of some of these acts is given later on in this monograph under specific themes. There are also some generally applicable laws, which do not contain specific provisions for religion, but indirectly affect both religious individuals and associations.

70. Religious associations have some privileges under tax law. However, in recent years there have been some small changes that have put religious associations on a more equal footing with all other non-profit organizations especially regarding exemptions from income tax. There is no longer an automatic exemption, as was the case before 2011. As of January 2011, religious associations have to apply for inclusion in the list of non-taxable organizations, as do other non-profit organizations.[121] Religious associations continue to be exempt from land (property) tax. Land tax is not imposed on land under the places of worship of churches and congregations.[122] This exemption does not apply to the properties of secular non-profit organizations. The issues related to financing of religious communities will be discussed later in Part VIII of this monograph.

71. Incitement to hatred, violence or discrimination on account of race, religion, nationality or sexual orientation, political ideas or economic or social status is forbidden by §151 of the Penal Code (*Karistusseadustik*) if the incitement has caused risk to person's life, health or property. Granting special privileges or restricting the rights of a person on religious grounds is forbidden in §152.[123] It should be mentioned that in Estonian law there is no provision *expressis verbis* prohibiting proselytism and there are no blasphemy laws. Not long ago, amendments to Penal Law regarding hate crimes were discussed. Religious organizations expressed their concerns about the future of the religious expression. The debates and penal law in relation to religion will be discussed in Part VII of this monograph.

72. Slaughter for religious purposes is regulated in the Animal Protection Act (*Loomakaitseseadus*), which came into force on 1 July 2001.[124] It needs to be noted, that at the time, the approval of specific provisions concerning religious slaughter was not accompanied by any public discussions (or substantial debate in the Parliament) on whether to forbid or permit slaughter for religious purposes. Details of slaughter for religious purposes are specified by the Regulation concerning the procedure for organizing and carrying out the killing of an animal for religious purposes.[125] The last-mentioned regulation entered into force on 1 January 2013. Before 2001, the Animal Protection Act, passed on 17 November 1992, and entered

---

121. Income Tax Act (Tulumaksuseadus), RT I 1999, 101, 903; RT I, 28.12.2020, 1 (last amended), https://www.riigiteataja.ee/en/eli/ee/511012021001/consolide/current, 28 Jan. 2021.
122. Land Tax Act (Maamaksu seadus), RT I 1993, 24, 428; RT I, 23.12.2020, 5 (last amended), https://www.riigiteataja.ee/en/eli/ee/528122020003/consolide/current, 28 Jan. 2021.
123. Penal Code (Karistusseadustik) RT I 2001, 61, 364; RT I, 10.07.2020, 1 (last amended), https://www.riigiteataja.ee/en/eli/ee/515072020011/consolide/current, 28 Jan. 2021.
124. Animal Protection Act (Loomakaitseseadus) RT I 2001, 3, 4; RT I, 30.12.2020, 3 (last amended), https://www.riigiteataja.ee/akt/130122020012?leiaKehtiv, 28 Jan. 2021.
125. RT I, 29.12.2012, 53; RT I, 04.11.2020 (last amended).

into force on 17 December 1992, permitted slaughter of a productive animal but did not specifically regulate religious slaughter.[126] Under this previous act requirements for protection of animals prior and during slaughter were milder than in the current legal acts. Tightening of the rules that regulate religious slaughter was due to the harmonization of Estonian laws with EU legislation prior to accession to the EU (Estonia became a member of the EU on 1 May 2004). Further changes to the rules were made in 2012 to comply with EU Regulation No. 1099/2009 on the protection of animals at the time of killing (the regulation came into force 1 January 2013). The changes in 2012 triggered some public and parliamentary debate.[127] Under the pressure of the Union for Animal Protection (*Eestimaa Loomakaitse Liit*) the Ministry of Agriculture proposed stricter rules (complete prohibition of religious slaughter) than proscribed in the EU regulation. These stricter rules were not approved by the Religious Affairs Department of the Ministry of Internal Affairs as they violated religious freedom. The contradictions in the proposal were also pointed out in the expert opinion[128] provided for the Religious Affairs department (some further details of the debate will be pointed out in Part V (Religion and Politics) of this monograph.

73. According to current law, slaughter of animals for religious purposes is allowed in Estonia. However, following the EU Regulation No. 1099/2009 the slaughter has to be carried out in slaughterhouses, before the law was amended this was not necessary. According to the regulation adopted by the Ministry of Agriculture detailing the procedures for ritual slaughter, the Veterinary and Food Board has to be informed in writing before the religious slaughter takes place. A supervisory official must be present in order to verify compliance with the binding animal protection rules.[129]

74. Only a person with the necessary skills may perform the slaughter. The carotid arteries and trachea of the restrained animal have to be cut with a sharp instrument and, immediately after the incision, the animal has to be stunned. The further handling of a slaughtered animal is prohibited until the death of the animal has been verified. In Estonia there have been no judgments regarding religious slaughter.

75. As to further acts directly concerning religion, the Identity Documents Act (*Isikut tõendavate dokumentide seadus*) sets forth *inter alia* requirements concerning the photos on identification documents (§9³).[130] According to the law a person

---

126. RT I 1992, 50, 617.
127. Riigikogu stenogramm: Loomakaitseseaduse muutmise ja sellega seonduvalt teiste seaduste muutmise eelnõu (288 SE) teine lugemine (Parliamentary debates) http://www.riigikogu.ee/?op=steno&stcommand=stenogramm&date=1353571171#pk11386, 1 May 2014.
128. M. Kiviorg, Religiooni puudutavate õigusaktide analüüs (Analysis of the Laws Regulating Religion) (Tallinn: Siseministeerium, 2012).
129. RT I, 29.12.2012, 53.
130. RT I 1999, 25, 365; RT I, 19.03.2019, 9 (last amended), https://www.riigiteataja.ee/en/eli/ee/528122020004/consolide/current, 30 Jan. 2021.

has the right, on religious grounds, to submit a photo with a head covering for identification documents. This specific provision was added to the law in 2009.[131] However, the face from mandible to upper forehead should be uncovered. This applies both to Muslim women and Christian nuns, as well as to the followers of other traditions for whom the head covering is mandatory. Interestingly, the law requires proof of the fact that the head covering is mandatory on religious grounds. According to the law, the Ministry of Internal Affairs has to provide a written opinion about this fact. For the purposes of obtaining this opinion the Ministry of Internal Affairs has to be provided with a person's name, date of birth and an identification code, but also with the name of the religious organization of which the person is a member. The Ministry of Internal Affairs may require the religious organization to provide data to prove the persons affiliation. However, these requirements of law somewhat contradict Article 42 of the Estonian Constitution, which provides that 'The State agencies, local governments, and their officials shall not gather or store information about the beliefs of an Estonian citizen against the citizen's free will.'[132] According to the Identity Documents Act, Estonian citizens have to have an identity card (§5). Thus, a citizen who has to have the identity card, but is also required by his or her religion to have a head covering, has no real choice other than to let the State agencies gather information about his or her beliefs. One could argue that in circumstances where keeping the face from mandible to upper forehead uncovered is enough for the purposes, for example, of the identity card, religious affiliation of the person is completely irrelevant.

76. There is no specific law solely regulating religious education. In addition to Article 37 of the Constitution, Article 2 of the Education Act (*Haridusseadus*) sets general objectives and levels of education, stating *inter alia* that the fundamental principles of education are based on the recognition of universal and national values of the individual and of freedom of religion and conscience.[133] The laws specifically relevant to religious education are the Education Act and The Act of Basic Schools and Gymnasiums (**BSG**, *Põhikooli- ja gümnaasiumiseadus*).[134] The curriculum is approved by the Ministry of Education and Research. The teachers of religion in public schools must have both pedagogical as well as religious training. Issues relating to religion and education will be discussed in Part IX of this monograph.

77. In Estonia, church-state relations are governed not only by general laws but also by formal agreements that are negotiated directly between the Government and religious institutions. Some of these agreements are considered to be international treaties (such as the agreement between the State and the Holy See for the Roman Catholic Church). The agreements between the State and religious organizations

131. RT I 2009, 27, 166.
132. For further contradictions with the Churches and Congregations Act *see* Part VII Ch. 1 Protection of Privacy.
133. RT 1992, 12, 192; RT I, 16.06.2020, 1 (last amended), https://www.riigiteataja.ee/en/eli/517072020006/consolide, 30 Jan. 2021.
134. RT I 2010, 41, 240; RT I, 16.06.2020, 1 (last amended), https://www.riigiteataja.ee/en/eli/ee/530062020003/consolide/current, 30 Jan. 2021.

may also have the nature of administrative agreements or cooperation agreements under civil law. The purpose of these agreements may vary from coordination and cooperation on issues of public interest to contracting for the specific religious needs of a religious community. Contractual relationship between religious communities and state will be discussed in more detail in Part II of this monograph.

Chapter 3. Typology of the System

78. The fact that the Estonian Constitution provides that there is no State Church and that the 2002 CCA addresses all religious communities equally has not been seen by the State as providing grounds for a rigorous policy of non-identification with religion. After Estonia regained its independence at the beginning of the 1990s, the historically dominant Evangelical Lutheran Church started to re-establish its position in society and in relation to the State, actively lobbying Government and Parliament for a more privileged position. In constitutional terms Estonia does not have a State Church; indeed, the present Constitution states *inter alia* that 'there is no state church' (Article 40). But the separation of State and Church (especially the Evangelical Lutheran Church) has not been interpreted in administrative practice strictly and inflexibly; as a consequence of this some have argued that Estonia has a de facto State Church. Although this is clearly an exaggeration, the EELC has, in fact, enjoyed a certain amount of preferential treatment from the State. This privileged position has been hotly disputed.

79. There are several other forms of preferential treatment of Christian Churches. The Estonian Council of Churches, which consists of ten Christian communities,[135] has been very active in determining relations between Church(es) and State. The State has treated the Council as a partner in decision-making on religious freedom questions in this country. The privileged position of the Council is visible, and perhaps most sensitive, in matters of financial support and education. On 17 October 2002, the Government and the Estonian Council of Churches signed the Protocol of Common Concerns. Although it has been argued that other religious organizations have in principle the right to seek the same type of cooperation, no other religious organization has yet been able (or expressly willing) to establish it. However, a step forward was made in 2005 when a commission consisting of state representatives, representatives of Native religion, and various other experts was formed to draft a state programme for the protection of 'Groves' and other natural sacral objects.[136] In the context of Estonia it is rather difficult to determine if there is a strong enough social need or tradition (including a legal tradition) in existence to justify differing legal treatment of religious organizations.

80. Estonia has so far been very liberal towards so-called non-traditional religious movements. Nevertheless, just before the adoption of the 2002 CCA by the Estonian parliament, the Estonian Council of Churches sent a letter to the parliamentary commission asking it to take measures in the new law to limit the activities of 'non-constructive religious communities'. Fortunately, these proposals were not enacted into law. The Council's intention was probably a good faith attempt to avoid harmful experiences to individuals, and raises questions about proselytism. Yet, raising this issue created alarm when seen against the larger Eastern European or even European context. Especially in Eastern Europe new religious movements and

135. The Council decides according to its own statutes, which churches to admit to membership.
136. Estonian Ministry of Culture, Directive of Minister of Culture, 11. 02.2005, No. 49.

minority religions have been persecuted. Estonia does not have cases with comparable severity. However, there is a visible tension in the triangle of Christian, non-Christian communities and the State, but also in the triangle of Christian Churches (primarily EELC), State and the secular community (these issues will be elaborated further in Part V of this monograph).

81. As to identifying where Estonia stands in terms of the classification of the Church and State relationship, it probably fits most comfortably into the category of cooperation systems. In cooperation systems the law separates but allows collaboration between state and religion.

Part II. Religious Freedom in General

Chapter 1. Individual Religious Freedom

§1. Legal Framework

82. Various national, international and supranational sources of law determine the normative framework for religious freedom. From international/regional human rights instruments the European Convention on Human Rights is the most influential along with the Charter of Fundamental Rights of the European Union. Both instruments are legally binding in Estonia. Individual religious freedom is also protected by Article 40 of the Estonian Constitution and Part II of the 2002 Churches and Congregations Act (CCA) sets further guarantees for this freedom. Like the international instruments the Constitution and the CCA protect both the right to have/choose and the right to manifest one's religion or belief. The CCA reiterates the right protected by Article 40 of the Constitution, although in somewhat different wording. §8(1) sets for that: 'Every person has the right to freely choose, profess and declare his or her religious beliefs unless it damages public order, health, morals, or the rights or freedoms of others.' §8(2) echoes Article 42 of the Constitution providing that: 'No one is required to provide information on his or her religion or membership in congregations, except a suspect, accused, accused at trial or victim in the course of criminal proceedings.' It should be pointed out that §8(2) provides a restriction on individual freedom which is not *expressis verbis* mentioned in Article 42 of the Constitution. As noted, Article 42 of the Estonian Constitution sets forth that the State agencies, local governments and their officials shall not gather or store information about the beliefs of an Estonian citizen against the citizen's free will. Thus, there is potentially a conflict between these provisions. There is no case law which would clarify how these provisions need to operate together.

83. §8(3) specifies the right to leave a religious community or monastery. A person has the right to leave a congregation if he or she notifies the management board of the congregation of his or her decision beforehand. A similar requirement applies to leaving a monastery. A person has the right to leave a monastery if he or she notifies the superior of the monastery of his or her decision beforehand. The guardian of a person who has been divested of active legal capacity does not have the right to change the religion or membership in a congregation of the person (§8(4)).

84. Members with active legal capacity and who are at least 18 years of age have the right to participate in the election of the management board and officials of a church, congregation or association of congregations, unless a different age limit is provided for in the statutes (§8(5)).

85. The Churches and Congregations Act sets forth that every person has the right to be buried according to his or her confession (§8(6)). In the absence of relatives, guardians or curators, and if it is known that a deceased person was a member of a congregation, the congregation of the deceased person is required to take care of the confessional funeral service (§8(7)).

86. The Churches and Congregations Act also specifies the rights of an individual in medical institutions, educational institutions, social welfare institutions, custodial institutions and military units. Persons staying in named institutions have the right to perform religious rites according to their faith unless this violates public order, health, morals, the rules established in these institutions or the rights of others staying or serving in these institutions.

87. The rights of children are addressed in §10 of the Churches and Congregations Act. Every person of at least 15 years of age may independently become a member of a congregation or leave a congregation pursuant to the procedure prescribed in the statutes of the relevant religious community. A child who is less than 15 years of age may be a member of a congregation with the permission of his or her parents or guardian. This corresponds with obligations of Estonia under the Convention on the Rights of the Child,[137] the Child Protection Act (*lastekaitseseadus*)[138] and with the principle of best interest of a child. However, the previous version of the Child Protection Act was somewhat more specific as to religious freedom explicitly emphasizing the right of a child to freedom of thought, conscience, religion and experience. It also set forth the right and opportunity of a child to seek, receive and impart 'diverse humanistic information' and to engage in organizations and movements.[139]

§2. Case Law

88. There have been only very few court cases involving individual freedom of religion or belief and only seldom a case has reached the Supreme Court. However, in recent years, there seem to have been an increase in certain type of court cases that will be discussed later on. From earlier cases, however, one can point out a case in the Supreme Court that clarified the meaning of conscientious objection in Estonian law. This case was decided by the Criminal Law Chamber of the Supreme Court. This case concerned a person who was avoiding conscription on religious

137. RT II 1996, 16, 56.
138. RT I, 06.12.2014, 1; RT I, 12.12.2018, 3 (last amended), https://www.riigiteataja.ee/en/eli/ee/506052015001/consolide/current, 30 Jan. 2021.
139. Eesti Vabariigi lastekaitse seadus, RT I 1992, 28, 370.

grounds. He refused to do both alternative and military service. The Court found that Article 40 (freedom of religion or belief) of the Constitution does not include the right to refuse alternative service.[140] The Court concluded that, in accordance with Article 124(2) of the Constitution, those who refuse service in the defence forces for religious or ethical reasons are obliged to participate in alternative service. Another case in the Supreme Court was decided in the Administrative Law Chamber. This case concerned a prisoner who demanded solitary confinement, among other things, on the basis of his religion (Buddhism). The Court found that religion, nationality or habits (in this case smoking) cannot be a sole ground for prison authorities to assume that there is a need for solitary confinement.[141]

89. One of the most recent cases in the Supreme Court of Estonia concerned denial of international protection/refugee status to a person who claimed he was religiously persecuted in Uzbekistan due to alleged membership in the Hizb ut-Tahrir.[142] The refusal was considered justified on national security grounds. As noted, Estonia is not yet facing any of the challenges related to the growing Muslim communities experienced in other European countries. However, this does not mean that there is currently no national debate relating to the possible effects of it. Besides legitimate concerns over the capability of the state and society to cope with increasing religious diversity and possible challenges to security, the theme has also been engaged by populists and far-right groups for their political purposes.

90. There seems to be a slight increase in court cases that involve denial of international protection to people who have claimed that they have been persecuted in their countries because of their religion or beliefs. As to lower courts, in 2020, there was a case concerning a Buddhist Sinhalese from Sri Lanka who claimed that he was persecuted in his country because of his support to other religious communities, especially Christians and for belonging to a group called *Sinhal Youth Community*.[143] The court did not find his claim convincing. Without taking a stance on this particular matter, one could notice that the court and authorities were somewhat superficially dealing with the international reports on religious freedom in Sri Lanka that do show serious problems with protecting this freedom.[144]

91. There also seems to be an increase in cases that involve religious freedom in prisons. There have been several cases involving religious dietary requirements. For example, in 2016, there was a case where prison authorities stopped provision of religiously acceptable meals to an inmate because he was seen buying pork meatballs in the prison shop.[145] Later, however, it turned out that the balls consisted of

140. Case No. 3-1-1-82-96, 27 Aug. 1996 (RT III 1996, 23, 312).
141. Case No. 3-3-1-76-11, 19 Jan. 2012.
142. Supreme Court of Estonia, Case No. 3-17-1026, 1 Oct. 2018.
143. Tallinna ringkonnakohus, Case No. 3-19-1901, 18 Jun. 2020.
144. *See*, e.g., Preliminary findings of Country Visit to Sri Lanka by the Special Rapporteur on freedom of religion or belief, 26 Aug. 2019, https://www.ohchr.org/EN/NewsEvents/Pages/DisplayNews.aspx?NewsID=24918&LangID=E, 30 Jan. 2021.
145. Tartu ringkonnakohus, Case No. 3-16-176, 15 Dec. 2016, https://www.riigiteataja.ee/kohtulahendid/fail.html?id=197216024, 30 Jan. 2021.

chicken meat that was in compliance with his religion. Although the authorities remedied the situation, the prisoner applied to the court for the violation of his religious freedom and filed for compensation. The court found his claim unfounded. Notwithstanding the result, the problematic aspect in this case was the fact that the first instance court interpreted freedom of religion to be a purely negative right, meaning no action from the state could be required. This understanding is not completely in line with international understanding of freedom of religion or belief.[146] The district court did not clarify the matter either. In that year there was another case where similar reasoning came up. The case concerned a prisoner who claimed that refusal to give him one day of rest for religious needs was not in compliance with his right to freedom of religion or belief.[147] In 2013 there was a case where a prisoner claimed that his religious freedom was violated by authorities refusing him a meat-free diet.[148] Analogous reasoning was used there as well. The interpretation of international human rights instruments reveals that today freedom of religion is also a positive right, which requires States to commit to something more than just leaving religious individuals or groups alone. What States have to commit themselves to exactly is, however, debatable.[149] Nevertheless, in the cases above, the courts do not seem to take into account developments, for example, in the European Court of Human Rights regarding positive duties and prisoner's rights.[150]

92. In 2007 there was a case decided by the Tartu District Court that concerned confiscation of candles from a prisoner.[151] The prisoner claimed that his religious belief (Buddhism) requires using (incense) candles. He claimed that prison authorities violated his rights under Article 40 of the Constitution and undermined his dignity. Prison authorities justified their actions on the grounds of prison security. Although not elaborated by the Court, prison security is not listed as one of the limitation grounds in Article 40. It is likely that the Court sees prison security as falling under the umbrella of 'public order' as listed in Article 40 of the Constitution. Furthermore, the District Court gave an opinion on what Buddhism requires. It stated that although candles are an important part of Buddhist rituals, Buddhism does not require a prisoner to burn candles in his cell. With this, it was established that no unreasonable damage was caused to the prisoner. The grounds for restriction (justifications) or proportionality of the measure were not discussed at all. One more observation needs to be added here, which stems from the membership of Estonia to the European Convention of Human Rights. The European Court of Human Rights has stated numerous times that the terms 'manifestation' or 'practice' do not

146. *See*, e.g., Council of Europe, *Guide on Article 9 of the European Convention on Human Rights, Freedom of Thought, Conscience and Religion*, 31 Aug. 2020, 19-20.
147. Tartu ringkonnakohus, Case No. 3-14-52503, 21 Jun. 2016.
148. Tartu ringkonnakohus, Case No. 3-11-2943, 15 Nov. 2013. *See also* Tartu ringkonnakohus, Case No. 3-10-1854, 4 Oct. 2011.
149. M. Kiviorg, *Freedom of Religion or Belief – The Quest for Religious Autonomy* (Oxford: Oxford Research Archive, University of Oxford), 107, https://ora.ox.ac.uk/objects/uuid:6c5916d8-d69d-4f2d-91e5-a5586f8abd4b, 30 Jan. 2021.
150. *See, e.g., Thlimmenos v. Greece* (App. No. 34369/97) (2001) 31 EHRR 411; *Jakóbski v.Poland* (App. No. 18429/06) ECHR 7 Dec. 2010; *Vartic v.Rumenia* (No 2) (App. No. 14150/08) ECHR 17 Dec. 2013. *See also* M. Olesk, 'Usuvabadus vanglas' 10 *Juridica* (2015).
151. Tartu ringkonnakohtu määrus haldusasjas 3-07-701 (2.5.2007).

cover every act which is motivated by religion or belief. Actions which do not actually express a belief cannot be considered to be protected by Article 9 of the European Convention of Human Rights.[152] However, it has also stated that a State's duty of neutrality and impartiality is incompatible with any power on the State's part to assess the legitimacy of religious beliefs or the ways in which those beliefs are expressed.[153] Some contradiction with this latter requirement can be seen in the aforementioned Estonian case. Although the outcome of the case would have probably been the same, instead of assessing what is required by Buddhist belief, the Estonian court should have focussed on the proportionality of the restriction vis-à-vis the protection of prison security/public order. Another case with the same matter came to court in 2010.[154]

93. As noted above, in addition to Article 40 of the Constitution, religious practices in prisons are regulated by the Churches and Congregations Act (§9). According to the Churches and Congregations Act, prisoners have the right to perform religious rites according to their faith unless this exercise violates public order, health, morals, the rules established in these institutions or the rights of others staying or serving in these institutions. §62 of the Imprisonment Act (*Vangistusseadus*) states that a prison board has to provide for the religious needs of a prisoner.[155]

152. *See* P. van Dijk & G.J.H. van Hoof, *Theory and Practice of the European Convention on Human Rights*, 3rd edn (The Hague: Kluwer Law International, 1998), 549.
153. *Church of Scientology Moscow v. Russia* (App. No. 18147/02) ECHR 24 Sep. 2007, para. 72; *Metropolitan Church of Bessarabia v. Moldova* (App. No. 45701/99) (2002) 35 EHRR 13, para. 123.
154. Tartu ringkonnakohus, Case No. 3-09-1822, 12 Nov. 2010; *see also* Tallinna ringkonnakohus, Case No. 3-08-286, 4 Mar. 2009.
155. RT I 2000, 58, 376; RT I, 06.05.2020, 1 (last amended), https://www.riigiteataja.ee/en/eli/ee/513052020005/consolide/current, 30 Jan. 2021.

Chapter 2. Collective Religious Freedom

94. As noted above, collective freedom of religion or belief is protected by Article 40 of the Estonian Constitution, which sets forth that everyone has the freedom to practise his or her religion, both alone and in a community with others, in public or in private, unless this is detrimental to public order, health or morals.[156] It should be emphasized that in order to enjoy collective freedom of religion or belief registration of the community is not required. There are religious communities which do not want to obtain legal personality. However, as a rule, most religious communities prefer to obtain some sort of legal personality. This option is seen as useful for everyday functioning of a religious community and for a meaningful and effective communal enjoyment of freedom of religion or belief. Ferrari points out that:

> As a rule, religious activities such as gathering for prayer etc. can be performed without the need for any legal organization: but … the inability to obtain legal personality can indirectly affect religious liberty when it prevents the religious community from owning or renting a place of worship, opening a bank account etc.[157]

95. In an Estonian context, there is no restriction as such on a non-registered religious community to conduct religious meetings or ceremonies at somebody's home or rented premises. According to the law, collective freedom of religion or belief can only be restricted if it is detrimental to public order, health or morals and violates the rights and freedoms of others.

96. One more issue in relation to protection of collective religious freedom and minority religions should be mentioned here, particularly in light of its close connection to the cultural autonomy of national minorities. When Estonia ratified the Council of Europe's Framework Convention on the Protection of National Minorities, it declared that members of the national minorities must be citizens of Estonia. In Estonia, minorities who are registered in the national register of national minorities may submit an application for national cultural autonomy (self-government).[158] The autonomy granted would include, in particular, the right to organize education in their mother tongue and form minority cultural institutions, and also the preservation of their distinctive religion. The monitoring bodies of the convention have suggested that the National Minorities Cultural Autonomy Act (*Vähemusrahvuse kultuuriautonoomia seadus*) contains elements that are not suited to the present situation of minorities in Estonia and needs to be revised or replaced in order for it to

156. *See* Part I, Ch. 1 above.
157. S. Ferrari, 'Religious Communities as Legal Persons: An Introduction to the National Reports', in *Churches and Other Religious Organisations as Legal Persons*, ed. L. Friender (Leuven: Peeters, 2007), 5.
158. National Minorities Cultural Autonomy Act (*Vähemusrahvuse kultuuriautonoomia seadus*), RT I 1993, 71, 1001; RT I, 13.03.2019, 2 (last amended), https://www.riigiteataja.ee/en/eli/ee/5040420 19005/consolide/current, 30 Jan. 2021.

be effective.[159] This pertains in particular to the application of the act only to citizens. Religious minorities can, however, also associate under the 2002 Churches and Congregations Act or the Non-profit Organizations Act in order to enjoy their collective freedom of religion or belief. The limitation of the right to form cultural autonomies only to citizens is controversial, especially in the context of Estonia where a significant number of non-citizens have been residing for a long time. However, one of the reasons for limiting cultural self-government only to citizens is probably a result of the loyalty concerns of the Russian-speaking population and from concerns of preserving the Estonian language. This limitation has caused frustration particularly among the Russian-speaking population and has definitely not contributed to the promotion of tolerance in Estonian society. It should be noted, however, that non-citizens can participate in the activities of national cultural autonomies. They cannot found cultural self-governments or actively participate in the election of governing bodies of the organization. More than 3000 persons are needed for the formation of a cultural autonomy.[160]

97. Interestingly, the first National Minorities Cultural Autonomy Act was adopted in Estonia as early as 1925[161] and was quite unique in Europe at that time. According to that law, all the largest minorities were entitled to form cultural autonomies (self-governing organizations). At that time the largest national minorities were German, Russian, Swedish and Jewish. The right to cultural self-government was granted to Germans in 1925, and Jews in 1926. Swedish and Russian communities did not manage to create their cultural self-governments before 1940.[162] However, as these communities were geographically located in certain areas, it was easy for them to manage problems related to their minority status through respective local governments (for the Russian community this holds true even today). All cultural self-governments were liquidated in 1940 by the Soviet authorities.

159. Advisory Committee on the Framework Convention for the Protection of National Minorities: Opinion on Estonia, Adopted on 14 Sep. 2001, Council of Europe, ACFC/INF/OP/I(2002)005.
160. For further discussion *see, e.g.*, A. Aidarov, W. Drechsler, 'The Law & Economics of the Estonian Law on Cultural Autonomy for National Minorities and of Russian National Cultural Autonomy in Estonia' *Halduskultuur* Vol 12, No 1 (2011), http://halduskultuur.eu/journal/index.php/HKAC/article/view/52, 30 Jan. 2021.
161. RT 1925, 31, 32.
162. Kultuuriministeerium, www.kul.ee/index.php?path=0x2x1424x1431, 1 May 2010.

Chapter 3. Organizational Religious Freedom

98. Organizational religious freedom is first of all protected by Article 40 of the Constitution. Article 9(2) of the Constitution specifies that the rights, freedoms and duties set out in the Constitution shall extend to legal persons insofar as this is in accordance with the general aims of legal persons and with the nature of such rights, freedoms and duties. In fact the constitutional protection enshrined in Article 9(2) extends to legal bodies which do not have full legal capacity as legal persons.[163] Thus the term 'legal person' in Article 9(2) may encompass religious communities without formal legal personality. This is in line with the interpretation of Article 34 of the European Convention on Human Rights,[164] which allows applications to the Court from any person, non-governmental organization or group of individuals claiming to be the victim of a violation of the rights set forth in the Convention or in the Protocols. Article 9(2) provides the same protection to Estonian and foreign legal persons.

99. As to the requirement that the rights set out in the Constitution shall extend to legal persons insofar as this is in accordance with general aims of legal persons, the 'general aims' does not refer to the aims set forth in the by-laws of religious organizations. The meaning of 'a general aim of legal persons' is broader and refers to the facilitation of individual freedoms through legal persons.[165]

100. As to the nature of rights which can be extended to religious communities, certain rights set forth in the Constitution do not apply to legal persons (including religious organizations). Rights such as the right to life and parental rights obviously do not apply to religious organizations. One can also argue that the right to freedom of conscience and thought cannot be enjoyed by a religious legal person.

163. K. Albi, '§ 9', in *Eesti Vabariigi Põhiseadus: Kommenteeritud väljaanne* [*Commentaries of the Estonian Constitution*], ed. Ü. Madise et al., 5 täiendatud trükk (Tallinn: Juura, 2020), https://pohiseadus.ee, 30 Jan. 2021.

164. European Convention on Human Rights and Fundamental Freedoms (adopted 4 Nov. 1950, entered into force 3 Sep. 1953) 213 UNTS 221 (ECHR).

165. *Eesti Vabariigi Põhiseadus: Kommenteeritud väljaanne* [Commentaries of the Estonian Constitution], 3 täiendatud trükk (Tallinn: Juura, 2012), Art. 9.

Part III. Legal Status of Religious Communities

Chapter 1. Formal Status of Religious Communities

101. The Churches and Congregations Act addresses five different types of religious organizations: (1) churches; (2) congregations; (3) associations of congregations; (4) monasteries; and (5) religious societies. Quite uniquely in Europe, the 2002 CCA gives legal definitions of all five categories of religious organizations. The 2002 CCA regulates the activities of only the first four. The first four are called 'religious associations'. The activities of religious societies are not regulated by the CCA (as special law), but by the Non-profit Organizations Act (*as lex generalis*). The following are the definitions of religious associations as specified by law.

§1. Church

102. A church (*kirik*) is an association of at least three voluntarily joined congregations which has an Episcopal structure and is doctrinally related to three ecumenical creeds or is divided into at least three congregations and which operates on the basis of its statutes, is managed by an elected or appointed management board and is entered in the register (§2(2)).

§2. Congregation

103. A congregation (*kogudus*) is a voluntary association of natural persons who profess the same faith, which operates on the basis of its statutes, is managed by an elected or appointed management board and is entered in the register (§2(3)).

§3. Association of Congregations

104. An association of congregations (*koguduste liit*) is an association of at least three voluntarily joined congregations which profess the same faith and which operates on the basis of its statutes, is managed by an elected or appointed management board and is entered in the register (§2(4)).

§4. MONASTERY

105. A monastery (*klooster*) is a voluntary communal association of natural persons who profess the same faith, which operates on the basis of the statutes of the corresponding church or independent statutes, is managed by an elected or appointed superior of the monastery and is entered in the register (§2(5)).

§5. RELIGIOUS SOCIETY

106. A religious society (*usuühing*) is a voluntary association of natural or legal persons the main activities of which include confessional or ecumenical activities relating to morals, ethics, education, culture and confessional or ecumenical diaconal and social rehabilitation activities outside the traditional forms of religious rites of a church or congregation and which need not be connected with a specific church, association of congregations or congregation (§4(1)).

107. In Estonia the term '*kirik*' (Church, *Kirche*) has been traditionally used for Christian organizations. The 2002 Churches and Congregations Act defines the term in line with the tradition. Only Christian organizations can use that term by-law. The reference to three ecumenical creeds (Apostles' Creed, Nicene Creed and Athanasian Creed) determines this clearly. The term '*kogudus*' (Congregation) has been traditionally used for congregations of a church. Before the adoption of the 1993 Churches and Congregations Act, there was a debate as to whether the extension of the term '*kogudus*' (congregation) to other faiths would be insulting for them. The same definition is included in the 2002 Churches and Congregations Act. A Congregation can be an association of natural persons confessing the Christian faith or any other religion or belief. It can be concluded that the law defines the term 'congregation' in contradiction with tradition. It should be noted, however, that the Ministry of Internal Affairs has been of the opinion that the term '*kogudus*' has a broad meaning and is adequate for non-Christian communities.[166]

108. The terminology used in the law was contested by non-Christian communities. After the adoption of the 2002 Churches and Congregations Act, accusations were made that the law employs Christian terminology even though such terminology does not directly apply and may be alien to non-Christian religious organizations. This was brought to the attention of the Chancellor of Justice by non-Christian religious organizations. They claimed that imposition of the terminology on non-Christian religions by the legislator is unconstitutional and restricts their

166. Official Correspondence between the Ministry of Internal Affairs and the Chancellor of Justice, Letter of Ministry of Internal Affairs to Chancellor of Justice, 4 Jul. 2002 No. 10.3-3-4-/6715.

freedom of religion.[167] It should be mentioned that this was also viewed as an intrusion into their autonomy in choosing their own name.[168] Although the law gives broader meaning to the term 'congregation', it has not changed its traditional connotation in society. The main problem was that, according to the Churches and Congregations Act, the official name of a religious association had to include the corresponding word '*kirik*' (church), '*kogudus*' (congregation), '*koguduste liit*' (association of congregations) or '*klooster*' (monastery).[169] The law was amended and religious associations are now entitled to use their historical names instead of Christian terminology imposed by the 2002 Churches and Congregations Act (§7(1)) before the amendment.[170]

109. During the first independence period (1918–1940), the legislature did not find it necessary to give definitions of different religious communities. The 1925 Religious Societies and their Associations Act simply divided all religious organizations into two categories: religious societies and associations of religious societies. Under that law, churches were associations of religious societies. Similarly, the 1934 Act did not try to give legal definitions of different religious organizations. It was up to each religious organization to decide whether it wanted to be a church, religious society or an association of religious societies and organize itself accordingly.[171]

110. The peculiar fact is that the purpose of the legal definitions of the 1993 Churches and Congregation Act was explained as educational. It has been argued that as Estonia had been a so-called atheist country for fifty years, people had forgotten the basic terms and it was necessary to educate them with the help of the law. The same explanation was put forward for including the definitions in the 2002 Churches and Congregations Act. The Ministry of Internal Affairs has stated that this is a transitional law and can be changed in the future when the legal definitions used have found acceptance in society.[172] However, it should be said that the necessity for the legal definitions and their purpose are dubious. The Ministry of Internal Affairs has also provided an additional, more adequate explanation for legal definitions. The purpose of legal definitions is also to distinguish religious organizations from other legal persons.[173] However, whether detailed definitions are necessary for that purpose is also debatable. Recently the detailed definitions have

167. Petition to Check the Constitutionality of §2, §7 and §11 of the Churches and Congregation Act, Registered No. 1-14/158, 22 May 2002, Office of Chancellor of Justice.
168. M. Kiviorg, *Expert Opinion on Compatibility of Provisions of the Churches and Congregation Act with the Estonian Constitution* (Office of Legal Chancellor, 2003); Letter of the Chancellor of Justice to the Ministry of Internal Affairs, Letter No 1-14/158 (25 Jun. 2002).
169. M. Kiviorg, Expert Opinion on Compatibility of Provisions of the Churches and Congregation Act with the Estonian Constitution (Office of Legal Chancellor, 2003).
170. RT I 2004, 54, 391.
171. W. Meder, 'Ülevaade Eesti kirikuõigusest' ['Overview of the Estonian Church Law'], *Õigus* 1 (1938): 14.
172. Official Correspondence between the Ministry of Internal Affairs and the Chancellor of Justice, Letter of the Ministry of Internal Affairs to the Chancellor of Justice, 4 Jul. 2002 No. 10.3-3-4-/6715.
173. *Ibid.*

been found unsatisfactory by existing religious associations.[174] Among the reasons is the fact that not all Christian Churches follow the three ecumenical creeds mentioned in the legal definition of a church.

111. A religious association acquires legal capacity when entered in the register of religious associations. As noted above, the law does not prohibit the activities of religious associations which are not registered. Rather, the main disadvantage for these unregistered entities is that they cannot present themselves as legal persons, and therefore cannot exercise their rights or seek the protections accorded to a religious legal entity. Nevertheless, they still enjoy their constitutionally protected collective freedom of religion as a religious group.

112. The register of religious associations is a distinct part of the non-profit associations and foundations register, with regard to which the provisions of legislation concerning the non-profit associations and foundations register apply with differences provided by the 2002 Churches and Congregations Act. Unlike religious associations (i.e., 'church', 'congregation', 'association of congregations' and 'monastery'), religious societies must be registered in the register of non-profit organizations and foundations. Religious societies are treated as regular non-profit organizations.

113. At least twelve adult members who have active legal capacity can found and register a congregation (Churches and Congregations Act, §13(1)). For instance, at least thirty-six members are needed to establish a church, as the legal definition of the church requires a church to have a minimum of three congregations.

114. Congregations which belong to a church or association of congregations need not have legal personality; it is up to the religious association to decide. Moreover, a religious association may have departments and agencies if this is prescribed in the statutes; such departments and agencies are not, however, legal persons. Their competencies are described in the religious associations' statutes.

115. In order to found a religious association, it is necessary for the founders to enter into a memorandum of association. The memorandum should specify the name, seat, address and objectives of the activities of the religious association. The memorandum of an association also has to list the names and residences and the personal identification codes or registry codes of the founders (§11). It should list the names, personal identification codes and residences of the members of the management board. According to the definitions, all religious associations need to have an elected or appointed management board (§23). The management board of a church, congregation or association of congregations should be located in Estonia regardless of the location of its spiritual centre (§6(2)).

174. M. Kiviorg, *Religiooni puudutavate õigusaktide analüüs* (*Analysis of the Laws Regulating Religion*) (Tallinn: Siseministeerium, 2012), https://www.siseministeerium.ee/sites/default/files/dokumendid/Uuringud/Usuyhendused/2012_religiooni_puudutavate_oigusaktide_analuus.pdf, 30 Jan. 2021.

116. Additionally, the founders need to approve the statutes (by-laws) of their religious association. The statutes are among the required documents for registration. The by-law has to specify the name and the seat (location) of the religious association. It also needs to clarify the objective and doctrinal basis of intended activities and list obligatory religious rites. As to the management of the religious association, the by-law needs to give the structure of management bodies and supervisory bodies and the procedure for the foundation, competence and terms of authority thereof. The procedure for the election or appointment of members of the management board and restrictions on the right of representation also need to be laid out in the statutes. The statutes need to describe the status, hierarchy, service relationships and professional attire of the ministers of religion (§12).

117. As to membership, the statutes need to provide the conditions of and procedure for membership in the religious association and for leaving and excluding from the religious association. Furthermore, it needs to specify the rights and obligations of members or the procedure for the establishment of obligations for members.

118. According to the Churches and Congregations Act the objective or main activity of churches, congregations, associations of congregations and monasteries should not be the earning of income from economic activity (§3(2)). For example, the minister whose area of government includes management of issues relating to religious associations will request compulsory dissolution of a religious association from a court if economic activity becomes the main activity of the religious association. In principle, it is possible for a religious organization to register itself as a profit-making organization. However, in that case, it would not be able to present itself as a religious association or religious society as defined in the Churches and Congregations Act. It would also not be able to enjoy benefits which follow from being a non-profit organization.

119. In the current law there is no difference in registration of emerging religious entities and historical majority churches. So far there have been no major problems in practice either. With one exception, there are no cases inhibiting registration or activities of so-called non-traditional or new religious movements (NRM) and there is only one case where a traditional religious community encountered problems with registration.

120. The problems related to registration of the Estonian Orthodox Church of Moscow Patriarchate were introduced in the General Introduction of this monograph. Another incident involved Satanists in Estonia. First, a couple of general remarks need to be made about this community. According to the census carried out in 2000, forty-three people declared themselves to be Satanists (out of forty-three there were thirty-six men, thirty of them under the age of 24). They lived mostly in urban areas and were native Estonians.[175] According to the 2011 census 120 people

175. Statistical Office of Estonia, 2000 Population and Housing Census: Education. Religion (Tallinn: Statistical Office, 2002), 292.

identified themselves as Satanists.[176] Ringvee points out that it is difficult to determine when Satanism emerged in Estonia, but it seems to relate to the heavy metal rock music scene in the mid-1980s and early 1990s.[177]

121. In the early 1990s, there were a few incidents of graveyard vandalism, and two more serious crimes alleged to be related to Satanism. Although Satanist symbols were used, these crimes were committed by youths without much knowledge of Satanism as a religion or belief. In the late 1990s, a more organized form of Satanism started to emerge, partly to counter public opinion which linked Satanism to those crimes earlier in the decade. It seems that the Satanist community clearly wanted to distance itself from these incidents. In 1999, for the first time, the Estonian Satanist Church, Musta Veenuse Ordu (that's how they identified themselves) made enquiries about official registration. This triggered a lively debate in the media. As Satanists did not proceed with the official registration the public lost interest until 2001 when the group expressed their interest to register their community for the second time. When the news about possible registration hit the media in 2001 Christian organizations and some political parties reacted negatively to the possibility of registration of the Satanist community. For example, the Estonian Council of Churches announced already in 1995 that destructive communities including Satanists should be banned in Estonia.[178] The same year the former prime minister expressed his opinion in an interview that if Satanist sects are going to emerge he would not call them a 'religion' and would draw a clear line in this case.[179] These early reactions can also be attributed to general phobia against the emergence of so-called NRMs in Estonia after the collapse of the Soviet Union. Although no serious anti-cult movements appeared in Estonia there were negative responses to activities of NRMs similar to reactions in some other Western and Eastern-European states.[180] In this atmosphere certain paragraphs were added to the 2002 CCA, which was under preparation. As noted earlier, the 2002 law provides an option to suspend registration proceedings to request the opinion of the ministry with responsibility for those issues relating to religious associations or, in the alternative, the registrar may request an expert opinion from another competent agency. According to the explanatory note, which accompanied the law when it was sent to Parliament, the necessity for this *ex ante* control stems from the spread of fundamentalist and secularized religious organizations in the world. In the course of drafting the law another safeguard was felt to be necessary. Namely, the 2002 CCA repeats the limitation clauses built into the Estonian Constitution.

---

176. Population and Housing Census 2011, http://www.stat.ee/phc2011, 1 May 2014.
177. R. Ringvee, 'Satanism in Estonia', in *Contemporary Religious Satanism: A Critical Anthology*, ed. J. Aagaard Petersen (Surrey: Ashgate, 2008), 130.
178. *Ibid.*, 135.
179. A. Türnpu, 'Interview with Mart Laar', *Elu Sõna Leht. Valimiste Extra*, February 1995.
180. The expression 'New Religious Movements (NRM)' here does not mean necessarily absolute or world novelty, but rather novelty in Estonia or Europe (in this sense it includes, for example, nineteenth-century communities such as Jehovah's Witnesses or the Bahá'í. It is not used as a pejorative term. The choice of the term seeks to emphasize neutrality and is preferred to terms such as 'sects' or 'cults' which seem to have clearly negative connotation in Europe.

122. During the unofficial consulting process the Satanist community submitted their registration documents and by-laws for review by the Religious Affairs Department of the Ministry of Internal Affairs. The Religious Affairs Department pointed out some of the contradictions of their-by law with the Churches and Congregations Act. For example, in their early by-law they used the term '*kirik*' (Church) in their name.[181] As described above, this term is reserved only for Christian churches. It was suggested that they would use the term '*kogudus*' (Congregation) instead, as it has a broad meaning in the law. The Religious Affairs Department was not against the registration as such. The head of the department, Mr Au expressed his view that the community should better be registered than non-registered, adding that it is better to have the community out in the open than underground.[182] In 2002 the Estonian Satanist Congregation filed official registration application with the Ministry of Internal Affairs Department of Religious Affairs. As noted above, before the adoption of the 2002 CCA the department was in charge of the registry. The Ministry of Internal Affairs pointed out some formal deficiencies in the by-laws, but did not *per se* refuse to register the congregation. After the strong public reaction, the Satanists decided not to go ahead with their application. However, in 2003 the group decided to proceed with official registration as an ordinary non-profit organization. This registration failed. The registration department of the Tallinn City Court came to a controversial conclusion that the name of the organization was misleading.[183]

123. In 2005 the Congregation applied to the Tallinn City Court to be registered as a religious association. This application also failed. The reasons given, however, were very different from the previous instances. The court argued that the Satanist Congregation is established with the aim to unite people with criminal intent; its existence endangers public order and national security. The court found that beliefs of the Congregations are in contradiction with the Penal Law and Article 48 (freedom of association) of the Constitution. The court based its arguments mainly on the fact that the basis of the Congregation's beliefs is Anton Sandor LaVey's Satanic Bible and Eleven Satanic Rules. Both of which, in the court's view, are provocative and include texts which incite hatred and violence. The court emphasized that according to the Estonian Constitution it is prohibited to incite religious violence or hatred, incite hatred or discriminate between different segments of society. It also pointed out that refraining from torture, inhuman and degrading treatment or punishment is valued in democratic society. It found that Satanic ideology does not respect other people's freedoms and rights as set forth in the Constitution (namely dignity, prohibition of torture and cruelty). Satanists contested the decision. The review of the initial decision did not give different results and the court's argument remained the same, however, there were some additional points. The court substantiated its arguments with expert opinions from the University of Tartu and from the Ministry of Justice, the first of which pointed out that Satanic Bible has a chapter on human sacrifice. The court generalized, without concrete examples, that although

181. 'Satanistid tahavad end legaliseerida', *Eesti Päevaleht (ETA)*, 23 Apr. 2001. www.epl.ee/ artikkel /157410, 1 May 2010.
182. *Ibid.*
183. Musta Veenuse Ordu, http://liin.saadanas.org, 1 May 2014.

human sacrifice is very rare in the Satanist community, it has happened. It also agreed with the concern expressed in the expert opinion that the philosophy of Satanism may be destructive to mentally unstable people making them potentially dangerous to themselves and others. The Congregation contested these arguments by pointing out that their by-law *expressis verbis* states respect to laws of the Estonian Republic. They also tried to repute the argument on alleged human sacrifice cases by pointing out crimes that have been committed by Christian communities. This counterargument was seen by the court as irrelevant. The congregation did not appeal the decision.

124. It took several years before the registration issue emerged again. The latest attempt to register was made in 2013 when the Congregation submitted their application to Tartu County Court. The application failed again. However, this time around, the Congregation exhausted all domestic remedies available to them to contest the refusal. It appealed to Tartu District Court[184] and eventually to the Supreme Court,[185] which found their application inadmissible. The Tartu District Court followed the same lines of argumentation as the Tallinn City Court in 2005. The court resorted to literal interpretation of the Satanic Bible and Declarations and found that registering the Congregation may endanger public order, health, morals and rights and freedoms of others. This time the court proceedings were accompanied by three expert opinions written by Dr Merilin Kiviorg from the University of Oxford, Prof. Tarmo Kulmar from the University of Tartu Theology Faculty and Estonian Council of Churches. The court mainly relied on the negative opinion provided by the Estonian Council of Churches. The court came to the conclusion that the word 'Satan' ('saatan') in Estonian cultural and linguistic environment means evil and this meaning does not change when the congregation itself does not associate the word with any wrongdoing. It also pointed out that nowhere in Europe are Satanist's organizations registered. It needs to be noted that the congregation has existed in Estonia at least since 1999. It has been carrying out its activities without legal personality. There have been no criminal cases attributable to its members or to the organization itself. It is a very small community following rational Satanism (as opposed to acidic or theistic Satanism). As emphasized above, religious communities without legal personality are not prohibited under Estonian law. Interestingly, the latest registration cases did not trigger much media attention. There is no public debate currently on this matter. Compared to the early 2000s a change in public attitude appears to have occurred, with acceptance/tolerance or indifference towards Satanists. After exhausting all domestic remedies the Congregation submitted their application to the European Court of Human Rights, which also failed.

125. There are several advantages to being registered as a religious association. Religious associations have more autonomy in their internal affairs than other nonprofit organizations. There are also several financial advantages, which will be described in more detail in Part VIII of this monograph. There are specific advantages regarding religious marriages. Only ministers from churches, congregations

184. Tartu Ringkonnakohus, Kohtumäärus, 25. Nov. 2013, nr. 2-13-24298.
185. Riigikohus, Tsiviilkolleegium, Kohtumäärus, 10. veebruar 2014, nr. 3-7-1-2-1023-13.

and associations of congregations registered under the Churches and Congregations Act may apply for authorization to perform civil marriages. There is also a certain amount of additional autonomy as regards labour laws (this will be discussed in Part VI of this monograph).

126. A further specific advantage in being registered as a religious association regards clothing. The law provides protection of the attire of the ministers and restricts the use of this attire by others. Only a person to whom a religious association has granted corresponding permission has the right to wear the professional attire of a minister of religion prescribed in the statutes of the religious association. The specified restriction does not apply if ordinary clothing is the professional attire of the minister of religion. A religious association whose interests are damaged by the unauthorized use of the professional attire of its minister of religion may demand termination of the unauthorized use of said attire and compensation for any damages caused thereby.

Chapter 2. Autonomy of Religious Communities

127. As stated in Part I, the general right to self-determination of persons (both individuals and groups) stems from Article 19 of the Estonian Constitution. Article 19(1) sets forth that all persons should have the right to free self-realization. It was also noted that the right to religious autonomy is considered to be an essential part of collective freedom of religion. This was explicitly stated in the presidential decision to veto the 2002 Churches and Congregations Act after it was passed for the first time in the Parliament. As explained above, the Churches and Congregations Act regulates activities of religious bodies in Estonia.[186] The presidential decision concerned a provision (Article 14(3)) in the law prohibiting registration of religious communities whose administrative or economic governance takes place or whose decisions are approved by a body outside Estonia. The veto act stated that this provision is not in conformity with Article 40 (freedom of religion or belief) of the Estonian Constitution. It pointed out that there are many religious communities in Estonia, with established hierarchical structures, which would be adversely affected by this provision. It further explained that collective religious autonomy is clearly considered an important part of freedom of religion or belief. The restrictions on this freedom may be implemented only insofar as they are necessary in a democratic society, and their imposition may not distort the nature of the rights and liberties. As many religious communities have a strongly hierarchical structure, imposition of the above restrictions profoundly changes the nature of these communities and thus the nature of collective freedom of religion or belief. It was further pointed out that the previous law[187] did not prohibit registration of such religious communities and there are no obvious reasons to introduce this restriction. The law was subsequently amended by Parliament.[188]

128. As mentioned above, the 2002 Churches and Congregations Act gives considerable leeway for religious associations (churches, congregations and associations of congregations) to organize themselves in accordance with their own teachings and structures.[189] The statutes of a religious association may differ from the provisions of the Non-profit Organizations Act concerning membership and management if such differences arise from the historical teaching and structure of the religious association (§5(2)). Other associations and religious societies registered under the Non-profit Organizations Act do not have the same amount of freedom. The Non-profit Organizations Act prescribes a structure and a mode of (democratic) governance for the organization. Thus, religious associations and religious societies have different degrees of autonomy as to their internal affairs, specifically in their structure and management.[190] Religious societies are treated as

186. RT I 2002, 24, 135.
187. RT I 1993, 30, 510.
188. However, before it came into force on 1 Jul. 2002 it was vetoed once more on different grounds (RTL 2002, 7, 65).
189. *See* Part I, Ch. 2 above.
190. For the definitions of the terms 'religious association' and 'religious society' *see* Part III, Ch. 1 above.

regular non-profit-making organizations and enjoy considerably less autonomy in their internal affairs than do religious associations.

129. Autonomy of religious associations in their internal affairs is generally respected. Obviously there are limits to this autonomy. Some of them are determined by laws applicable to all (such as the Penal Code). There are also some specific restrictions in Estonian law that set limits to appointment of ministers and management boards of religious associations. The law requires that a minister of a religious association be a person who has the right to vote in local government elections (§20(1)). According to the Municipal Council Election Act (*Kohaliku omavalitsuse volikogu valimise seadus*),[191] an Estonian citizen or citizen of the EU has the right to vote if he or she has attained 16 years of age by Election Day and resides permanently in the territory of the local government (§5(1)). An alien has the right to vote if he or she has attained 16 years of age by Election Day, resides permanently in the territory of the local government and resides in Estonia on the basis of a permanent residence permit. The law was changed in 2016.[192] Previously the age limit for all categories of voters at local government elections was 18 years.

130. The requirement for a minister of a religious association to be eligible to vote in local government elections set forth in §20(1) of the CCA is to some degree mitigated by allowing the management board of a religious association to invite a minister of religion from outside Estonia as long as they apply for a work and residence permit for the alien minister of religion pursuant to the provisions of the Aliens Act (*Välismaalaste seadus*).[193] Thus, even if the person does not have the right to vote in the local government elections, he or she may be appointed as a minister if he or she acquires a work or residence permit. Other requirements regarding ministers are set by the religious association itself (Churches and Congregations Act §20(1)).

131. Similarly, until 2012 the law set forth that board members of a religious association have to be people who have the right to vote in local government elections. This provision was pointed out to be in contradiction with the Non-profit Organizations Act and EU law.[194] The Parliament has now adopted necessary amendments. Currently the residence of at least one-half of the members of the management board must be in Estonia, in another Member State of the European Economic Area or in Switzerland (§ 23(2)).[195]

---

191. RT I 2002, 36, 220; RT I, 03.01.2020, 2 (last amended), https://www.riigiteataja.ee/en/eli/ee/521122020001/consolide/current, 30 Jan. 2021.
192. RT I, 22.01.2016, 7.
193. RT I 1993, 44, 637; RT I, 10.07.2020, 4 (last amended), https://www.riigiteataja.ee/en/eli/ee/521072020002/consolide/current, 30 Jan. 2021.
194. *See* M. Kiviorg, *Religiooni puudutavate õigusaktide analüüs* (*Analysis of the Laws Regulating Religion*) (Tallinn: Siseministeerium, 2012), https://www.siseministeerium.ee/sites/default/files/dokumendid/Uuringud/Usuyhendused/2012_religiooni_puudutavate_oigusaktide_analuus.pdf, 30 Jan. 2021.
195. RT I, 18.12.2012, 3 – entry into force 19.12.2012.

132. Another area to which autonomy of religious organizations does not extend is related to accounting and control over financial means. Religious communities do not have exemptions from general accounting obligations and requirements for annual financial reports. Moreover, a review or audit may be called for, pursuant to the procedure established in the statutes. The members of the management board and of other bodies must allow controllers or auditors to examine all documents necessary for conduct of a review or audit and must provide necessary information (Churches and Congregations Act, §26). However, the privacy of members is respected: Article 42 of the Estonian Constitution states that 'state agencies, local governments, and their officials shall not gather or store information about the beliefs of an Estonian citizen against the citizen's free will'.

133. Religious communities have autonomy to regulate their own affairs and their membership. As a rule, religious acts do not have a civil legal effect. Historically, the possibility of enforcing decisions by secular institutions (Ministry of Internal Affairs and the Court) existed under Articles 24 and 25 of the 1934 Act on Churches and Religious Societies.[196] Today this kind of option is not provided by law.

134. The Gender Equality Act (*Soolise võrdõiguslikkuse seadus*) does not apply to the professing and practising of faith, or persons working as ministers of a religion in a registered religious association (§2(2)).[197] Application of the Gender Equality Act will be discussed later on in this monograph.

196. RT 1934, 107, 840.
197. RT I 2004, 27, 181; RT I, 10.01.2019, 2 (last amended), https://www.riigiteataja.ee/en/eli/ee/516012019002/consolide/current, 30 Jan. 2021.

Chapter 3. Fundamental Rights and Religious Communities

135. As specified above, Article 9(2) of the Estonian Constitution sets forth that the rights, freedoms and duties set out in the Constitution extend to legal persons insofar as this is in accordance with the general aims of legal persons and with the nature of such rights, freedoms and duties.[198] Both collective and institutional religious freedom are protected in Estonia (possible tensions between individual and collective rights will be briefly addressed in Part VII of this monograph).

136. A more general observation, however, is necessary here. There is very little case law involving rights of (religious) individuals or religious communities in Estonia. Thus, in many areas of law only speculative observations can be made as to the possible conflicts of interests in the triangle of state, religious communities and/or individuals. However, the lack of cases probably indicates that there are not yet many problems with freedom of religion or belief in Estonia.

137. There have been only very few cases in the Supreme Court of Estonia which have involved fundamental rights of religious communities. One of the first cases to reach the Supreme Court (1993) was the legal succession and property case of the Orthodox community in Estonia (the substance of the conflict was described in the General Introduction of this monograph).[199] The second case was decided by the Constitutional Review Chamber. This case concerned a review of the petition by the President of the Republic to declare the Non-profit Association Act (passed on 1 April 1996) unconstitutional.[200] The third case involved freedom of religion or belief of the community representing Estonian indigenous beliefs and was decided by the Administrative Law Chamber of the Supreme Court.[201] As mentioned before the registration case of Satanist also reached the Supreme Court but did not get permission for litigation.[202]

138. The case in the Administrative Law Chamber dealt with the claim by a religious association called House of Taara and Native Religions (*Härjapea Taarausuliste ja Maausuliste Koda*) that their freedom of religion or belief was restricted by a local government decision to allow wind turbines to be built on their sacred land. The land itself belonged to the local government; however, it was known to be an ancient sacred place of Estonian indigenous believers, and a part of

198. *See* Part II, Ch. 3 above.
199. Eesti Vabariigi Ülemkohus (Supreme Court of Estonia) 1.09.1993. Tsiviilasi nr. 2-3/92 1993, Ülemkohtu tsiviilasjade kohtukolleegium (Civil Chamber), järelvalveprotest Tallinna Linnakohtu otsusele 29.06.1992.a.
200. Riigikohus (Supreme Court of Estonia), Case No. 3-4-1-1-96, 20 Dec. 1996, http://www.nc.ee/?id =471, 1 Sep. 2014. This case was described in Part I, Ch. 2 above.
201. Case No. 3-3-1-39-07, 17 Oct. 2007 (RT III 2007, 36, 291).
202. Riigikohus, Tsiviilkolleegium, Kohtumäärus, 10. veebruar 2014, nr. 3-7-1-2-1023-13.

this area is also listed in the National Register of Cultural Monuments (*Kultuurimälestiste riiklik register*) according to the Heritage Conservation Act (*Muinsuskaitseseadus*) in force until 2019.[203] The main issue regarding freedom of religion or belief was the fact that the local government did not provide reasons for its decision with respect to why it was necessary to limit freedom of religion or belief of this religious community. The Supreme Court decided in favour of the religious community. It found that the local government did not take into consideration proposals made by the community for alternative solutions, it did not provide reasons for its decision and therefore did not substantiate why it was necessary to limit freedom of religion or belief as stipulated in Article 40 of the Estonian Constitution. The Court also found the Court of Appeal observation that the community did not at the time actively carry out religious activities on that sacred land irrelevant.

139. The majority of cases concerning religious communities in lower court instances have been related to land reform and restoration of illegally expropriated property as a result of the land reform initiated at the beginning of the 1990s. As mentioned above, this land reform provides for restitution of property, which was illegally expropriated by the Soviet regime, to individuals and legal entities (including religious communities) who owned the property before 1940 or for adequate compensation.[204] These cases have dealt with injustices caused during the Soviet times and legal disputes regarding claims on property. As a rule, no claims have been raised as to freedom of religion or belief. No reference to Article 40 (freedom of religion or belief) of the Estonian Constitution or international instruments, for example, Article 9 of the ECHR, has been made in these cases. The property dispute between two Orthodox Churches, which was described earlier in this monograph, was only partly resolved in the Court.[205]

140. Collective freedom of religion or belief and the right to assembly were addressed in a case decided by the Harju County Court (local court of first instance, *Harju Maakohus*) in 2006. This case concerned restricting freedom of religion and freedom of assembly on grounds of public order.[206] The case involved a small group of believers who gathered near the Tallinn railway station. They were singing religious songs using microphones and loudspeakers. The organizers of the event did not notify local authorities of the event and did not have permission to carry out this meeting. Although the religious meeting had a peaceful character, it was established that they were obstructing traffic coming into the railway station and that they were disturbing people selling flowers at the market nearby. Organizers of the event were

---

203. RT I 2002, 27, 153; RT I, 21.03.2011, 4 (last amended). The new law adopted in 2019 facilitates the same type of protection to the historical natural sacred sites. Heritage Conservation Act, RT I, 19.03.2019, 13; RT I, 10.12.2020, 1 (last amended), https://www.riigiteataja.ee/en/eli/ee/5131220 20003/consolide/current, 30 Jan. 2021.

204. *See* General Introduction, §2 Social Facts about Religion.

205. *Ibid.*

206. Harju Maakohus, Case No. 4-05-936/1 (25 Oct. 2006).

asked to stop singing; when they disobeyed, six people were arrested. Their activities were found contrary to §7 (1 and 2) of the Public Meetings Act (*Avaliku koosoleku seadus*),[207] in force until 2014,[208] as they were violating public order and obstructing traffic. Neither Article 9 or 11 of the ECHR nor Article 40 or 47 (right to assembly) of the Estonian Constitution was invoked. Article 47 of the Constitution sets forth the right to peaceful assembly and meetings without prior permission. However, this right can be restricted in accordance with the law in order to ensure national security, public order or morals, traffic safety and the safety of the participants in such meetings or to prevent the spread of infectious diseases. There was no elaboration on justifications for and/or proportionality of the restriction. This seems to be the tendency in the case law relating to freedom of religion or belief, at least in the lower courts.

207. RT I 1997, 30, 472; RT I, 23.02.2011, 3 (last amended).
208. RT I, 13.03.2014, 4.

Chapter 4. Contractual Religious Freedom

141. State and Church relations in Estonia are governed not only by general laws but also by formal agreements that are negotiated directly between the Government and religious institutions.[209] Such agreements appear to be becoming an increasingly important way of regulating the relationship between religious communities and the State. As a relatively new way of approaching this relationship in Estonia, this practice is not without difficulties and controversies – mainly as it concerns the equal treatment of religious communities. However, it is important to emphasize that although there is an ongoing tension between Christian, non-Christian communities and secular society, there have been no court cases alleging violation of the principle of equal treatment or state neutrality. In fact there have been no cases involving contractual relationships between state and religious communities.

142. The majority of specific contracts deal with financing of specific projects of religious communities. Generally, these contracts are for fulfilling some public function or goal (e.g., running a kindergarten, training chaplains for public institutions, preservation or research on religiously culturally important objects). Thus, at the basis of the contracts there is some common interest which both the State and religious communities share. However, in some cases, this common interest is only tentative or at least questionable in terms of the principles of state neutrality and non-discrimination. A more detailed account of these contracts will be given in Part VIII (Church Financing) of this monograph.

143. A more general agreement has been concluded between the Estonian Council of Churches and the Estonian Government. This agreement provides a broad basis for specific contracts and cooperation in fields of common interests (education, preservation of culturally important objects, financing, international relations, chaplaincy, etc.). The preamble of the agreement makes some general observations concerning the need for such cooperation. It emphasizes the fact that because of the tragic past of Estonia and atheistic propaganda during the Soviet occupation there is a serious lack of knowledge about and interest in spiritual matters. The role of education about different religions and the importance of integration of different segments of society are also stressed, and ecumenical/Christian cooperation is seen as a leading force in helping to solve many of these problems. A more scientific goal is also put forward, namely to conduct research on the current state of and changes in religious/spiritual needs and values of the Estonian population. The preamble declares that the future of the State and the nation depend on the quality of the next generation, and in this regard devotion to family and working with youth carries special importance. Hence it is quite a significant agreement, which involves cooperation in citizenship building. This agreement has not been favourably looked upon by non-Christian communities. Political debates over this cooperation will be discussed in Part V below.

---

209. *See* Part I, Ch. 2 above.

144. The activities of the Roman Catholic Church in Estonia are regulated by international treaty between Estonia and the Holy See. On 2 May 1995, the Apostolic Administration of the Roman Catholic Church was entered onto the church register with the Religious Affairs Department of the Ministry of Internal Affairs. The Ministry of Foreign Affairs in cooperation with the Religious Affairs Department of the Ministry of Internal Affairs prepared an agreement between the Republic of Estonia and the Holy See on the legal status of the Catholic Church, which came into force via an exchange of notes on 12 March 1999.[210] The agreement sets the legal arrangement between Estonia and the Vatican. In order to resolve some issues that became apparent when the 2002 Churches and Congregations Act entered into force, the Ministry of Internal Affairs developed an amendment to the law, which came into force on 12 February 2011.[211]

145. A few cooperation agreements have been concluded at the local government level with different religious communities (mainly with Christian churches) mostly in the area of social care and renovation of sacral objects. Interestingly it has been pointed out that at the local level agreements very much depend on the personal relationships between representatives of local churches and governments. These relationships may have both negative and positive impact on achieving agreements or cooperation at the local level.[212]

210. RT II, 22. 04.1999, 7, 47.
211. Rooma – Katoliku Kirik, https://www.katoliku.ee/index.php/et/uudised/vaelismaa/193-vatikan-pueha-tool-diplomaatilised-ja-kultuurisuhted-pueha-tooli-ning-eesti-vahel, 1 Apr. 2021.
212. R. Ringvee, Riik ja relgioon nõukogudejärgses Eestis 1991-2008 (Dissertationes Theologiae Universitatis Tartuensis, 2012), 51; S. Grasmann, Religioossete organisatsioonide roll tänapäeva Eesti kodanikuühiskonnas, Empiiriline uuring (Bakalaureusetöö, Tartu Ülikool, 2007).

Part IV. International, Transnational, Regional Effects on Religious Communities

Chapter 1. International Law Effects on Religious Communities

146. Article 3 of the Estonian Constitution stipulates that universally recognized principles and norms of international law shall be an inseparable part of the Estonian legal system.[213] The prevailing view among scholars is that Article 3 of the Estonian Constitution adopts the universally recognized principles and norms of international law into the Estonian legal system and makes them both superior in force to national legislation and binding on the exercise of legislative, administrative and judicial powers.[214] Article 3 incorporates only international customary norms and general principles of law into the Estonian legal system.

147. As mentioned above, international treaties ratified by parliament are incorporated into the Estonian legal system by Article 123(2) of the Constitution.[215] According to Article 121 the Parliament ratifies treaties:

(1) which alter state boundaries;
(2) the implementation of which requires the passage, amendment or repeal of Estonian laws;
(3) by which the Republic of Estonia joins international organizations or unions;
(4) by which the Republic of Estonia assumes military or proprietary obligations; and
(5) in which ratification is prescribed.

148. Article 123(2) also establishes the hierarchy of these treaties, stating that if Estonian acts or other legal instruments contradict foreign treaties ratified by the *Riigikogu* (Parliament), the provisions of the foreign treaty shall apply. This rule of superiority of foreign treaty law over domestic legislation also applies to internal

213. *See* Part I, Ch. 1 above.
214. K. Merusk & R. Narits, *Eesti Konstitutsiooniõigusest* [*About Estonian Constitutional Law*] (Tallinn: Juura, 1998).
215. *See* Part I, Ch.1I above.

laws enacted after the ratification of the treaty. The Constitution does not say anything about the legal position in the hierarchy of norms of international treaties concluded by the Estonian government, but not ratified by the Parliament. In practice, many such international treaties exist and the majority view among legal scholars is that these treaties have the same position in the norm hierarchy as international treaties ratified by Parliament. This interpretation is also in conformity with the international obligations of Estonia under the 1969 Vienna Convention on the Law of Treaties.[216]

149. Implementation of international norms in Estonia can take place in three different ways: (1) international norms are directly applied; (2) international norms and their interpretation on the international level are used for interpretation of similar norms in domestic law; (3) international law is used to check the conformity of domestic norms with international norms. A fourth option – permitting executive acts to be taken directly on the basis of international law – is not permitted by the Estonian Constitution.[217] The Constitution establishes the principle of legality. All executive acts have to be based on the Constitution and laws; the Executive Branch enforces the laws and the Executive Branch only has a law-making function if one is delegated to it by the Parliament (Articles 87(6) and 94(2)).

150. Article 123(1) of the Estonian Constitution forbids the Estonian Republic to conclude treaties which contradict the Constitution. The constitutional review of Estonian laws or foreign treaties is carried out by the Supreme Court of Estonia, either in the constitutional review chamber or by the Court in plenary session. A constitutional review of Estonian legal acts can be started by ordinary courts as well as by the President, Chancellor of Justice, and the councils of local governments. A constitutional review of international treaties before enforcement of their ratification laws can be started by the President. A constitutional review of enforced international treaties, ratified by Parliament or concluded by the Estonian Government, can be started by the Chancellor of Justice or by any ordinary court.

151. According to Article 15(3) of the Constitutional Review Act (*Põhiseaduslikkuse järelevalve kohtumenetluse seadus*), if the Supreme Court of Estonia finds that an international treaty or any provision is in contradiction with the Constitution, the executive agency that concluded the treaty must, if possible, withdraw from the treaty or initiate the denunciation or an amendment to the treaty in order to conform to the Constitution (§15(3)).[218] An international treaty in violation of the Constitution cannot be applied domestically.[219] As Estonia is a party to the 1969 Vienna Convention on the Law of Treaties, national law cannot be invoked as a reason for

216. L. Mälksoo et al, .'Välissuhted ja välislepingud' in Ü Madise jt (toim), *Eesti Vabariigi põhiseadus. Kommenteeritud väljaanne* (Juura 2017) paras 5–6; K. Merusk & R. Narits, *Eesti Konstitutsiooniõigusest* [*About Estonian Constitutional Law*] (Tallinn: Juura, 1998), 26–32.
217. M. Kiviorg, et al., *Rahvusvaheline õigus* [Public International Law] 4th edn (Tallinn: Juura, 2010), 64–70.
218. RT I 2002, 29, 174; RT I, 07.03.2019, 1 (last amended), https://www.riigiteataja.ee/en/eli/ee/512122019006/consolide/current, 30 Jan. 2021.
219. *Ibid.*

failure to perform a treaty obligation as part of Estonia's foreign affairs.[220] A treaty proclaimed unconstitutional will thus remain internationally binding on Estonia until the withdrawal from the treaty in accordance with international law or the conclusion of negotiations amending the treaty.

152. As mentioned above, Estonia is a member of many international organizations, including the United Nations, Council of Europe, OSCE and NATO, and has ratified key conventions protecting freedom of religion or belief.[221] In the European context the most important instrument guaranteeing freedom of religion or belief is probably the ECHR. Estonia became a member of the Council of Europe on 14 May 1993. The same day Estonia signed the European Convention for Fundamental Rights and Freedoms. The Estonian Parliament ratified the ECHR on 13 March 1996.[222] The letters of ratification were deposited on 16 April 1996. The Convention became legally binding for Estonia from that date.

153. The ECHR is part of the Estonian legal system and is directly applicable. Prior to ratification of the ECHR, the courts had already used the ECHR and its practices for interpretation of domestic legislation or even in obiter dictum.[223] There is also a growing number of cases involving Estonia coming before the European Court of Human Rights. However, none of these cases have been concerned with freedom of religion or belief under Article 9 or under related articles of the Convention.

154. The ECHR is the international treaty most frequently referred to in Estonian courts. In the Supreme Court of Estonia references to the ECHR constitute approximately 60% of the total references in the court's decisions on international treaties. However, in freedom of religion cases, Article 9 or related articles of the Convention have not been directly invoked. As was discussed above, there have been only a few cases directly or indirectly involving freedom of religion or belief. In comparison with the references to the ECHR and also EU law, UN human rights treaties have been referenced seldom. No reference to Article 18 of the ICCPR or other relevant articles has been made.[224] In addition to international treaties, the human rights documents of international organizations have also been referred to in court cases.[225] None of these references have involved freedom or religion or belief. However, the quality of application of international law by the Supreme Court has increased from year to year.

---

220. Vienna Convention on the Law of Treaties, RT II 1993, 16.
221. *See* General Introduction, §1 General Background of the Country.
222. RT II 1996, 11/12, 34.
223. H. Vallikivi, 'Euroopa inimõiguste konventsiooni kasutamine Riigikohtu praktikas' ['Use of the European Convention on Human Rights in the Practice of the Supreme Court'], *Juridica* IV (2001): 401.
224. *See also* M. Kiviorg, 'Estonia', in *The impact of the United Nations Human Rights Treaties on the Domestic Level*, ed. C. Heyns & F. Viljoen (The Netherlands: Brill, 2021, forthcoming).
225. *See, e.g.*, Constitutional Review Chamber of the Supreme Court of Estonia, Case No. III-4/A- 5/94, 30 Sep. 1994, www.nc.ee/english/, 1 May 2010.

155. Thus, in principle, religious communities can take advantage of the protection provided by international law, including the European Convention of Human Rights. Although international law has been used in litigation, it seems however that the knowledge and availability of international norms that communities can refer to for the protection of their freedom of religion or belief is still not sufficient.[226] This can be one of the reasons why almost no cases on freedom of religion or belief refer, for example, to the ECHR. It could also be one of the reasons that there are only a few cases involving freedom of religion or belief generally. People simply are not aware of their rights. Moreover, since regaining independence international law training of the legal community has been a high priority. However, the application of international norms in litigation has come about gradually. This can also be explained by the rapid and constant changes in domestic legislation in all fields of law.[227] The legal community, which could be of help to people in the protection of freedom of religion or belief, has simply been overburdened keeping up with changes in domestic law. Additionally, it is not customary to resort to the court: most problems tend to be solved through negotiation and in administrative practice. Thus, there are many factors which influence the application of international norms. However, the lack of usage or interest in international law may also indicate that there are no major problems regarding freedom of religion or belief in Estonia.

226. This in principle, has been pointed out also in the latest concluding observations on Estonia of the UN Human Rights Commitee. *See* HRC, CCPR/C/EST/CO/4, 26 Mar. 2019.

227. *See* Part I, Ch. 2 above.

Chapter 2. Transnational Law Effects on Religious Communities

156. Estonia joined the EU on 1 May 2004. Prior to joining the EU, Estonia needed to amend its Constitution. With the referendum on 14 September 2003, the people of Estonia adopted the following amendments to the Estonian Constitution:

> Estonia may belong to the European Union in accordance with the fundamental principles of the Constitution of the Republic of Estonia. The Constitution of the Republic of Estonia applies taking account of the rights and obligations arising from the Accession Treaty.[228]

157. This means, in principle, that the law of the EU takes precedence over Estonian law, as long as it does not contradict the Estonian Constitution's basic principles. Before 1 May 2004, European law affected Estonia by means of the association agreement (Europe Agreement) concluded between the European Community (and its Member States) and the Estonian Republic, which came into force on 1 February 1998.[229] Because it was ratified by the Parliament, the Europe Agreement, according to Article 123(2) of the Constitution, took precedence over domestic legislation. It was viewed as an ordinary international treaty.[230] Apart from the agreement, European Community law was not directly applicable before Estonia achieved membership status in the EU. Nevertheless, even before membership in the EU was finalized, Estonia assumed the obligation to bring Estonian law in line with European Community legislation, making decisions of the European Court of Justice an important consideration.[231]

158. The effects of EU law in specific areas will be discussed when necessary under relevant themes in this monograph.

228. Amendments to the Constitution of the Estonian Republic, RT I 2003, 64, 429.
229. Europe Agreement, RT II 1995, 22–27, 120.
230. *See* J. Laffranque, 'Eesti assotsiatsioonileping Euroopa Liiduga' ['Estonia's Association Agreement with the European Union: Legal and Constitutional Aspects'], *Juridica* IV (2000): 233.
231. The decisions of the European Court of Justice were considered persuasive (but not binding) authority and a source of legal values.

Chapter 3. Regional Law Effects on Religious Communities

159. As Estonia is a politically unitary state, the law governing religious communities is adopted at the state level. However, decisions of local governments may affect the everyday life of religious communities, for example, regarding planning permissions, renovation of sacral objects and social work.

Part V. Religion and Politics

Chapter 1. Religious Influence in Politics

160. As indicated at the very beginning of this monograph, when the Estonian Constitutional Assembly held heated discussions over each provision and meaning of the draft Constitution of the Republic of Estonia (after the collapse of the Soviet Union), there were no real discussions about the provisions relating to freedom of religion or belief and State and Church relationships. It was not considered one of the priorities. However, clerics and lay members of different denominations were politically active in the process of regaining independence and they contributed to the re-building of the Estonian legal system (it has been observed, however, that hardly any EELC leaders directly participated in this process; at the same time Orthodox leaders were directly involved in it[232]). It is probably correct to say that at the time contribution of religious leaders in politics was very much appreciated and not disputed at all. Social attitudes at the beginning of the 1990s were generally more favourable to religion. As noted previously, after regaining independence Estonia experienced what can be called a 'return of religion' or 'church boom', which was partly an expression of national identity and partly a reaction to suppression of freedom of religion by the Soviet regime. Many joined religious organizations at that time. This enthusiasm, however, did not last long. The period of religious enthusiasm and growth of membership of religious communities in the first half of the 1990s was followed by relative indifference to religion, a high level of secularization, as well as growing individualization of religious beliefs (as mentioned above, according to recent statistics about 58% of people questioned say they have individual beliefs non-dependent on any religious community). There has been growth in the number and diversity of registered religious organizations, but not in the overall religious affiliation of the population. Against this background it should not be surprising that political parties with clear identification with ethos or beliefs of any religious community have had very low impact in politics and government. Furthermore, for example, during the period leading up to 2013 local government elections and 2014 European Parliament elections religious affiliations or beliefs of candidates were not emphasized or discussed. This in fact could be said to be a general trend at any elections up to now. Political parties' manifestos, apart from one, do not mention or emphasize Christian or other religious traditions when proposing solutions to specific problems that Estonian society faces. However, certain issues

232. R. Saard, 'Eestlane ja luterlus II', *Akadeemia* 7 (2007): 1436.

involving human rights protection such as same-sex marriage, hate speech, new religious movements, immigration and asylum policies (e.g., in connection with events in Ukraine and Syria), have been hotly disputed both within different parties and religious circles. The input of religious organizations and party members personal beliefs into these disputes has been highly visible.

161. Today, clerics participate in different political parties. It is considered a normal aspect of democratic society. The membership of clerics and church leaders in political parties does not seem to depend on whether the party has a religious ethos or not. They have been represented on the lists of different parties at local government elections (e.g., in October 2005[233], October 2009[234], October 2013, October 2017) and Parliament elections. Thirteen clerics were elected to local governments in 2009[235] and fifteen in 2013. There were no clerics elected to the Parliament in 2014 elections.[236] Only a few clerics have been elected to leading positions in local governments.[237] In comparison with the 1990s there seems to be a decline in the number of clerics who are willing to be elected to representative bodies. Some previously politically active clerics have themselves noted that there is a need to keep neutral to give a message to people that everybody is welcome in the church.[238]

162. Before returning to the question about religious influence in politics, more information is probably needed as to the political landscape of Estonia. Pursuant to the Riigikogu Election Act (*Riigikogu valimise seadus*),[239] a required 5% threshold was exceeded by four political parties at the March 2011 elections: (1) Estonian Reform Party (*Eesti Reformierakond*);[240] (2) Estonian Centre Party (*Eesti Keskerakond*);[241] (3) Res Publica and Pro Patria Union (*Erakond Isamaa ja Res Publica Liit – IRL*);[242] and (4) Social Democratic Party (*Sotsiaaldemokraatlik Erakond*).[243] The Estonian Peoples Union (*Eestimaa Rahvaliit*) and Estonian Green Party (*Erakond Eestimaa Rohelised*), represented in the previous parliament did not manage to gain the 5% threshold. The Estonian Reform Party acquired the majority of seats in the Parliament, a fraction behind was the Centre Party. At these elections, of the 575,133 citizens who voted, the Reform Party gathered 28.6% and Centre Party 27.8% of the votes.[244] The resultant coalition Government consisted of two political parties: the Estonian Reform Party and the Union of Pro Patria and Res Publica.

233. S. Tamm, 'Vaimulikud ei jää valimistest kõrvale', *Eesti Kirik*, 6 Oct. 2005.
234. M. Paenurm, 'Hulk vaimulikke tegevad nii kirikus kui poliitikas', *Eesti Kirik*, 21 Oct. 2009.
235. *Ibid. See also* National Electoral Committee, www.vvk.ee/varasemad/kov09/detailed.html, 1 May 2014.
236. Riigikogu, www.riigikogu.ee/index.php?id=31678, 1 May. 2014.
237. L. Jürgenstein, 'Jumalariigi kodanikud riigi poliitikas', *Eesti Kirik*, 28 Nov. 2007.
238. I. Karlep, 'JAAN TAMMSALU: Öelge tänusõnu inimese eluajal, mitte peielauas!', *Pealinn*, 2 Mar. 2020. https://www.pealinn.ee/newset/jaan-tammsalu-oelge-tanusonu-inimese-eluajal-mitte-peielauas-n250921, 1 Mar. 2021.
239. RT I 2002, 57, 355; RT I, 03.01.2020, 2 (last amended).
240. Reformierakond, www.reform.ee, 1 May 2014.
241. Keskerakond, www.keskerakond.ee, 1 May 2014.
242. Erakond Isamaa ja Res Publica Liit, www.irl.ee, 1 May 2014.
243. Sotsiaaldemokraatlik Erakond, www.sotsdem.ee, 1 May 2014.
244. The Parliament of Estonia, 'Elections', www.riigikogu.ee/index.php?id=41593, 1 May 2014.

In spring 2014, the government went through a major reorganization resulting in a new very young and popular prime minister and with a coalition of the Estonian Reform Party and Social Democrats. This reshuffling was partly a response to the plummeting trust in established and traditional parties and to the dissatisfaction of people regarding social policies in the aftermath of the financial crisis. This distrust also influenced the local government elections in 2013. The Centre Party gained the majority (32%) of votes, the Union of Pro Patria and Res Publica came second (17.2%), Reform Party gained 13.7 and Social Democrats 12.5%. The success of the Centre Party was high in cities with a Russian-speaking majority population and membership in the Russian Orthodox Church. The popularity of the Centre Party was partly influenced by its support to building a new Russian Orthodox Church in the capital city (Tallinn). In rural areas election coalitions with no clear political or religious affiliation were dominant.

163. In 2019 significant changes took place in the composition of Parliament and in political directions generally. In 2019 elections 5% threshold was gained by the following parties: Reform Party (27.7% of votes), Centre Party (23.1% of votes), Conservative People's Party (*Konservatiivne Rahvaerakond, EKRE*) gained 17.8% of votes, Pro Patria 11.4% and Social Democrats only 9.8% votes. The right-wing, nationalist, populist Conservative People's Party improved significantly its positions. Although the Reform Party won the election the coalition government was somewhat surprisingly formed by an unusual and uncomfortable team led by the Centre Party in cooperation with Conservative People's Party (*EKRE*) and Pro Patria. While in the coalition EKRE pushed forward its negative views on immigration policies, same-sex unions and abortion. The EKRE also controversially supported giving public funding for an anti-abortion NGO. The party is also known for its populist statements and hate speech. Their statements on aforementioned sensitive issues (same-sex unions, abortion, migration) caused frictions not only between the parties but also proved very divisive in society. These controversies and also a corruption scandal eventually led to demise of the coalition at the end of 2020 and appointment of the new government with the leadership of the Reform Party in cooperation with Center Party and with Estonia's first female prime minister – Kaja Kallas.

164. The Reform Party (currently in majority in the Parliament) classifies itself as liberal. They aim to apply liberal democratic ideas and traditions. In the centre of their ideas is individual liberty, which is also reflected in their economic policies. The Reform Party has carried out active cooperation with Christian Churches, most importantly with the Estonian Council of Churches and the EELC. The previous Reform Party Prime minister (Andrus Ansip) regularly took part in public events organized by the Church. However, this has been common practice throughout Estonian recent history, and cannot be attributed solely to the policies of one party or government.

165. The Social Democrats, not currently in the coalition, emphasize solidarity, justice, tolerance and freedom in their manifestos. Support for education is in a prominent place in their programme. They also emphasize that besides the need to develop Estonian culture, the State needs to protect the identity and cultures of minorities as well. There is no explicit mentioning of any religious tradition.[245]

166. Of the other parties represented in the Parliament, the Pro Patria (Res Publica and Pro Patria Union until June 2018) unites conservatives, right-wing and Christian democratic politicians. They determine their policies as relying clearly on individual freedom and responsibility, Estonian culture and European Christian traditions. They value patriotism and the patriotic upbringing of young people.[246] Although other parties represented in the Parliament, including the Centre Party, indicate in their programmes that one of their priorities is the preservation of the Estonian nation and culture (there are variations in wording of course), they do not have any expressed (or tacit) link to the Christian religion. It needs to be noted that the rhetoric of preservation of the Estonian nation and culture is dominant in everyday political life and also in the programmes of political parties. As Estonian society can be described as secular and highly individualistic, nationalism (*rahvuslus*) seems to be the glue binding this society and giving it identity. It has been argued that quite uniquely in Estonian political culture, identity building is not based on emphasizing positive achievements in the past or present but primarily on negative, opposition to the 'other'. The strong emphasis on nationalism has sometimes produced intolerance towards 'foreign and other'.[247] In some respects this kind of identity building was reflected in the handling of the conflict between two Orthodox Churches (Estonian and Russian) and in strict immigration policies.

167. The Estonian Christian Democrats Party (*Erakond Eesti Kristlikud Demokraadid – EKD*)[248] was declared bankrupted by court in 2012 and was never represented in the Parliament. The party has ceased to exist and was officially deleted from the list of registered parties in 2017. According to the Central Commercial Register (*Äriregistri teabesüsteem*) it had only 1,669 members in 2014, which placed it then among the smallest political parties in Estonia.[249] It was registered in 1998 and it grew out of the Association of Estonian Christian Businessmen. The *EKD* tried to join forces with the Estonian National Movement (*Eesti Rahvuslik Liikumine*),[250] which was not registered as a political party, but as a nonprofit organization. In this way it was intended to meet the threshold for the Parliamentary elections in March 2011. However, it was not successful. The *EKD* and the Estonian National Movement both had conservative views as to, for example,

245. E.g. Sotsiaaldemokraatlik Erakond, www.sotsdem.ee, 1 May 2014; SDE programm 2019. aasta Riigikogu valimisteks, https://www.sotsid.ee/liikmele/dokumendid/, 29 Mar. 2021.
246. Erakond Isamaa, www.irl.ee/en/Our-Policies, 1 Mar. 2021.
247. L. Kalev, M.-L. Jakobson & T. Saarts, 'Eesti poliitiline kultuur: alusväärtused', 18 *Riigikogu Toimetised,* 2008.
248. Erakond Eesti Kristlikud Demokraadid, www.ekd.ee, 1 Mar. 2021.
249. Data updated to 1 May 2014. Central Commercial Register, https://ariregister.rik.ee/ erakonnad.py /liikmed_list, 1 May 2014.
250. Eesti Rahvuslik Liikumine, https://www.facebook.com/pages/Eesti-Rahvuslik-Liikumine/114401031913318, 1 May 2014.

abortion and homosexuality.[251] The Estonian National (Patriotic) Movement did not identify itself as having a Christian ethos.[252] Their main aim was the preservation (and growth) of the Estonian indigenous population and its culture, security and patriotic education. They also supported strict immigration policies as necessary considering the small size of the Estonian population. In March 2012, the movement merged with the People's Union Party (*Rahvaliit*) into the Conservative People's Party of Estonia (EKRE). The party that can be considered being a far-right and populist, similar to many others that have emerged in Europe, acquired 8.1% of the vote and seven seats in the *Riigikogu* in 2015 Parliament election. As mentioned above, in 2019 Parliamentary election its support had grown to 17.8% of the vote.

168. Thus, apart from *Pro Patria* who emphasizes Christian values there is no party in Estonia at the moment that can be directly or explicitly identified with any particular religion. However, there is cooperation and some members of clergy have been participating in local and parliamentary elections.

169. Historical ties between religion and politics had been closer during the first independence period.[253] According to the 1938 Constitution, the leaders of the two largest churches (the EELC and the EAOC) gained ex officio membership of the *Riiginõukogu* (Upper House of Parliament).[254] Although the constitutions of the first independence period were consulted for drafting the 1992 Constitution, this particular practice was not followed. Moreover, the Parliament today does not have two chambers. However, establishing a two-chamber Parliament has been discussed.[255]

170. The public resentment to the political influence of religion has been most visible in debates over the different treatment of Christian and non-Christian religions in Estonia, religious education and financing of religious communities. However, criticism in this regard (with some exceptions) is usually targeted at the Government rather than religious institutions or their members. As hinted before, regarding certain sensitive issues there is a visible tension in the triangle of Christian, non-Christian communities and the State, as well as in the triangle of Christian Churches (primarily EELC), State and the secular community.[256] The Government has been accused of favouring Christian religions. Recently topics such as abortion, same-sex unions and hate speech have contributed to social divisions and fierce public debate.

---

251. 'EKD teeb koostööd ERL-ga' [The EKD cooperates with ERL], *Infoleht: Eesti Kristlike Demokraatide tegevust kajastav leht* 1 (2010): 4.
252. Eesti Rahvusliku Liikumise programmilised seisukohad, www.rahvuslikliikumine.ee/dokumendid/ERL_programm.pdf, 1 Jun. 2010.
253. For detailed history of religious life in Estonia within 100 years *see* P. Rohtmets, *Eesti usuelu 100. aastat. Rahvakirikust uue vaimsuseni* (Tartu: Post Factum, 2019).
254. RT 1937, 71, 590.
255. T. Koch, 'Kahekojaline parlament vähendaks parteide osakaalu', *Positmees*, 25 Nov. 2009. It has been suggested that the two-chamber parliament would be able to reduce the importance of political parties and would give candidates with no party affiliation a real opportunity to be elected. It has also been suggested that the two-chamber Parliament would connect members better with reality.
256. *See* Part I above.

171. As noted above, compared to Lithuania or Poland, historic religious traditions and national identity have been weakly connected for Estonians.[257] However, debates over identity still seem to be nationally vibrant. There is ongoing debate regarding the preferential treatment of traditional religious communities. These debates are related to wider questions about the re-building of Estonian identity after the collapse of the Soviet Union, and more recently in the context of membership in the EU. The role of the Government in this process has been criticized for having forced one brand of religion on Estonians. The above-mentioned debates illustrate the reality that for many Estonians the question about religion or identity is probably a bizarre mixture of acknowledgements: the cultural influence of the Christian Church since the thirteenth century, opposed, sometimes, by feelings of it being a religion of occupying foreigners, topped up with atheistic education during the soviet times, traditional pagan beliefs and a general indifference of Estonians towards organized religion as a whole. These are just a few variables which influence the attitudes towards religion and politics in Estonia (the past and present myths and narratives about the identity of Estonians will be to some degree discussed in Part XI (Religion and Culture) of this monograph). Active endorsement of one brand of religion is a sensitive issue for many in this country.

172. Kilp has rightly generalized that whichever way you count Christians in Estonia; they form a minority in Estonian society. Thus, it is not surprising that Christian values do not play a significant role and are not a unifying factor in society.[258] Due to cultural traditions and history, religion does not have a significant role in politics (both believers and non-believers in Estonia do not consider religion important in political decision-making). This does not mean, however, that the participation of religious organizations in politics needs to be treated as something negative in a democratic society.[259] This, as noted above, is to a certain extent acknowledged in society. As to the cooperation between Church and State and the role of Government, Kilp notes that far too close a cooperation may be tempting. In addition to its spiritual goals the Church has institutional interests. It needs to pay the bills. Dependence on allocations from the State budget may turn the Church into a timid domestic animal who does not want to disagree with its sponsor. The State, on the other hand, has always sought support from the Church and religious ceremonies for the legitimacy of its government and for trust in its policies by society.[260] These observations are to a large degree very true in Estonia. It can be added that the State also seems to aim at citizenship building in Estonia via cooperation with Christian Churches and the EELC specifically.

257. A. Kilp, 'Secularisation of Society after Communism: Ten Catholic-Protestant Societies', in *Religion and Politics in Multicultural Europe*, ed. A. Saumets & A. Kilp (Tartu: Tartu University Press, 2009), 226. *See also* General Introduction, §2 Social Facts about Religion above.
258. A. Kilp, 'Religiooni ja poliitika vahekorra põhimõtetest Euroopa demokraatiates', paper given at the EELC Conference on Christian Valuesi in Estonian Politics (Tallinn, 2008).
259. *Ibid.*
260. *Ibid.*

173. As to direct political influence of religion in politics and law-making, religious organizations and clerics have expressed their views about abortion, euthanasia and homosexuality. Recently, homosexuality has been in the spotlight because of the heated debates laws of co-habitation and hate speech. Previously, several positive changes in laws have been carried out with the initiative of religious organizations. For example, family law now allows authorization of clergy to register marriages, alternative service for conscientious objectors to military service was re-organized with an input from religious institutions (including Jehovah's Witnesses); and the chaplaincy service has been introduced in the armed forces, prisons and police.

174. As to other specific examples of religious influence in politics, the former Archbishop of the EELC has criticized the State for trying to treat all religions and ideologies equally and for passing far too liberal laws.[261] In his vision the Church needs to become an inseparable part in the life of the Estonian nation. However, he makes the express distinction between becoming a State Church and becoming a National Church, referring to the latter as being the aim of the Church. The model of the State Church as subjecting the Church under the State control is seen as not desirable. He envisaged the future of the State and Church relationships in long-term bilateral agreements. He also criticizes the Church itself as sometimes hoping for too much support from the State (he labels it as the mentality of thinking in favour of State Church), and for a too passive attitude as to the development of the church and its relationship to the Estonian people. The Archbishop also points out that it is unrealistic today to talk about the National Church comprising the entire Estonian population, but encourages church members to be active. Thus, he calls for real public involvement of the Church. However, from his speech it can also be discerned that there are different understandings of the State and Church relationship within the Church itself. Roughly speaking, the conservative wing of the Church sees its future in a closer relationship with the State and more progressive wing in an active mission among the Estonian population. The elections of the new Archbishop were in November 2014. The discussions over candidates reflected the divisions in the church. The less conservative members of the church suggested that the church has to reform, decentralise and perhaps allow diversity within the church itself to accommodate different approaches to disputed issues such as homosexuality or women priests.[262] This debate in the church is still very vibrant also under new leadership of Archbishop Urmas Viilma.

175. The Estonian Council of Churches has also been very active in contributing to policies and projects, for example, regarding religious education, media, the chaplaincy service, training, crime prevention and youth work. The Council decides according to its own statutes which churches it admits. The members of the Council

---

261. A. Põder, 'Tulevikupeegeldusi kirikust', Paper given at the Scientific Conference: The Estonian Evangelical Lutheran Church on the Way to Tomorrow [Teaduskonverents Eesti Evangeelne Luterlik Kirik – teel homsesse] (Tartu, 2007).

262. *See*, *e.g.*, V. Vihuri, 'Ettepanek Eesti Evangeelse Luterliku Kiriku Reformimiseks', *Eesti Kirik*, 26 Mar. 2014.

are as follows: (1) the EELC; (2) the Roman Catholic Church; (3) the EAOC; (4) the Estonian Orthodox Church of Moscow Patriarchate; (5) the Estonian Christian Pentecostal Church; (6) the Estonian Methodist Church; (7) the Estonian Union of Evangelical Christian and Baptist Congregations; (8) the Seventh-day Adventist Church; (9) the Charismatic Episcopal Church of Estonia; and (10) the Estonian Congregation of St. Gregory of the Armenian Apostolic Church. The Estonian Council of Churches is a rather unusual ecumenical organization (registered as a non-profit organization) which has members who normally are not interested in ecumenical cooperation. It also includes churches with a relatively short history. The Council of Churches represents the majority of believers in Estonia and has definitely contributed to conflict avoidance between different communities. This organization was established in 1989 and its political importance may be seen in its contribution to Estonian independence. As mentioned earlier in this monograph on 17 October 2002, the Government and the Estonian Council of Churches signed the Protocol of Common Concerns. This protocol provides a broad basis for specific contracts and cooperation in fields of common interests (education, preservation of culturally important objects, financing, international relations, chaplaincy, etc.). It clearly makes statements which go beyond simple recognition of the importance of religious organizations in fulfilling public functions. It can be argued that it sees the role of churches in contributing to social cohesion, nationhood, and the national conscience.[263] Cooperation between the State and Christian Communities will be further discussed in Chapter 3 below and under specific themes throughout the monograph.

176. Before the 2019 parliamentary elections the Estonian Council of Churches sent several proposals to political parties, including some very dividing and controversial ones, for example, terminating national health funding for abortions (they proposed channelling the money into counselling and support of parents instead). They also demanded changing the constitutional provision on marriage to clearly state that it can only be concluded between a man and a woman. Less controversially, they proposed, for example, extending non-confessional religious education (teaching about religions) at schools. As noted later in this monograph, it is not available in all schools. They also insisted on continuing the support for cultural/ sacred objects (including church buildings) that is discussed further in the chapter on financing of churches.[264]

177. As mentioned above, public criticism about the political involvement of religion in politics has focused mostly on the role and attitudes of the State in this involvement. However, there are other examples as well. Most recently the involvement of religious organizations in the debate over the co-habitation law has been criticized. However, this debate has also made more visible the tensions inside the

263. M. Kiviorg, 'The Mutual Roles of Religion and State in Estonia' in *The Mutual Roles of Religion and State in Europe*, ed. B. Schanda (Trier: European Consortium for Church and State Research, 2014).
264. Estonian Council of Churches, http://www.ekn.ee/inc.uudis.php?id=372, 1 Mar. 2021.

religious communities and specifically EELC itself. Some of the prominent members of the church, for example, a former Estonian President, have expressed opinion of leaving the church due to statements against same-sex unions by some conservative members.[265] The tensions were addressed by the Archbishop of the EELC Urmas Viilma calling for open discussion on this issue and for unity of the church.[266] The Church is planning to form a commission for furthering this open discussion.

178. Another example is from not too long ago where several church leaders expressed their negative views about the political advertising of the Centre Party (at the time an opposition party). This triggered a lively debate in media. Some academics expressed their opinion that the Church has called for restraint from criticizing the current government.[267] Toots pointed out that this undermines democracy.[268] She also makes a tentative link between the attitude of the Church and political cowardliness of the younger generation. On the basis of recent research she suggests that a significant part of the younger generation thinks that criticizing the government is not good for democracy. Kilp expressed his view that the opinion expressed by clerics is not impartial as it is focused solely on the political advertisement for the Centre Party. He suggests that views about boundaries between ethical and non-ethical campaigns are not objective, but are part of the political battles. Although the views expressed by clerics did not explicitly state their political preferences, these views can be interpreted as such in reality. He also points to a more general question as to the role of clerics in politics.[269] His observations are correct as several political parties are guilty of controversial (and publicly criticized) political manoeuvring, which have slipped the attention of clerics. However, the President of the Estonian Council of Churches was also right to point out that everybody has a right to freedom of speech in Estonia. In his opinion, although the note focused on the Centre Party it carried a message for all political parties calling for more ethical behaviour from them in relations with each other.[270] Kuuskemaa (minister of one of the EELC congregations) criticized Toots for reducing the message of clerics to merely an everyday political battle.[271] He also makes a more general suggestion as to the possibility that politicians want to monopolize politics and are not open to wider political participation in society. All in all, the above-mentioned incident seems to have illustrated that political involvement of clergy as such is not considered a problem. However, questions and frustration start when their involvement provides real or assumed support to ruling political parties.

179. Non-Christian communities and especially the religious community representing Estonian indigenous beliefs have also been active in politics to a certain extent. With their initiative the Round Table of Religious Organizations (*Usuliste*

265. EELK peale solvunud Ilves plaanib kirikust välja astuda, *Meie Kirik,* 26 Jan. 2021.
266. U. Viilma, 'Kiriku diskussioonikübsusest ja ühtsusest', *ERR* 26 Jan. 2021.
267. A. Toots, 'Jumalik demokraatia' [Divine Democracy], *Postimees*, 5 May 2010.
268. *Ibid.*
269. V. Pesur, 'Politoloog: kirikuõpetajate pöördumine on tavatu', *Postimees*, 3 May 2010.
270. V. Pesur, 'Einar Soone: kõigil on õigus oma arvamusele', *Postimees*, 3 May 2010.
271. T. Kuusemaa, 'Vaimulikud närigu muru?!', *Delfi*, 13 May 2010.

Ühenduste Ümarlaud) was established in April 2001. The Round Table comprises non-Christian movements in Estonia and was established with the aim to present their views more successfully in their relationships with the State. It was created in consideration of the fact of State favouritism of Christian religions. When the Round Table was initiated, new proposals about religious education were hotly disputed in society. Today, the initiative and especially the community representing Estonian indigenous beliefs (House of Taara and Native Religions) have been able to contribute to policies on the environment and historical/cultural heritage.[272]

180. The Muslim community in Estonia has never been politically very active. However, in 1994 the Estonian Islamic Congregation made a statement concerning the situation in Chechnya giving support to the president at the time, Dzhokhar Dudayev.[273] Ringvee also points out that several Muslims have been active in political life via their national cultural societies, while their registered religious communities tend to abstain from the political arena.[274] The Chairman of the Islamic Congregation Timur Seifullen has been the president of the Estonian Union of National Minorities. His work for national minorities was recognized by the State. He was rewarded with Estonian State Honour in 2004 (5th Class order of the White Star).[275]

---

272. *See* Part VIII below for further developments of the cooperation.
273. R. Linnas, 'Islam Eestis' [Islam in Estonia] in *Mitut usku Eesti II. Valik usundiloolisi uurimusi: kristluse eri*, ed. L. Altnurme (Tartu: TÜ Kirjastus, 2007), 62.
274. R. Ringvee, 'Islam in Estonia', in *Islam v. Európe* (Centrom pre európsku politiku: Bratislava, 2005), 245.
275. *Ibid.*

Chapter 2. Political Influence in Religion

181. Historically, there have been only a couple of incidents of direct political influence in religion. At the end of the 1930s, the Minister of Internal Affairs suspended activities of the governing body of the EELC. The Minister of Internal Affairs acted upon the request from eight EELC ministers. In 1938 they requested the State to solve their internal conflict according to the law. The conflict evolved from the fact that the EELC bishop at the time (H. B. Rahamägi) wanted to divorce. The conservative members of the Church were very much against it.[276] The Estonian Government supported the opposition in the church and suspended the activities of the bishop and governing bodies of the EELC according to Article 20 of the Act of Churches and Congregations on grounds of public order and peace. According to the 1934 Churches and Congregations Act the Minister of Internal Affairs had the discretion to prohibit ministers from performing their activities if it was in the interest of the State and public order. The relationship between State and Church in the 1930s was close to the State Church model. The second incident took place at the beginning of the 1990s and involved conflict between two Orthodox Churches (the EAOC and the Estonian Orthodox Church of Moscow Patriarchate) and their registration. The latter incident was discussed above.[277]

182. There is the possibility that because of the financing religious organizations receive from the State, churches tend to restrain themselves from public criticism of government policies. In this regard, there is an opportunity for political influence in religion.

183. Other examples illustrate not so much political influence in religion, but rather political influence regarding freedom of religion or belief. At the beginning of the 1990s there was an influx and increase in activity of so-called New Religious Movements (NRMs). It is probably right to say that there was a phobia against these movements in society and correspondingly in politics. As emphasized before, the expression 'new' in 'NRM' here does not necessarily mean absolute or world novelty, but rather novelty in Estonia or Europe. In this sense it includes, for example, nineteenth-century communities such as Jehovah's Witnesses and the Bahá'í. NRM is not used as a pejorative term. The choice of the term seeks to emphasize neutrality and is preferred to terms such as 'sects' or 'cults' which seem to have clearly negative connotations in Europe. However, these movements were popularly considered dangerous, particularly in the 1990s. According to one of the surveys in 1998, both Estonians and Russians in Estonia had the most negative views about

276. M. Kiviorg, *Kirikuõigus avaliku õiguse osana Eesti Vabariigis* (võrdlev analüüs 1918–1940.a. ja 1991–1996.a.) [*Law on Religions in Estonia: Comparative Analysis of the Periods 1918–1940 and 1991–1996*] (Tartu: Tartu Ülikool, 1996), 36–37; S. Luiga, *Eesti Vabariigi territooriumil asuvate usuorganisatsioonide õigussubjektsus* [*Legal Status of Religious Organisations in the Estonian Republic*] (Tartu: Tartu Ülikool, 1992), 26–27.

277. A description of this conflict was provided in the General Introduction (§2 Social Facts about Religion) above.

Jehovah's Witnesses.[278] To be frank, on the one hand, this was related to ignorance about different religious beliefs generally, and on the other, it showed that Estonian society was not used to active proselytizing. The activities of the NRMs were simply different from the activities of traditional religious communities known to Estonians.

184. Some examples of political reaction to the activities of the NRMs can be given here. According to the 1993 Churches and Congregations Act permission from a local government or relevant agency was needed to conduct religious services in public institutions (including prisons). The law potentially gave considerable leeway to local governments and agencies to decide over these matters. The head of the Religious Affairs Department of the Ministry of Internal Affairs at the time expressed her view that this was needed to stop the spread of all sorts of Americanisms (in her wording referring to NRMs coming from overseas) in prisons.[279]

185. At the first reading/discussion of the 1993 Churches and Congregations Act in Parliament concern was raised as to the influx of the NRMs to Estonia. It was pointed out that the ideological background of many of these organizations is unknown in Estonia. It was suggested to include in the law a provision which would allow a government official to suspend activities of a religious person or organization on the suspicion of illegal activities (this had an analogy in the 1934 Churches and Congregations Act).[280] Eventually the provision was not included in the 1993 law.[281] The matter was/is in the competence of the Estonian courts and is regulated by generally applicable criminal law.

186. It is probably right to say that by 2002 wide spread phobia in society against the NRMs was over. Accordingly, this view was reflected in politics as well. As mentioned in Part I above, before the adoption of the 2002 Churches and Congregations Act by the Estonian Parliament, the Estonian Council of Churches sent a letter to the parliamentary commission asking it to take measures in the new law to limit the activities of 'non-constructive religious communities'. This proposal did not get political support. Despite the past phobia, it needs to be emphasized that Estonia has so far never been a place of serious anti-cult movements.

187. As to other religious communities, the Muslim community came into the spotlight in 2000 when plans to build a mosque received media attention. This created some reaction from political parties. A relatively small and marginal Estonian

278. R. Liiman, *Usklikkus muutuvas Eesti Ühiskonnas* [*Religiosity in Changing Estonian Society*] (Tartu: Tartu Ülikooli Kirjastus, 2001), 84. They were negative towards Muslims and Hindus as well (Estonians were slightly more negative regarding Muslims than Russians).

279. M. Kusnets, 'Kirikute ja koguduste seadusest' ['About the Churches and Congregations Act'], *Eesti Kirik*, no. 22 1993; *see also* M. Kiviorg, *Kirikuõigus avaliku õiguse osana Eesti Vabariigis* (võrdlev analüüs 1918–1940.a. ja 1991–1996.a.) [*Law on Religions in Estonia: Comparative Analysis of the Periods 1918–1940 and 1991–1996*] (Tartu: Tartu Ülikool, 1996), 32.

280. 'Kirikute ja koguduste seaduse esimene lugemine (A. Veidemann)', Riigikogu stenogramm, II Istungjärk, 4 Apr. 1993.

281. RT I 1993, 30, 510.

Christian People's Party (since 2006, the Estonian Christian Democrats Party until it was officially liquidated in 2017) started to collect signatures for prohibiting the planned building.[282] Reactions from other political parties were more moderate.[283] The representatives of the conservative Pro Patria Party (*Isamaliit*) expressed their view that they are not against the mosque per se, however, it should not be built in Tallinn's historical city centre. They further emphasized that the mosque should not dominate the silhouette of Tallinn.[284] The Estonian Council of Churches, the largest ecumenical organization in Estonia, stated that they had no objections against building the mosque. However, they stated that they do not actively support it either.[285] The plans to build this mosque have not materialized yet (mostly because of financial reasons). However, as mentioned above, since 2009 there is a prayer hall in the Islamic Cultural Centre 'Turath', which serves as a mosque for the Islamic community in Tallinn. Across Estonia there are also several other converted premises for serving the religious needs of Muslims.

282. 'Tatarlane Timur unistab pisikesest pühakojast' [Tatar Timur is Dreaming about a Small Sanctuary], *Eesti Päevaleht*, 9 May 2002.
283. R. Ringvee, 'Islam in Estonia', in *Islam v. Európe* (Bratislava: Centrom pre európsku politiku, 2005), 245.
284. 'Mośee tekitab vaidlusi' ['The Mosque Is Provouking Debates'], *Eesti Päevaleht*, 26 Jan. 2001; *see also* M. Huang, 'A Mosque with a View', *Central European Review* 3, no. 3 (2001).
285. 'Kirikud ei ole mośee rajamise vastu' ['Churches are not against the Mosque'], *Eesti Päevaleht*, 11 Jan. 2001.

Chapter 3. Interaction Between Religion and State on a Political and Legal Level

188. The political and legal interaction between religion and State was to a certain degree addressed above. Some additional observations as to the broader theoretical framework of this interaction should be made here.

189. Article 10 of the Estonian Constitution sets forth that Estonia is a State based on social justice. This brings the ideas of welfare state into the Estonian legal system. The provision is located in the Chapter of Fundamental Rights, Freedoms and Duties. This has importance regarding its interpretation. The actual wording of this provision is as follows:

> The rights, freedoms and duties set out in this Chapter shall not preclude other rights, freedoms and duties which arise from the spirit of the Constitution or are in accordance therewith, and conform to the principles of human dignity and of a state based on social justice, democracy, and the rule of law.

190. The scope of the positive duties of the State in relation to the welfare state concept enshrined in Article 10 of the Constitution is debatable. Saaremäel-Stoilov notes on the basis of the practice of the Supreme Court of Estonia that it may mean just providing the absolute minimum which is required for the preservation of human dignity.[286] Her observations are related to the justiciability of social and economic rights in the courts. Estonia also has international obligations (e.g., Estonia is a party to the International Covenant on Social, Economic and Cultural Rights) to provide (at least gradually) for the enjoyment of social, economic and cultural rights. The Estonian Constitution also enables cooperation with private institutions (including religious organizations) in carrying out its goals and obligations.

191. However, the welfare state concept embodied in the above constitutional provision is not usually discussed when the relationship between the State and religion (religious communities) is addressed. However, the cooperation between State and Church (religious communities) has been accepted to a certain extent in many areas of common social concern (education, health, rehabilitation, unemployment, crime prevention, etc.). There is an established committee of experts for development of cooperation between the Estonian Government and the EELC. The committee consists of members of the Estonian Government administration and representatives of EELC.[287] On 17 October 2002, the Government and the Estonian Council of Churches signed the Protocol of Common Concerns (the content of the Protocol was described above in Part III, Chapter 4: Contractual Religious Freedom). Religious communities and specifically Estonian Council of Churches have been consulted in lawmaking.

---

286. K. Saaremäel-Stoilov, 'Sotsiaalriigi põhimõtte elementide kaitse Eesti Vabariigi Riigikohtu põhiseaduslikkuse järelevalve praktikas', paper given at the International Conference related to 15th Anniversary of the Estonian Constitution (Tartu, 2007).
287. RTL I 1999, 15, 250; RTL 2010, 16, 298 (last amended).

192. The themes discussed in this chapter will be further elaborated in Part XI, Chapter 3: Religion and Civil Society.

193. To conclude this part, it is probably right to say that Estonia is still looking for an adequate balance for political interaction between State and religion. This process is influenced by Estonian history and culture, but also by similar processes and debates throughout Europe and beyond. The ongoing debates can only be considered healthy and normal for a democratic society.

Part VI. Labour Law Within Religious Communities

Chapter 1. Scope of Application of Labour Law

194. Labour relations were re-organized at the beginning of the 1990s after the regaining of independence. The first Employment Contracts Act (*Töölepingu seadus*) was adopted on 15 April 1992.[288] According to §7 of that act, labour law did not apply to persons who conducted religious activities in religious organizations, unless it was prescribed in the by-laws of the religious organization. The latter would have been the case when the by-laws prescribed entering into an employment contract with these persons. Different religious organizations have had different approaches. For example, in the EELC ministers do not have labour contracts. Their stipends are generally determined by the board of a congregation. Thus, the protocols of the board meetings are the main ground for paying social tax and income tax. The purpose of the law was to give more autonomy to religious organizations in employment decisions.

195. As to the general application of labour law, the 1992 Employment Contracts Act prohibited discrimination on the grounds of religion or belief and/or on the ground of membership in a religious association (§10(3)). This applied to ordinary employers other than religious communities and was targeted to protect individual freedom of religion or belief in employment relations. The Act prohibited both direct and indirect discrimination (§10^2).[289] From 1 May 2004 the Employment Contracts Act also specified that allowing a suitable working and rest time regime which satisfies the religious requirements of an employee was not deemed to be discrimination (§10^1(5)).[290] These provisions were the result of Estonia joining the EU and implementation of the EU Employment Directives.[291]

196. A new Employment Contracts Act was adopted on 17 December 2008 and it came into force on 1 July 2009.[292] The new law replaced the previous Act and introduced significant changes in employment law. The act aims to make working

288. RT I 1992, 15, 24.
289. RT I 2004, 37, 256.
290. *Ibid.*
291. Council Directive (EC) 2000/78 on Employment Equality [2000] OJ L 195/16; Council Directive (EC) 2000/43/ on Racial Equality [2000] OJ L 180/22.
292. RT I 2009, 5, 35; RT I, 29.12.2020, 2 (last amended).

relations more flexible by giving more room for negotiations and agreements between employers and employees. This new law was seen as necessary in order to stimulate the Estonian economy (the 1992 law was considered to be outdated and too rigid/formalistic for economic development). It was also necessary for the harmonization of employment law with other private law acts, most importantly with the Law of Obligations Act (*Võlaõigusseadus*).[293]

197. As there have been no court cases regarding application of labour law within religious communities it is still not clear how exactly the law may affect religious communities. However, a few remarks can be made on the basis of the Parliamentary debates and Explanatory Notes accompanying the law. The Explanatory Note from 10 December 2008 states that it was considered unnecessary to include in the new law the list of occupations to which the Employment Contracts Act does not apply.[294] Thus the explicit provision that labour law does not apply to persons who conduct religious activities in religious organizations has been dropped. It is further noted that it is important to determine the actual nature of the contract. For example, the law specifies that the provisions concerning employment contracts do not apply to contracts where the person obligated to perform the work is to a significant extent independent in choosing the manner, time and place of performance of the work (§1(4)). The Explanatory Note states that if a minister of a religious community has said degree of independence then the law does not apply.

198. The Ministry of Social Affairs has subsequently explained that, as a rule, work is normally done on the basis of an employment contract, but it can also be based on an authorization agreement, a contract for services or other similar agreements (as specified, e.g., in the Law of Obligations Act). Compared to other contracts, an employment contract guarantees the employee greater rights and better protection, which is why from the perspective of an employee it is recommended that an employment contract be stipulated wherever possible. Moreover, in the event of a dispute as to whether the agreement in question constitutes an employment contract, it is always assumed that the parties have entered into an employment contract.[295]

199. Thus, it seems that it is still possible for religious communities to arrange their employment or service relations according to their own needs. However, in the case of a conflict it is always assumed that an employment contract has been concluded between a minister or another person and the religious community. Although the new labour law has been in force since 2009, its actual application and possible problems which may arise concerning religious communities are a still matter of speculation. So far there is no case law regarding employment relations between

293. RT I 2002, 53, 336; RT I, 04.01.2021, 2 (last amended), https://www.riigiteataja.ee/en/eli/ee/512012021002/consolide/current, 8 Feb. 2021.
294. 299 SE II, Töölepingu seaduse eelnõu seletuskiri eelnõu teise lugemise juurde, 10 Dec. 2008, Riigikogu, www.riigikogu.ee, 1 May 2010.
295. Sotsiaalministeerium, www.sm.ee, 1 May 2010.

religious communities and their ministers or other employees. There are many aspects of the new regulation which await clarification.

200. For example, in preparing to enter into an employment contract (e.g., during interviews or in job advertisements), the employer does not have the right to request personal information about which they can have no justified interest. As a rule, employers have no right to ask about family planning, religious or political views, sexual orientation, personal beliefs, etc. If the employer requests such information, they must explain why they need to know it and how it is connected to the job in question.[296] Religious communities are presumably able to ask necessary questions before entering into employment contracts with persons.

201. In relation to requests for personal information, two other acts need to be mentioned here: the Estonian Gender Equality Act (*Soolise võrdõiguslikkuse seadus*)[297] and the Equal Treatment Act (*Võrdse kohtlemise seadus*),[298] which prohibit discrimination on the basis of sex, race, age, nationality, command of language, disability, sexual orientation, duty to serve in the defence forces, family status, family-related duties, social position, representation of the interests of employees or membership in workers' associations, political views or membership in a political party, religious or other beliefs.

202. These two acts have general application and are not only restricted to employment situations/contracts. The Equal Treatment Act applies, for example, to membership of, and involvement in, an organization of employees or employers, or any organization whose members exercise a particular profession, including the benefits provided for by such organizations, social protection, including social security and healthcare, and social advantages (§1). It also states that discrimination against persons on the grounds of religion or other beliefs, age, disability or sexual orientation is prohibited in relation to conditions for access to employment, to self-employment or to occupation, including selection criteria and recruitment conditions, whatever the branch of activity and at all levels of the professional hierarchy, including promotion.

203. Religious communities are allowed certain exemptions from the Equal Treatment Act. In the case of occupational activities within religious associations and other public or private organizations, the ethos of which is based on religion or belief, a difference in treatment based on a person's religion or belief shall not constitute discrimination where, by reason of the nature of these activities or of the context in which they are carried out, a person's religion or belief constitutes a genuine, legitimate and justified occupational requirement, because it is directly related to the organization's ethos (§10(2)). The law also does not prejudice the right of these

---

296. Sotsiaalministeerium, www.sm.ee, 1 May 2010.
297. RT I 2004, 27, 181; RT I, 26.04.2013, 2 (last amended).
298. RT I 2008, 56, 315; RT I, 26.04.2017, 6 (last amended).

organizations to require individuals working for them to act in good faith and with loyalty to the organization's ethos (§10(3)).[299]

204. The Explanatory Note states that these exceptions are based on EU anti-discrimination directives. Namely the Council Directive (EC) 2000/78 on Employment Equality and the Council Directive (EC) 2000/43/ on Racial Equality.[300] It also refers to Declaration No. 11 on the status of churches and non-confessional organizations, which was added to the Amsterdam Treaty.[301]

205. However, at the second reading of the Equal Treatment Act in the Parliament, the head of the Constitutional Law Commission pointed out that the exemptions in law primarily relate to specific occupational requirements, noting that occupations such as church cleaner and secretary are not directly connected to the manifestation of religion or belief.[302] It thus appears that the Equal Treatment Act is applicable when the occupational requirements are not directly related to the manifestation of religion or belief.

206. The Gender Equality Act (*Soolise võrdõiguslikkuse seadus*) does not apply to the professing and practising of faith or working as a minister of a religion in a registered religious association (§2(2)).[303] However, commentaries to the Gender Equality Act (commissioned by the Ministry of Social Affairs) state that it would be reasonable, in the future, to extend the application of the law to religious organizations.[304]

207. International and transnational developments in anti-discrimination law have become increasingly (and potentially) challenging for religious communities. However, the effects of the interplay between anti-discrimination legislation and collective freedom of religion or belief in Estonia remain to be seen. Currently there is no case law in relation to this matter, nor is there any case law regarding the exemptions discussed above. In short, the scope or the future application of current anti-discrimination laws in relation to religions and religious communities is not entirely clear in Estonia.

208. Although there have been no court cases yet in relation to employment disputes there was an incident involving application of the Equal Treatment Act within religious communities. In 2010 the Estonian Evangelical Lutheran Church decided

299. RT I 2008, 56, 315; RT I, 26.04.2017, 6 (last amended).
300. Council Directive (EC) 2000/78 on Employment Equality [2000] OJ L 195/16; Council Directive (EC) 2000/43/ on Racial Equality [2000] OJ L 180/22.
301. The Declaration stated that: 'The European Union will respect and does not prejudice the status under national law of churches and religious associations or communities in the Member States. The European Union will equally respect the status of philosophical and non-confessional organisations'.
302. XI Riigikogu stenogramm, IV Istungjärk, 21. oktoober 2008, Võrdse kohtlemise seaduse eelnõu 262 SE teine lugemine, www.riigikogu.ee, 1 May 2010.
303. *See* Part I, Ch. 2 above.
304. K. Albi et al., Soolise võrdõiguslikkuse seadus, Kommenteeritud väljaanne (Tallinn, 2010), 23.

to exclude from the ranks of priesthood a minister who had openly expressed his views in support of gays and had become a board member of the association for Gay Christians. The incident fuelled some internal discussions in the church, but also attracted public attention. The minister turned to the Gender and Equal Treatment Commissioner to investigate the matter. The post of Gender Equality and Equal Treatment Commissioner has been established to monitor compliance with the requirements of the Gender Equality Act and the Equal Treatment Act. Some church members were furious about the enquiries and demanded resignation of the Commissioner for violating church autonomy.[305] In its official response the consistory of the EELC explained that the minister's sexual orientation as such was not the ground for the dismissal but the fact that he broke his oath by not following and obeying internal regulations of the church (including its 2009 declaration on homosexualism).[306] No legal action was taken by the church or the Commissioner. An analogous incident happened regarding a female priest of the EELC expressing her support for same-sex unions in a television talk show. Consequently, Archbishop of the EELC expressed his disapproval. He noted that the priest expressed opinion which is in contradiction to the church's official position.[307] However, times have moved on from 2011. Although there were calls to dismiss her form her position, it never came to it. In 2021 she was cautioned again, but not dismissed.[308]

305. 'EELK praost nõuab võrdõiguslikkuse voliniku ametist lahkumist', *Delfi*, 7 Nov. 2011.
306. 'EELK selgitas soovolinikule, miks tagandati üks vaimulik ametist' Meie Kirik, 11 Oct. 2011.
307. H. Mihelson, 'Risti koguduse õpetaja kaitses kooseluseadust, peapiiskop on nördinud', *Postimees*, 5 Oct. 2017, https://www.postimees.ee/4266051/risti-koguduse-opetaja-kaitses-kooseluseadust-peapiiskop-on-nordinud, 30 Jan. 2021. M. Kiviorg, P, Roosma, '§ 40 - 41' (freedom of religion and conscience) in *Eesti Vabariigi põhiseadus. Kommenteeritud väljaanne*. Viies, täiendatud väljaanne (5th edn, Commentaries to Estonian Constitution), ed. Ü. Madise et al. Tallinn: Juura, 2020.
308. A. Ladva, 'Risti koguduse õpetaja Annika Laats sai abielu kohta öeldu eest piiskopilt noomida', *Õhtuleht*, 15 Jan. 2021.

Chapter 2. Religious Ministers and Labour Law

209. As described above, according to the 2009 Employments Contract Act[309] the labour law may apply to religious ministers. This depends on the contract concluded between the religious organization and the specific minister. The Estonian Gender Equality Act and Equal Treatment Act provide an exemption from anti-discrimination regulation as regards relationships between the religious minister and his or her community, also discussed above.

210. The salaries of priests and other people working for the Church or other religious communities are paid by the religious communities themselves (financial matters will be addressed in more detail in Part VIII of this monograph).

309. RT I 2009, 5, 35; RT I, 29.12.2020, 2 (last amended).

Chapter 3. Other Church Employees and Labour Law

211. As noted above, it is not entirely clear how labour law and anti-discrimination laws should apply in relation to other church employees other than religious ministers. There is no case law as yet.

Part VII. Religious Communities and Protections of the Individual

212. As elaborated above, both individuals and religious communities are protected under the Estonian Constitution. Thus, in the case of a conflict, rights of individuals need to be balanced against the autonomy and rights of religious communities. As emphasized already, there is no case law dealing with a conflict between individual rights and collective freedom of religion or belief in Estonia. If such a conflict were to come before the Estonian courts, it is likely that the case law of the European Court of Human Rights would be referred to. The ECHR is part of the Estonian legal system and is directly applicable. It is also possible that the decisions of the UN Human Rights Committee under the International Covenant for Civil and Political Rights or other international instruments would be used for interpretation, as well as emerging case law from the European Court of Justice. As to the ECHR, there is an increasing amount of case law, which essentially concerns conflicts between individual rights and autonomy of religious communities.[310] For some time the approach taken by the ECtHR indicated that individual rights, in the case of conflict, were primarily protected by leaving the community (let's call it the principle of voluntarism).[311] It could be argued that there is evidence of a new contextual (substantive) approach in Strasbourg, which does not focus on voluntarism, but on the balancing of different rights in given factual circumstances.[312] However,

310. It needs to be noted that it is not possible to bring a case against a private person (e.g., religious community) under the ECHR. It is possible to lodge complaints only about violations of the Convention by one of the contracting States. However, the ECtHR has recognized the positive obligations of States to protect individuals or communities in their enjoyment of their convention rights against third parties. Thus, the State becomes responsible under the Convention for the way it has dealt with the private conflictual relationship, but it is not liable for the private violation itself.

311. *X v. Denmark* (App. No. 7374/76) (1976) 5 DR 157. *See also E/GR v. Austria* concerning the levying contributions from church members, *E/GR v. Austria* (App. No. 9781/82) (1984) 37 DR 42; *Williamson v. UK* concerning Church of England priest opposing the decision of the Church to ordain women, *Williamson v. UK* (App. No. 00027008/95) 17 May 1995; and *Karlsson v. Sweden* in which the applicant priest's views on the priesthood of women were incompatible with the view generally held by the Church. In consequence, the Church was not obliged to accept the applicant's candidacy for a post of vicar, *Karlsson v. Sweden* (App. No. 12356/86) (1988) 57 DR 172.

312. For example, *Rommelfanger v. the Federal Republic of Germany* (App. No. 12242/86) (1989) 62 DR 151; *Pellegrini v. Italy* (App. No. 30882/96); *Schüth v Germany* (App. No. 1620/03) ECtHR 23 Sep. 2010; *Obst v. Germany* (App. No. 425/03) ECtHR 23 Sep. 2010; *Siebenhaar v. Germany* (App. No. 18136/02) 3 Feb. 2011; *Lombardi Vallauri v. Italy* (App. No. 39128/05) ECHR 20 Oct. 2009; *Baudler v. Germany* (App. No. 38254/04) ECtHR 6 Dec. 2011; *Reuter v. Germany* (App. No. 39775/04) ECtHR 6 Dec. 2011; *Müller v.* Germany (App. No. 12986/04) ECtHR 6 Dec. 2011;

the way this new approach is applied in different circumstances and how it affects diversity and the internal life of religious communities (right to collective freedom of religion or belief) is not clear. Religious liberty is one right among several strongly advocated in liberal democratic states, most notably freedom of speech, privacy and equality. There is increased attention and pressure at least by part of the human rights community to protect human rights and liberal values within religious communities or in their affiliated institutions. It remains to be seen how the ECtHR will react to this pressure to protect individual rights within religious communities in different cases. The pressure can be felt in Estonia as well. This was obvious in recent debates over amendments to the criminal law regarding hate speech and the co-habitation law.

213. A couple of brief theoretical remarks should be made here. The fundamental rights listed in the Estonian Constitution are primarily subjective rights of individuals, but also of legal persons (including religious communities), against abuses by the State. Human rights are traditionally understood as rights against State interference and the abuse of power by governments. Maruste has observed that: 'If a person violates another person's rights and this constitutes violation of human rights, then according to currently prevailing opinions, it is not an issue of human rights law, but is an issue of criminal law, family law, procedural law or another specific branch of law depending on the content of the violation.'[313]

214. However, protection of fundamental rights extends to some degree to relations between private parties. According to Article 19 of the Estonian Constitution, everyone shall honour and consider the rights and freedoms of others, and shall observe the law in exercising his or her rights and freedoms and in fulfilling his or her duties. Muda insists that we must acknowledge the opinion that the question about private persons as addressees of fundamental rights cannot be disregarded only because a particular tradition exists.[314] She observes that fundamental rights are not exclusively about an absolute relationship between the State and the citizen but also about relations between citizens. Moreover, as Clapham contends, in a broader context a case can be made that, as a rule, human rights are to be respected

---

Sindicatul 'Păstorul cel Bun' v. Romania (App. No. 2330/09) ECHR Grand Chamber 9 Jul. 2013; *Fernández Martínez v. Spain* (App. No. 56030/07) ECtHR 12 Jul. 2014 (Grand Chamber); *KárolyNagy* v. *Hungary* (App. No. 56665/09) ECHR, 14 Sep. 2017; *Tothpal ja Szabo* v. *Rumenia* (App. No. 28617/13 ja 50919/13), ECHR 19 Feb. 2019.

313. R. Maruste, Inimõigused ja ausa õigusemõistmise põhimõtted: Euroopa Inimõiguste Konventsioon, Euroopa Sootsiaalharta (Tallinn: Juura, 1993), 11.

314. M. Muda, 'Regulation of Gender Equality as a Fundamental Right in Estonia', *Juridica International* VII (2002): 106.

by all persons, groups and States.[315] He argues that 'to insist on the exclusive applicability of human rights law to governments generates a dangerous sense of impunity for those who are undermining people's rights'.[316] Moreover, the fundamental status and importance of human rights adds more weight to the argument for their applicability to a broader range of subjects other than States. Thus, one can argue that at least theoretically both religious individuals and communities have human rights, but also an obligation to respect the human rights of others. A similar idea is also enshrined in Article 30 of the Universal Declaration of Human Rights.

215. Merusk and Narits have also explained that fundamental rights in the Estonian Constitution are, by nature, not simply a part of positive law, but also principles that are valid in law as such.[317] Ernits adds that, as a result, the private person is not subjected to correlative duties arising from fundamental rights but as a member of a society he or she is obliged to honour the fundamental rights of others.[318] He further notes that the private person is not the direct addressee of fundamental rights and freedoms, but his or her rights and freedoms are still influenced by the third-party application of fundamental rights that is mediated by the State (*Drittwirkung*).[319]

216. Moreover, private persons fulfilling public obligations/tasks may be addressees of fundamental rights and freedoms.[320] Thus, it is possible that when religious communities are fulfilling public obligations they can be addressees of fundamental rights. However, the actual application of the above theoretical observations to the relationship between individual rights and collective autonomy in Estonia remains to be seen.

---

315. A. Clapham, *Human Rights Obligations of Non-State Actors* (Oxford: OUP, 2006), 35. It has to be noted that Clapham does not specifically address the issue of religious communities. He focuses on non-state actors like international organizations, transnational corporations and armed opposition groups. However, he makes statements, which could be argued, are applicable to a wider group of non-state actors and individuals.
316. *Ibid.*, 54.
317. K. Mersuk & R. Narits, *Eesti konsitutsiooniõigusest* [*About Estonian Constituional Law*] (Tallinn: Juura, 1998), 177.
318. M. Ernits, 'Holders and Addressees of Basic Rights in the Constitution of the Republic of Estonia', *Juridica International* IV (1999): 24, 27–29.
319. *Ibid.*
320. *Eesti Vabariigi Põhiseadus: Kommenteeritud väljaanne* [*Commentaries of the Estonian Constitution*], 2 täiendatud trükk (Tallinn: Juura, 2008), Art. 14.

Chapter 1. Protection of Privacy

217. As to the protection of privacy of individuals, Article 26 of the Constitution sets forth that everyone has the right to the inviolability of private and family life. There is no case law as to the protection of the privacy of individual's vis-à-vis religious communities. Only a couple of remarks can be made on the basis of the laws directly regulating freedom of religion or belief. As discussed above, while employers do not have the right to request personal information in which they can have no justified interest, religious communities are probably able to ask necessary questions before entering into employment contracts with persons.

218. Privacy issues in relation to identity cards were described above.[321] Some further notes should be made here. The Ministry of Internal Affairs may require religious organizations to provide data to prove the person's affiliation when the identity cards are at issue. However, these requirements somewhat contradict Article 42 of the Estonian Constitution, which prohibits the State agencies and local governments from gathering or storing information about the beliefs of an Estonian citizen against the citizen's free will. Requiring data from religious organizations also contradicts the 2002 Churches and Congregations Act which states that nobody is required to provide information on his or her religion or membership in congregations, except a suspect, accused, accused at trial or victim in the course of criminal proceedings (§8(2)).[322] Thus, the Constitution and the 2002 Churches and Congregations Act have much more restrictive approach as to the possible range of circumstances in which State officials can collect data on an individual's religious affiliation than does the Identity Documents Act.[323] In some cases a religious community may face a legal dilemma in determining whether to provide the requested information to State officials or to respect the privacy of an individual as set forth in the 2002 CCA.[324]

219. All in all, the major problem with the right to privacy, as in other areas, appears to be the fact that different legal acts which regulate the same issue contradict each other in wording and in substance. As explained above, this has been the result of constant changes in the course of re-building the Estonian legal system after the collapse of the Soviet Union. How particular contradictions should be solved in the case of a conflict between individual rights and collective autonomy is a matter for future legislation or court practice.

---

321. *See* Part I, Ch. 2 above.
322. RT I 2002, 24, 135; RT I, 30.12.2017, 1 (last amended).
323. RT I 1999, 25, 365; RT I, 19.03.2019, 9 (last amended).
324. The EU General Data Protection Regulation (GDPR), which entered into force on 24 May 2016 and is applicable from 25 May 2018 may be relevant in this context.

Chapter 2. Freedom to Marry

220. Celebration of religious marriage before civil marriage is not an offence. In accordance with the Family Law a clergyman who has received authorization from the Minister of Regional Affairs is entitled to perform civil marriages. The State has not recognized the concept of religious marriage per se but, rather, has established the possibility of delegating the obligations of the register office to a clergyman of a church, congregation or association of congregations.[325] Without this authorization religious marriage simply does not have civil consequences.

221. As will be described in Part X below, an authorized minister can refuse to perform a marriage if those being married oppose the conditions set for marriages by the beliefs of his or her community. The minister has a right, but not an obligation, to refuse registration according to his or her own religion. This right may come into play in cases where one of the persons is divorced – unacceptable in some religious traditions. In an Estonian context, this would mostly apply to Roman Catholics and Orthodox believers. There may be other circumstances as well when the minister may feel compelled to use this right. The law gives considerable autonomy in this regard and does not explicitly require the minister to justify or prove the reasons for the refusal.

222. However, it is possible that if the refusal is based on religious prescription which contradicts some fundamental values in a democratic society it could be contested, if not on the basis of family law then on the basis of criminal law or anti-discrimination law. For example, it is possible that when the refusal is based solely on racial grounds the law and the courts may need to react to it. There is no case law clarifying this yet.[326]

325. Religious marriage will be discussed in Part X of this monograph.

326. *See, e.g.*, controversial case about admission policy of the Jewish Free School in the UK Supreme Court. *R (on the application of E) (Respondent) v. The Governing Body of JFS and the Admissions Appeal Panel of JFS and others (Appellants)* [2009] UKSC 15.

Chapter 3. Freedom of Expression

223. Freedom of expression is protected by Article 45 of the Estonian Constitution, which sets forth that everyone has the right to freely disseminate ideas, opinions, beliefs and other information by word, print, picture or other means. This right may be restricted by law to protect public order, morals, and the rights and freedoms, health, honour and good name of others.

224. As noted above, the Equal Treatment Act does not prejudice the right of religious communities to require individuals working for them to act in good faith and with loyalty to the organization's ethos (§10(3)).[327] There is no domestic case law to provide any guidance in these matters. As noted above there was an incident where an EELC priest had openly expressed his views in support of gays and had become a board member of the Association for Gay Christians. The priest turned to the Gender Equality and Equal Treatment Commissioner who made enquiries about the matter. The case was not taken further and did not reach the court. In the case of a conflict of interests some help may be discerned from the practice of the ECtHR. For example, in the admissibility case of *Rommelfanger v. the Federal Republic of Germany*[328] the European Commission of Human Rights dealt with the question of State responsibility to protect freedom of expression (under Article 10) of a physician who was dismissed from a Catholic hospital for publicly expressing support for women's right to abortion. The main focus in this case was on the question of whether by entering into an employment contract the applicant waived his right to freedom of expression. As mentioned above, this was at the crux of the response provided to the Commissioner's enquiry by the consistory of the EELC. The consistory explained that sexual orientation as such was not the ground for the dismissal but the fact that the dismissed priest broke his oath by not following and obeying internal regulations of the church (including its 2009 declaration on homosexualism).[329]

225. In the *Rommelfanger* case the European Commission agreed with the decision made by the German Federal Constitutional Court. The Constitutional Court took a broad view of interpreting the constitutional right to church autonomy and found that the constitutional guarantee was applicable not only to recognized churches, but also to institutions affiliated with them which in the understanding of the church fulfilled religious functions. The churches could create employment relationships in the exercising of their private autonomy. Nevertheless, the Federal Constitutional Court held that there were limits to the right of the church to impose its views on its employees. The European Commission of Human Rights concluded that there is no basis for the assumption that the applicant waived his freedom of expression as such (by entering into an employment contract). The fact that he accepted the status of a doctor employed by a Catholic hospital could not deprive

327. RT I 2008, 56, 315; RT I 2009, 48, 323 (last amended). *See* Part VI, Ch. 1 above.
328. *Rommelfanger v. the Federal Republic of Germany* (App. No. 12242/86) (1989) 62 DR 151.
329. 'EELK selgitas soovolinikule, miks tagandati üks vaimulik ametist' Meie Kirik, 11 Oct. 2011. *See also* Part VI (Labour Law within Religious Communities) above.

him of the protection afforded by Article 10.[330] Moreover, the Commission emphasized that it was the responsibility of the courts to ensure that no unreasonable demands of loyalty were made. However, in this case the requirement to refrain from making statements on abortion in conflict with the church's views was not seen as an unreasonable demand because of the crucial importance of this issue for the church. The Commission concluded that the application had to be rejected as manifestly ill-founded.

226. Thus, it appears that there are at least two main factors to take into account. First, the demands of loyalty have to be reasonable. The proximity of the matter to the core doctrinal issues or simply crucial importance of the matter to a religious community is another factor to take into account. It is possible that the Estonian courts will follow the reasoning put forward by the Strasbourg court. The exact outcome of a particular case will obviously depend on facts. The case law which in principle concerns the conflict between individual rights and autonomy or religious communities is on the increase in the ECtHR as well as in the European Court of Justice. This case law will inevitably have an effect on how matters are addressed in Estonian courts.

330. *Rommelfanger v. the Federal Republic of Germany* (App. No. 12242/86) (1989) 62 DR 151.

Chapter 4. Due Process Norms and Religious Groups

227. There are no legal provisions or case law in Estonia which explicitly deal with this matter. There is no provision in law which explicitly deals with applicability of due process norms within religious communities. However, as noted above, autonomy of religious associations means the right to self-administration in accordance with religious law and prescriptions.[331] In the case of a legal dispute it is also possible to resort to the practice of the ECHR. For example, in the case of *Ahtinen v. Finland* the Court dealt with the application of a priest who refused to transfer from one parish to another against the orders of his Church.[332] He claimed under Article 6 of the Convention (right to a fair trial) that the real reasons for his transfer had not been properly heard and that the Cathedral Chapter had been partial. The Court pointed out the most important reasons to uphold religious association autonomy in this case as follows:

> As for the position of the Evangelical Lutheran Church under Finnish law, the Court notes that it has the right to administer its own affairs ... It is independent in matters such as the appointment of its priests and the latter's service. The relevant legislation leaves it to the Church as an employer to determine the period and place of pastoral activity. The Court notes that when accepting ecclesiastical employment, parish priests are aware of the possibility that they may later be transferred to another post ... the applicant by agreeing to serve as a parish priest within the Church, undertook to abide by the rules of his church.[333]

228. The Court referred to its previous decisions in *Duda and Dudová v. the Czech Republic,* [334] where priests of the Czechoslovak Hussits Church challenged the termination of their clerical services by the authorities of their church. Here the Court concurred with the domestic courts' findings that the judicial determination of issues such as the continuation of a priest's service within a church 'would be contrary to the principles of autonomy and independence of churches guaranteed by, *inter alia* the Charter of Fundamental Rights and Freedoms'.[335] The Court concluded in the *Ahtinen* case that the applicant did not have a right within the meaning of Article 6. Article 6 was non-applicable to the present case. Article 6(1) secures everyone the right to have any claim relating to his or her civil rights and obligations brought before a court or tribunal. In the *Ahtinen* case the Court decided there was no civil right involved as the matter fell within the church's exclusive autonomy in Finland. Another deciding factor was that Mr Ahtinen knew about the possibility of transfer when he accepted the post (principle of voluntarism). However, it is probably right to say that the European Court of Human Rights has not

331. *See* Part I, Ch. 1 and Part III, Ch. 2 above.
332. *Ahtinen v. Finland* (App. No. 48907/99) ECHR 23 Sep. 2008.
333. *Ibid.*, para. 41.
334. *Duda and Dudová v. the Czech Republic* (App. No. 40224/98) ECHR 30 Jan. 2001.
335. *Ahtinen v. Finland* (App. No. 48907/99) ECHR 23 Sep. 2008, para. 42.

excluded State responsibility completely in regard to claims against religious communities under Article 6. For example, one can mention three subsequent cases in the ECtHR.[336] *Baulder v. Germany* and *Reuter v. Germany* concerned decisions by the Protestant Church to place one clergyman on leave of absence and to oblige another to take early retirement. The third case, *Müller v. Germany* concerned a decision by the Salvation Army to terminate the missionary service of two officers. In the cases of *Baudler* and *Reuter* the Court observed that the impugned measures relating to ecclesiastical appointments had been based on the rules of the respective Churches governing the service of members of their clergy. They had therefore not been governed by the law of the State, but solely by ecclesiastical law. In the *Müller* case the Court accepted that the German Court of Appeal and the Federal Court of Justice had found that they had limited powers to review the decision of the Salvation Army to dismiss the applicants, by examining whether the decision had been compatible with fundamental principles of the German legal order such as the general prohibition on arbitrariness and the principles of public morals and public policy. The ECtHR concluded that, unlike in *Baudler and Reuter*, the applicants could rely on a right recognized under German law, and that Article 6 of the Convention was therefore applicable. However, the court agreed with the domestic court's finding that there were no grounds for finding that the Salvation Army's decision had been arbitrary or contrary to public morals or public policy. There are no similar cases in Estonian court practice.

336. *Baulder v. Germany* (App. No. 38254/04) 6 Dec. 2011; *Müller v. Germany* (App. No. 12986/04) 6 Dec. 2011; *Reuter v. Germany* (App. No. 32741/06) 17 Jan. 2012. *See also Lombardi Vallauri v. Italy* (App. No. 39128/05) ECHR 20 Oct. 2009 where the ECtHR found violation of Art. 6.

Chapter 5. Professional Secrecy

229. The Code of Criminal Procedure (*Kriminaalmenetluse seadustik*),[337] which came into force on 1 July 2004, sets forth the right of the clergy to keep confessional secrecy. This Code obviously aims to find a compromise between the right of a defendant to a fair trial and the clergy's freedom of religion. According to the Code, ministers of religious organizations registered in Estonia have the right to refuse to give testimony as witnesses concerning circumstances which have become known to them in the course of their professional activities (§72(1)). The same right, according to the law, applies to the professional support staff of the ministers (§72(2)). This right of ministers and their support staff is qualified by the requirement to give testimony if their testimony is requested by the suspect or the accused. Moreover, when a court is convinced that the refusal to give testimony is not related to ministerial or professional activities of support staff, the court may require a person to give testimony. The latter provisions may conflict not only with ecclesiastical law but also with §22 of the 2002 CCA. This provision categorically declares that a minister of religion shall not disclose either information which has become known to him or her in the course of a private confession or pastoral conversation, or the identity of the person who makes a private confession or has a pastoral conversation with a minister of religion. Thus, according to the 2002 Churches and Congregations Act, the minister of a religion has an obligation to maintain confessional secrecy. This requirement does not extend to other personnel of religious communities.

230. Although there has been no case law in this regard, there is again a contradiction in law which subjects religious ministers to two conflicting obligations: to maintain secrecy and to disclose information if their testimony is requested by the suspect or the accused (hopefully, this contradiction in Estonian law will eventually be addressed).

337. RT I 2003, 27, 166; RT I, 29.12.2020, 1 (last amended).

Chapter 6. Medical Deontology

231. With the exception of conscientious objection of Jehovah's Witnesses to some medical treatments the issues related to medical deontology and religion have not yet emerged as an issue in Estonia. Apart from a couple of criminal cases described below there is also no court practice to refer to. The majority of hospitals do not have any particular religious ethos which may potentially conflict with individual freedoms of their employees. There are also no known incidents regarding conscientious objection of doctors, for example, to abortion or provision of certain pharmacological products by pharmacists, as known in some other European states. It is difficult to predict under the current law where the balance would be drawn in any case of conflict of interest.

232. As to the law that has relevance in the conscientious objection cases regarding Jehovah's Witnesses the relationships between a provider of health care services (e.g., a hospital or a doctor) and a patient are, first of all, regulated by the Law of Obligations Act (*Võlaõigusseadus*).[338] According to §766(3) of this act a patient may be examined and health care services may be provided to him or her only with his or her consent. A patient may withdraw his or her consent within a reasonable period of time after granting consent. At the request of a provider of health care services, such consent or an application to withdraw such consent shall be in a format which can be reproduced in writing.

233. The Law of Obligations Act further provides that in the case of a patient with restricted active legal capacity (e.g., a child), the legal representative of the patient has the right to be informed about the treatment and to consent insofar as the patient is unable to consider the pros and cons of the treatment responsibly. If the decision of the legal representative appears to damage the interests of the patient, the provider of health care services shall not comply with the decision. The patient with restricted active legal capacity also has to be informed of the circumstances personally to a reasonable extent (§766(4)). Nõmper and Sootak have noted that the law makes it clear that the health care provider first of all needs to consider what is best for the patient, despite the opinion of his or her legal representatives (including parents).[339]

234. Compared to the previous regulations the current law does not state, for example, at what age a child is competent to make a decision over what kind of health care should be provided to him or her. In the ESSR the age limit was 16. The draft of the Patient Rights Act (*Patsiendi õiguste seadus*),[340] which was submitted to the Parliament in 2000 and never materialized as a law, set the age limit at 15. Under current law the doctor needs to establish whether the patient is capable of weighing the pros and cons of proposed treatment responsibly. If an under aged person is acknowledged as capable of doing it, then the patient can independently

338. RT I 2002, 53, 336; RT I, 04.01.2021, 2 (last amended)
339. A. Nõmper & J. Sootak, *Meditsiiniõigus* (Tallinn: Juura, 2007), 72.
340. Patient Rights Act (*Patsiendiseadus*), 1009 SE II, www.riigikogu.ee, 1 May 2010.

decide over the treatment provided to him or her. In this case the doctor should not involve parents unless he or she has the patient's consent. Involving parents contrary to the consent would breach the confidentiality requirement.[341]

235. Nõmper and Sootak in their comprehensive textbook for students, but also for practitioners (lawyers and health care providers alike), suggest that the law is clear as to what doctors need to do in the case of Jehovah's Witnesses who object to a desperately needed blood transfusion for their child. Even if the child is not, legally speaking, capable of deciding over the treatment and theoretically parents' consent is necessary, doctors should ignore the parents' objections. Refusing the blood transfusion in this case would not be in the best interest of the patient.[342]

236. Conscientious objection to medical treatment has occasionally captured media attention. In this regard, cases around the world involving Jehovah's Witnesses have been in the spotlight quite frequently.

237. However, there are only a very few actual cases in Estonia involving medical practice and religion. All these cases have involved Jehovah's Witnesses. The first case was a criminal case[343] concerning doctors who followed the request of parents not to give medical help to their new-born child. The baby died. In the course of proceedings, the criminal charges were dropped by the prosecutor (on 15 March 2000) on the ground that, at that time, there existed a widespread misconception among doctors, who believed that they could not go against the will of the parents in such cases.

238. The follow-up of the same incident was a criminal case against the parents of the new-born child. The charges were dropped on 14 March 2001 after it was found that there was no causal link between the refusal of the blood transfusion and baby's death. The death was predicted earlier during the pregnancy (for that reason doctors recommended abortion). Saving a child's life in this case would have been impossible with or without a blood transfusion.

239. This case triggered lively debates in society and in the legal community. The draft of the Patient Rights Act,[344] which was debated in the parliament at that time, reflected the concerns expressed in society. According to the act no one could, on behalf of other persons, refuse or prevent indispensable medical aid. The express purpose of this provision was to prevent persons from hindering indispensable medical aid to other persons on religious grounds. The Explanatory Note to the legislation stated expressly that this bill addresses the prevention of blood transfusion.[345] According to the draft, in other cases the consent of the person was

341. A. Nõmper & J. Sootak, *Meditsiiniõigus* (Tallinn: Juura, 2007), 72.
342. A. Nõmper & J. Sootak, *Meditsiiniõigus* (Tallinn: Juura, 2007), 72.
343. Criminal Case No. 98110537. For the detailed analysis of the case *see* A. Nõmper, 'Jehoova tunnistajate lapse arstide kriminaalasjast' ['About the Criminal Case Against Doctors of Jehovah's Witnesses Child'], *Juridica* IV (2000): 212–223.
344. Patient Rights Act (*Patsiendiseadus*), 1009 SE II, www.riigikogu.ee, 1 May 2010.
345. *See* Explanation note to the Draft No. 1009 SE II, www.riigikogu.ee, 1 May 2010.

necessary. The draft act also required doctors to take into account as much as possible the will of an under aged patient. As mentioned above, the Patient Rights Act never materialized as a law. The current regulation differs from the draft law in wording and is to a certain degree more flexible regarding a child's rights to make decisions about health services provided to him or her.

240. Today, alternative medical treatments to blood transfusion have been gradually accepted and applied by doctors and hospitals. When the treatment is not available in Estonia, the help of hospitals abroad has been procured. In this case the Estonian Health Insurance Fund (*Eesti Haigekassa*)[346] may compensate the patients' expenses in some cases. The Jehovah's Witnesses have been active in cooperating with medical institutions to solve religiously sensitive issues. In many cases this cooperation has been successful.[347]

241. Since 2001 there have been a few other incidents where a conflict of interests has occurred between health care providers and parents of an under aged child. All these incidents were solved without legal consequences. It is a common practice that adult Jehovah's Witnesses carry with them documentation which indicates in detail what type of treatment they refuse. These documents also provide names and contact details of two other witnesses in case the patient is not capable of expressing his or her own will under any circumstances.

242. As noted above, there was a general phobia against the NRMs, especially in the 1990s.[348] Ignorance and prejudice guided some of the public and media reaction. Gradually the attitude seems to be changing and efforts have been made to find reasonable solutions, which satisfy all parties as far as possible within the limits of the law and keeping in mind the best interests and autonomy of the patient.

346. Eesti Haigekassa, www.haigekassa.ee/eng/ehif, 1 Jun. 2010.
347. Interview with Aarne Naaber from the Estonian Jehovah's Witnesses Association of Congregations, 25 Aug. 2010.
348. *See* Part V, Ch. 2 above.

Chapter 7. Non-discrimination

243. As stated in the Chapter 1 of Part I of this monograph, the principle of equality is anchored in the first sentence of the first paragraph of Article 12 of the Estonian Constitution. Article 12 states that all persons shall be equal before the law. The second paragraph of Article 12 of the Constitution sets forth the principle of non-discrimination, prohibiting discrimination *inter alia* on the basis of religion or belief. It was also noted before that there are two further pieces of anti-discrimination legislation in Estonia: the Equal Treatment Act[349] and the Gender Equality Act.[350] These acts are the result of anti-discrimination legislation at the EU level and the application of both of these acts extends to relationships between private parties. The Gender Equality Act does not apply to the professing and practising of faith or working as a minister of a religion in a registered religious association (§2(2)). The Equal Treatment Act allows exemptions for religious communities.[351]

244. International and transnational developments in anti-discrimination law have become increasingly (and potentially) challenging for religious communities. The effects of the interplay between anti-discrimination legislation and collective freedom of religion or belief in Estonia remain to be seen. Currently there is no case law in relation to this matter. Issues arising from employment situations were described above.[352]

---

349. RT I 2008, 56, 315; RT I, 26.04.2017, 6 (last amended).
350. RT I 2004, 27, 181; RT I, 26.04.2013, 2 (last amended).
351. *See also* Part VI (Labour Law within Religious Communities).
352. *See* Part VI above.

Chapter 8. Penal Law and Religion

245. The current Penal Code (*Karistusseadustik*)[353] was adopted on 6 June 2001 and entered into force on 1 September 2002. It repealed the earlier code which was in force since 1 June 1992.[354] The new Penal Code introduced two principal changes. First, both criminal offences and some misdemeanours are dealt with in the same law. A criminal offence is an offence for which the principal punishment prescribed is, in the case of natural persons, a pecuniary punishment or imprisonment, and, in the case of legal persons, a pecuniary punishment or compulsory dissolution (§3(3)). A misdemeanour is an offence which is provided for in the Penal Code or another Act, and the principal punishment prescribed for which is a fine or detention (§3(4)). If a person commits an act which falls under the criteria for both a misdemeanour and a criminal offence, the person shall be punished only for the criminal offence. If a punishment is not imposed for the criminal offence, the same act may be punished for the misdemeanour (§3(5)). It should also be specified that only intentional acts are punishable as criminal offences, unless a punishment for a negligent act is provided by the Penal Code. An act is also deemed to be intentional if it comprises the necessary elements of an offence in the case of which intent is presumed with regard to the act, and negligence is deemed to be sufficient in the case of grave consequences. Intentional and negligent acts are both punishable as misdemeanours (§15).

246. Second, the 2002 Penal Code introduced the concept of criminal liability of legal entities into Estonian law.[355] Before the 2002 Code legal persons were only liable for administrative offences. Since 1 September 2002, in the cases provided by law, a legal person can be held responsible for an act which is committed by a body or senior official thereof in the interest of the legal person (§14(1)). Prosecution of a legal person does not preclude prosecution of the natural person who committed the offence (§14(2)). Legal persons cannot be held liable for every offence listed in the Penal Code, such as murder, manslaughter, theft and assault. But it can be held liable for crimes like fraud, tax evasion, bribes, and also war propaganda and acts of terrorism. Only registered legal persons with legal capacity and rights can be held liable. The state, local governments and legal persons in public law cannot be held criminally liable. Religious associations registered under the CCA are legal persons in private law. Thus, in principle, a religious community can be held responsible in certain circumstances. In some cases a religious community may even be subjected to compulsory dissolution. The basis for this may be found in Article 48(3) of the Estonian Constitution: 'associations whose aims or activities violate criminal law

353. RT I 2001, 61, 364; RT I, 10.07.2020, 1 (last amended).
354. RT I 1992, 20, 287 ja 288.
355. For an overview of criminal liability of legal persons in Estonia *see* J. Ginter, 'Criminal Liability of Legal Persons in Estonia', *Juridica International* XVI (2009): 151–156.

are prohibited'.[356] In 2012 the Ministry of Justice initiated major amendments/ revisions of the Penal Code. The amendments entered into force on 1 January 2015.[357]

247. Only a very few cases related to religion have been decided by courts generally. There have been no cases dealing with criminal responsibility of religious communities. There have been a couple of cases dealing with an offence committed by a religious individual.[358] However, not all of these cases directly concerned religion or religious freedom. In 2016 two men were prosecuted for facilitating terrorism, by funding or organizing funding for a friend to join ISIS.[359] According to the Estonian Internal Security Service (KAPO) there were about twenty individuals associated with Estonia who are or have been in the Syria-Iraq conflict zone in 2019. Similar to previous years, in 2019 KAPO identified nearly fifty individuals linked to Islamic extremism or forty-one terrorist organizations who either arrived in or transited Estonia.[360]

248. Paragraph 154 of the Penal Code (*Karistusseadustik*)[361] deals specifically with violation of freedom of religion. It lays down the penalty (a pecuniary punishment or up to one year of imprisonment) for knowingly interfering without legal grounds, with acknowledgement or declaration of religious beliefs or the absence thereof, or exercise of religion or religious rites, is punishable by a pecuniary punishment or up to one year imprisonment. This crime can be attributed to a legal person. The Penal Code also sets forth punishment for violation of freedom of association. According to the Code, violation of freedom of founding of a religious or freedom of membership in such association is punishable by a pecuniary punishment or up to one year imprisonment. Legal person can face pecuniary punishment for the same act (§155). It is not entirely clear when acts of persons compelling another person to join a religious community are attributable to the legal person. Concerning this crime, so far there have been no cases involving either an individual or a religious community. It also has not become a provision which is abused, for example, towards new religious movements.

249. Up to 2015, §159 of the code set forth that interference with the foundation of, joining or membership in a non-profit association, if the foundation or activities of the association do not violate the conditions or restrictions provided by law in the interests of the protection of the security of the state and the society, public

356. The major amendments to the Penal Code, currently under discussion in the Parliament, exclude dissolution as a form of punishment because the dissolution is sufficiently covered by civil and administrative law.
357. RT I, 12.07.2014, 1.
358. Supreme Court, Criminal Law Chamber, Case No. 3-1-1-82-96, 27 Aug. 1996 (RT III 1996, 23, 312.
359. They committed a crime provided in § 2373 (1) of the Penal Code (financing and supporting an act of terrorism and activities directed at it).KAPO Aastaraamat 2016 (Annual Review of the Estonian Internal Security Service), https://www.kapo.ee/en/content/annual-reviews.html, 8 Feb. 2021, 26.
360. KAPO Aastaraamat 2019-2020 (Annual Review of the Estonian Internal Security Service), https: //www.kapo.ee/en/content/annual-reviews.html, 8 Feb. 2021, 41.
361. RT I 2001, 61, 364; RT I, 10.07.2020, 1 (last amended).

order, morals or the rights of other people, and if joining or membership in the association does not violate the conditions or restrictions provided by law for persons in public service, is punishable by a fine or by detention. A legal person could not be held liable for this offence. According to the explanatory note to the amendments to the Penal Code criminal punishment for this offence is not justified. This provision was removed from the penal code during the aforementioned revision.[362] The change entered into force in 2015.

250. Interference with or violent dispersion of a lawfully organized public meeting is punishable by a pecuniary punishment or up to one year of imprisonment (§158). The change that entered into force in 2015 introduced criminal liability of legal persons for these acts. The wording of paragraph 262 of the Penal Code, which establishes crime for breaching public order, was also changed in 2015. It reads now as follows: 'Violation of the general requirements for behaviour in public places is punishable by a fine of up to one hundred fine units or by detention.'

251. Breach of public order, if committed by using violence, or by using threat with a weapon, any other object used as a weapon, an explosive device or explosive substance, is punishable by a pecuniary punishment or up to five years' imprisonment (§263, 'Aggravated breach of public order'). Since the amendments entered into force in 2015 these two offences can be attributable to a legal person.

252. There are no provisions specifically dealing with 'blasphemy' or defamation. Previous (1992) Criminal Code had a provision on defamation (§129). Drafters of the new law were of the opinion that defamation is sufficiently covered by other provisions which deal with specific circumstances. For example, activities which publicly incite hatred, violence or discrimination on the basis of religion (among other grounds) if this results in danger to the life, health or property of a person are punishable by a fine or by detention (§151(1)). In certain circumstances such behaviour may result in more severe punishment. This crime can also be attributable to a legal person, for example, to a religious community, which can be fined. In 2013 the draft amendments to the current Penal Code envisaged broadening the applicability of criminal liability for incitement to hatred. According to the draft act then, hate speech did not necessarily have to result in danger to the life, health or property of a person. The proposed amendments (the broadening of the scope of the provision) caused intense negative response from the Estonian Council of Churches. The Council feared that any religious speech from the pulpit or otherwise concerning objection to abortion or homosexuality could have been termed as a hate crime. The amendments were not included among the ones that entered into force on 1 January 2015. However, the debates are still ongoing. Only at the beginning of 2021 another attempt was made to change the provision. The narrow scope of the provision has been, over the years, criticized by multiple international human rights

---

362. Seletuskiri karistusseadustiku ja sellega seonduvalt teiste seaduste muutmise seaduse eelnõu juurde (SE 554), http://www.riigikogu.ee/?op=ems&page=eelnou&eid=78433b29-8b2f-4281-a582-0efb9631e2ad&, 6 Jun. 2014.

monitoring bodies (e.g., by UN Human Rights Committee in its 2019 concluding observations on Estonia) and by the European Union.[363]

253. There is no provision specifically dealing with proselytizing. It is not as such an offence. General provisions on offences against persons apply to 'improper proselytising' (this term is not used in the Penal Code).

254. No provisions are specifically dedicated to deal with sects in the Penal Code. If a religious person or a minority religious group commits a crime it will be tried under the provisions applicable to all.

255. The chapter on 'Offences Against Political and Civil Rights' has a specific division dealing with offences against equality. Article 152 of the Penal Code provides the penalty for the violation equality. 'Unlawful restriction of the rights of a person or granting of unlawful preferences to a person on the basis of his or her nationality, race, colour, sex, language, origin, religion, sexual orientation, and political opinion, financial or social status is punishable by a fine or by detention.' The same act, if committed at least twice, or if significant damage is caused to the rights or interests of another person protected by law or to public interests, is punishable by a pecuniary punishment or up to one year of imprisonment. Since 2015 a legal person can be punished for acts provided in Article 152.

256. Misuse of religious garments could be an aggravating circumstance: 'taking advantage of an official uniform or badge in order to facilitate commission of the offence' (§58). Only a person to whom a religious association has granted the corresponding permission has the right to wear the professional attire of a minister of religion as prescribed in the statutes of the religious association concerned. The specified restriction does not apply if the professional attire of the minister of religion is ordinary clothing (2002 Churches and Congregations Act, §21).

257. Ritual homicide is not a specific crime or an aggravation. Female genital mutilation is not a special crime or a form of aggravated assault. These cases would be dealt under provisions covering offences against persons.

258. In accordance with the Law on Narcotic Drugs and Psychotropic Substances (*Narkootiliste ja psühhotroopsete ainete ning nende lähteainete seadus*), consumption of drugs without prescription of a doctor is strictly prohibited (§15^1).[364] Illegal manufacture, acquisition and possession of narcotic drugs or psychotropic substances in a small quantity are punishable by fine or detention. According to the §183 of the Penal Code illegal trafficking or mediation of small quantities of narcotic drugs or psychotropic substances, or illegal manufacture, acquisition or possession of small quantities of narcotic drugs or psychotropic substances with the intention of trafficking, is punishable by a pecuniary punishment or up to three years

363. J. Värk, 'ERR Brüsselis: Eesti pole koos Rumeeniaga ainsana EL-is vihakõnet kriminaliseerinud', *ERR*, 16 Nov. 2020.
364. RT I 1997, 52, 834; RT I, 08.01.2020, 2 (last amended).

of imprisonment. What constitutes a small or large quantity of drugs is regulated by the Government regulation in force since 1997. For example, 10 grams of opium is considered to be a large quantity.[365] Illegal possession, acquisition, trafficking, mediation, transportation, import, export, transit or other illegal handling of large quantities of drugs is punishable by up to five years' imprisonment (Penal Code, §184). The same act, if committed by a group or a criminal organization, or at least twice, is punishable by up to ten years' imprisonment. Criminal liability follows also, for example, from the illegal inducement of a person to the use of drugs (up to three years of imprisonment – §186). Up to ten years imprisonment is prescribed for inducing a person under 18 to use drugs (§187).

259. As noted above, the 2002 Penal Code introduced into Estonian law the possibility of criminal liability upon legal entities. For the illegal handling of large quantities of drugs, a legal entity (including a religious organization) can be fined. In certain circumstance a religious organization can be subjected to compulsory dissolution.

260. Religious motivations do not figure in the specific list of aggravating (§57) or mitigating circumstances (§58). No provision concerning individual offences has listed religious motivations as specific aggravating or mitigating factor. Moreover, Article 41(2) of the Estonian Constitution specifically stipulates that 'beliefs shall not constitute an excuse for a legal offence'. However, no person can be held legally liable just because of his or her beliefs.

261. There is no case law on the use of drugs in religious ceremonies in Estonia. However, recently, Estonian media pointed out that the use of Ayahuasca (native North American ritual drug) has been on the increase in Estonia. Allegedly the practice arrived here in the end of the 1980s and has gained momentum. It has not captured interest of regular drug abusers, but rather ordinary people looking for new spiritual experiences and healing.[366] In Estonia this hallucinogen is on the list of prohibited drugs. It is doubtful whether individual or collective religious autonomy extends so far in Estonia as to allow the use of drugs in religious practice. Taking into account how the law stands at the moment, growing drug-related problems and the current climate of zero tolerance to drugs, an Estonian court and legislator would most likely find the prohibition of using drugs in religious practice justified. However, there is no court case yet to refer to.

---

365. RT I 1997, 83, 1416.
366. K. Aasma, '"Pealtnägija": Eestis on plahvatuslikult levinud ayahuasca rituaalid' *Õhtuleht*, 9 Oct. 2013; H. Kaasik, 'Ayahuasca Rituaalne kasutamine Eestis', *Usuteaduslik Ajakiri* 2 (75) (2019): 118–146.

Part VIII. Church Financing

262. The fact that the Estonian Constitution provides that there is no State Church, and that the 2002 CCA addresses all religious communities equally, has not been seen by the State as providing grounds for a rigorous policy of non-identification with religion. As noted before, in terms of the classification of the Church and State relationship, Estonia probably fits most comfortably into the category of cooperation systems (in cooperation systems the law separates but allows collaboration between state and religion). In Estonia, alongside religious leaders participating in certain state/local government ceremonies, the cooperation manifests itself most notably in the form of State financing of religious organizations and projects where religious communities and the State have mutual interests (education, social care, preservation of culturally important objects, chaplaincy, etc.). Like in most European states this financing is based on the implicit understanding that it facilitates the citizens' exercise of religious freedom and helps to strengthen the positive role that religion plays in society. In Estonia, however, this financial cooperation could be said to have also a very pragmatic nature, aiming at consolidating limited human and financial resources for common good.

Chapter 1. Direct Financing of Religious Communities

263. There is no direct and automatic financing of religious communities (including churches) in Estonia. There are no church taxes. However, the distinction between direct and indirect financing can only be tentative. For the sake of convenience all types of financing will be considered in the next section.

Chapter 2. Indirect Financing of Religious Communities

264. One could consider tax exemptions to be a form of indirect financing of religious communities. In Estonia religious communities enjoy several tax exemptions. However, recently there have been some changes, which indicate a move towards less automatic exemptions and more equality between taxing religious communities and other non-profit organizations. For example, there is no longer an automatic exemption from income tax, as was the case before 2011. Before 2011 religious associations registered in Estonia were automatically included into the list of non-taxable organizations, ordinary non-profit organizations (including religious societies[367]) had to apply for it. When the law was changed a sort of compromise was made. Namely, all religious associations, which already were in the list of non-taxable organizations by 31 December 2010, were automatically included in the list from 1 January 2011. As of January 2011, newly established religious associations have to apply for the inclusion in the list of non-taxable organizations, as do other non-profit organizations.[368] This also means that this status can also be refused on certain grounds. There have been no reports of abuse of this provision oppressing activities of newly established religious communities. However, in 2013 there were two cases where two foundations that are running Christian schools (Tallinna Toomkooli Sihtasutus and Püha Johannese Kooli Sihtasutus) had to establish through the court that they had a right to be included in the list of non-profit organizations. According to the Estonian Tax and Customs Board these two organizations were making profit. As a result of the court case in the Tallinn Administrative Court both foundations were included in the list in 2013.[369]

265. However, several religious associations previously in the list were excluded in 2013 because of the non-compliance with the Income Tax Act. Some have expressed dissatisfaction with the complexity of writing annual financial reports and with bureaucracy related to complying with tax obligations. Religious organizations, like other entities, have to submit an annual fiscal report to the Estonian Tax and Customs Board. Failure to provide it can be a sole ground for exclusion from the list of non-taxable organizations. In 2012 there was a case where this failure eventually resulted in dissolution proceedings against a congregation.[370] One could argue that this dissatisfaction is mainly related to incapacity of smaller congregations (also within churches) to deal with financial issues. The problem could be solved inside religious communities. There is no oppression of religious organizations by the state in financial matters. The above-mentioned dissatisfaction is also partly related to a more general criticism from some religious organizations not satisfied with laws, as they see it, allegedly treating religious organizations as ordinary

367. One should keep in mind the legal distinction between religious associations and religious societies in Estonian law.

368. Income Tax Act (*Tulumaksuseadus*), RT I 1999, 101, 903; RT I, 23.12.2013, 3 (last amended).

369. RT III, 21.12.2013, 13.

370. *See* correspondence between Ministry of Internal Affairs and Harju County Court (Harju Maakohus) June 2012 (Siseministeeriumi arhiiv).

non-profit making organizations.[371] The latter criticism does not have a solid ground. This issue was taken up again by the Estonian Council of Churches before the 2019 elections in its letter to political parties.[372]

266. As to other taxes, religious associations had certain privileges concerning value added tax until 2007. These usually figured as discounts against the ordinary tax rate. For example, until 1 July 2007, religious organizations could buy electricity attracting a rate of 5% VAT (instead of the normal 18%).[373] The same did not apply to most non-profit-making organizations, including religious societies. This privilege does not exist anymore.

267. Religious associations continue to be exempt from land (property) tax. Land tax is not imposed on land under the places of worship of churches and congregations (*Maamaksuseadus,* Land Tax Act, §4(1)(5)).[374] This exemption does not apply to the properties of secular non-profit-making organizations. Thus, regarding land tax there is a distinction in the treatment of religious associations and other non-profit making organizations, including religious societies. In addition, there have been debates over tax on land under natural sacral objects. The religious association called House of Taara and Native Religions has been trying to achieve changes in law to extend the exemption from land tax to the land under these objects. The debate is ongoing and has not been solved yet.

268. In addition to tax exemptions there are other more direct ways to finance religious communities. Taking into account the fact that sacred church buildings usually have historical, cultural and artistic value, the State is obliged, according to law, to find additional finances to support the churches and other religious communities in the preservation of these buildings. The money, however, depends on available resources. On 11 March 2003 the Estonian government approved a programme/ policy paper '*Pühakodade säilitamine ja areng*' (Preservation and Development of Sacred Buildings). Although not a law, the paper provides a basis for several legislative and financial actions to support development of churches over the period from 2004 to 2013 (the programme was renewed and revised for 2013-2018[375]). Although among the others Estonian Council of Churches has proposed continuation of the programme,[376] it has not been renewed by the time of the revision of this monograph. On the basis of this policy paper, which recognized the historic, cultural and communal importance of Christian Churches, allocations were made every year from the State budget. In total EUR 9.23 million were given towards the project between 2004 and 2013 which, however, was only 22.8% of the initially

371. *See, e.g.*, '"Kirikute ja koguduste seaduse" muutmise kohta saabunud ettepanekud. Saadetud kuni 31.03.2012' (Siseministeeriumi arhiiv). *See also* M. Kiviorg, *Religiooni puudutavate õigusaktide analüüs* (Analysis of the Laws Regulating Religion) (Tallinn: Siseministeerium, 2012).
372. Estonian Council of Churches, http://www.ekn.ee/inc.uudis.php?id=372, 1 Mar. 2021.
373. RT I 2001, 64, 368.
374. RT I 1993, 24, 428; RT I, 23.12.2020, 5 (last amended).
375. 'Progrmm 'Pühakodade säilitamine ja areng' 2013-2018', kinnitatud kultuuriministri käskirjaga nr. 371, 28.11.2013 (Tallinn: Kultuuriministeerium, 2013).
376. Estonian Council of Churches, http://www.ekn.ee/inc.uudis.php?id=372, 1 Mar. 2021.

planned contribution. The immediate aim has been to restore culturally and artistically important buildings. The majority of churches having historical value belong to Evangelical Lutheran Church and EAOC, but also to other minor communities. In total, between 2004 and 2018 approximately EUR 13 million was given by state for achievement of the goals of the programme.[377]

269. However, this policy paper had a wider purpose, as it envisaged Christian Churches to be partners to the State. For example, it stated that churches have an important role in preserving national identity and cultural heritage, but also in carrying out social work, educating the young, fostering regional development and community life in the countryside with high unemployment and even in providing people with spiritual guidance by educating them on religious matters after the vacuum caused by Soviet times, in doing so giving them support in a globalizing world. Thus, financial contributions were envisioned to extend beyond the mere preservation of sacred buildings. As stated in the policy document, the basis of this wider goal was the aim expressed in the Estonian Constitution to preserve the Estonian nation and culture.

270. The document raised a range of interesting questions concerning the general role of today's state in preserving (or shaping) national identity, maintaining a coherent society and protecting human rights and rights of minorities in a generally multi-religious and secularized context. There is a clear difference between cooperation with religious communities (not only churches) for the common good and active (financial) promotion by the State of one brand of religion. There has been a long running debate since the breakup of the Soviet Union in which some parties have argued that Estonia does not have a concept of the State and Church (religious communities) relationship. There has been hesitation on both sides. Even inside the Lutheran Church there have been conflicting ideas of how much involvement the Church should have with the State and to what extent the Church can use the tools of the State for the fulfilment of its purpose. In addition, it should also be said that no church has really won the hearts of Estonians. Although many may identify themselves as believers, most have remained indifferent to institutional expression of their convictions. However, in light of the above, a concept of a relationship between the State and Christian Churches seems to be gradually emerging.

271. From the wording of the policy paper it also appears that the State wants to take affirmative action/reverse discrimination to compensate for the sufferings of churches not only during Soviet times but throughout history. Here, the equality question should probably be treated with more care as all religions suffered during Soviet times and before. It is a tricky business to estimate who has suffered more in order to justify preferential treatment, especially when one goes beyond property matters. Collective/institutional freedom of religion is protected by the Estonian Constitution; in principle, it should be balanced against other freedoms and rights

377. Kultuuriministeerium, Pühakodade programmist on toetatud kirikuid ligi 13 miljoni euroga, 14 Dec. 2018, https://www.kul.ee/et/uudised/puhakodade-programmist-toetatud-kirikuid-ligi-13-miljoni-euroga, 1 Apr. 2021.

and principle of equality. The same applies to the extent of fulfilment of the State's positive obligations regarding religious freedom, including financial subsidies.

272. One of the main principles underlying financial arrangements with religious communities is captured in Article 40 of the Estonian Constitution: there is no State Church. However, this does not necessarily require strict separation of state and church (or other religious communities). Cooperation with religious communities and financial subsidies by the state for the common good has been accepted; however, how extensive such cooperation should be is hotly debated and has caused non-Christian communities to express concerns about equal treatment. These problems have also been pointed out by the Chancellor of Justice in one of his annual reports, where he has quite rightly observed that 'many of the issues in this field tend to remain outside the sphere of the Constitution and a debate and agreement in society is needed to find an answer to them'.[378] The statement also reflects the reality that Estonian national identity may not be so easily identified. Because of historical reasons, any ideological push to one direction will make large segments of society uncomfortable.

273. As pointed out above there are differences concerning financial policy between the religious communities in Estonia. The privileged position of the Estonian Council of Churches was mentioned before: the State has considered it a partner in making decisions on religious freedom questions in Estonia.[379] The privileged position of the Council is visible and perhaps most sensitive in matters of financial support and education. The trend towards allocating more funds to the council can be seen when State budgets over the last few years are compared. For example, EUR 695 372 in 2014; EUR 671 072 in 2013; EEK 7,420,000 (approximately EUR 476 000) in 2009; EEK 5,900,000 in 2006; EEK 4,900,000 (about EUR 314,103) was allocated from the 2004 State budget,[380] compared with EEK 1,945,000 in 2000.[381] It seems, however, that there has been a shift in wording the conditions for the allocation. Until rather recently the Estonian Council of Churches decided upon the usage of money by itself. The annual contracts signed between the Ministry of Internal Affairs and the ECC only defined the broad purpose of it: ecumenical cooperation of Christian churches for the development of Estonian society on the basis of Christian values. For example, the 2010 contract mentioned that the common interest of this agreement is furthering the cooperation between churches and the State. No specific targets or common goals were mentioned.[382] Since 2011 the terms of the contract have gradually become more detailed containing specific targets/projects or goals of common interests.[383]

378. The Annual Report 2003–2004 of the Chancellor of Justice of Estonia (Tallinn, 2005), 63; Chancellor of Justice www.oiguskantsler.ee/.files/37.pdf, 1 May 2010.
379. *See* Part I, Ch. 3 above.
380. RT I 2004, 1, 1.
381. RT I 2000, 1, 1.
382. Contract No. 7-4/30, 2010, Siseministeerium, www.siseministeerium.ee/30468/?highlight= lepingud, 1 May 2014.
383. *See* contracts signed between Ministry of Internal Affairs and Estonian Council of Churches, 2011, 2012, 2013, https://www.siseministeerium.ee/30468/?highlight=%2520lepingud, 1 Jun. 2014.

274. In addition, allocations have been made to support the publication of the newspaper of the EELC and Radio 7, which broadcasts programmes on Christianity and culture. The constitutionality of these allocations and preferential treatment of the Estonian Council of Churches and the Evangelical Lutheran Church have been questioned by non-Christian religious communities. Ringvee from the Ministry of Internal Affairs has suggested that if the non-Christian communities could establish themselves as a legal entity in a similar manner to the Estonian Council of Churches, further State subsidizes might be forthcoming for them too.[384] As noted above, in 2001, non-Christian communities themselves initiated the Round Table of Religious Organizations.[385] However, it has never been registered as a legal entity. Ringvee has also pointed out that it has not always been very active. Another initiative was taken in 2005 when a commission consisting of state representatives, representatives of Native religion, and various other experts was formed to draft a state programme for the protection of 'Groves' and other natural sacral objects.[386] There is a new initiative in the Parliament to adopt a policy document on preservation of natural sacral objects.[387] Recently some allocations have been made to non-Christian community. For example, in the 2009 budget allocations were made to the community representing the Estonian indigenous religion. The allocation was made for research on historical sacred sites of the indigenous religion and for the project aiming at raising awareness about the preservation of nature. The Ministry of Cultural Affairs initiated a development strategy for raising awareness about and preservation of sacred natural sites for the period of 2015–2020 (previous period was 2008–2012).[388]

275. In allocating funds, the government enters into a contract with the relevant community. The contract normally prescribes, among other things, control and reporting about the usage of said funds. There are also financial penalties for breach of contract (e.g., for not using the money purposefully). Some of the current contracts are for financing projects where the State and the community have common interests, for example, preparation of religious teachers or chaplains for public institutions. The financing of specific activities by the government appears to be on the increase. However, the current economic climate may hinder some of these projects. During the corona pandemic significant support was provided to religious communities.[389]

---

384. R. Ringvee, 'State, Religion and the Legal Framework in Estonia', *Religion, State and Society* 32, no. 2 (2008): 191.
385. *See* Part V, Ch. 1 above.
386. Estonian Ministry of Culture, Directive of Minister of Culture, 11 Feb. 2005, No. 49.
387. Riigikogus toimub looduslike pühapaikade avatud konverents, http://www.riigikogu.ee/index.php?id=176329, 1 Jun. 2014.
388. Kultuuriministeerium, 'Eesti looduslikud pühapaigad. Uurimine ja hoidmine. Arengukava 2015-2020' (Tallinn: Kultuuriministeerium, 2015), https://www.muinsuskaitseamet.ee/et/ajaloolised-ja-looduslikud-puhapaigad, 1 Mar. 2021.
389. Eesti Kirikute Nõukogu, Kogudused saavad sotsiaalse mõjuga tegevuste jätkamiseks ja koguduste majanduslike raskuste leevendamiseks toetust, 20 Apr. 2020, http://ekn.ee/inc.uudis.php?id=455, 1 Mar. 2021.

276. The salaries of priests and other people working for the Church or other religious communities are paid by the organizations themselves.

277. Army, prison and police chaplains are civil servants and are paid in full by the State budget. The prison chaplaincy is coordinated by the Ministry of Justice and the army chaplaincy by the Ministry of Defence. There is no chaplaincy system established in hospitals. In 2007 the chaplaincy service was established in the Estonian police force. Only people from the member churches of the Estonian Council of Churches are entitled to serve as chaplains. The institution of the chaplaincy is meant to be inter-denominational and ecumenical. Members of other religious organizations (including non-Christian) do have access to these institutions upon the request of the people staying there. These visits are privately funded. The chaplaincy service is not regulated by law and needs future development. It is mainly based on the cooperation agreement between the Estonian Council of Churches and the State (17 October 2002 Protocol of Common Concerns).

278. Private schools (including schools registered by religious associations) may receive subsidies for specific purposes from the state budget or local government budget (Private Schools Act, §22). However, financing of staff depends on the type of school and is provided only to the extent to which the school follows the curricula used by state or municipal schools. Teachers of religious studies at public schools are paid out of the state or municipal budget (religious education will be discussed in the following section).

Part IX. Education

Chapter 1. Religious Education in Public and Private Schools

279. Religious education has been one of the most contested issues regarding religion in Estonia today, and in fact, throughout its history as an independent State. To understand the controversies as they exist today it is important to take a brief look at the history of religious education in Estonia. This is also important because when Estonia regained independence in the early 1990s and started to re-build its legal order on the principle of restitution, it needed to look back at the legal framework of 1918–1940, while acknowledging new circumstances and developments in European legal order and thinking.

280. First, some historical points of reference are necessary. As mentioned above, after the conquest of Estonian territory by crusaders in the thirteenth century, cultural life in Estonia was divided along national and social lines.[390] Raun points out that, educational institutions in medieval times were those associated with the Church and monasteries. Instruction took place in German, and only a few Estonians were able to participate.[391] As to the actual completion of Christianization of Estonian people, the Moravian Brethren movement played a significant role in this in the eighteenth and nineteenth century.[392]

281. The first attempts to translate and publish biblical texts in Estonian date back to the early sixteenth century. There is some evidence of Catholic writings in 1517, and definite evidence of Lutheran texts in 1525 (unfortunately, no copies of these early writings have been found to date).[393] The first known surviving text is a fragment of Lutheran catechism by Simon Wanradt and Johann Koell, published in 1535 in Wittenberg. Some 1,500 copies were published. However, as a result of religious struggles this text was removed from sale two years later. The first Estonian language edition of the full Bible was translated by pastors Anton Thor Helle and Eberhard Gutsleff. It was finally printed in Tallinn in 1739.

390. *See* General Introduction, §3 Historical Background above. In fact, significant changes in this came only after abolishing the serfdom in 1816–1819.
391. T. Raun, *Estonia and Estonians*, 2nd edn (Stanford: Hoover Institution Press, 2001), 24.
392. *See* General Introduction, §3 Historical Background above.
393. T. Raun, *Estonia and Estonians*, 2nd edn (Stanford: Hoover Institution Press, 2001), 24.

282. In the seventeenth century, when Estonia came under the sovereignty of Sweden, a systematic reorganization of social and religious life under the Lutheran Church began.[394] Under Swedish rule from the middle of the seventeenth century to the beginning of the eighteenth century, the Lutheran Church enjoyed the position of being the State Church. One of the cornerstones of the Lutheran paradigm was the idea that people should be taught to read in order that they were able to read the Bible. To some extent one can say that the network of public schools that began to develop at the end of the seventeenth century was somehow an offshoot of the Lutheran Church – being to some degree an expansion of the confirmation school, where religious education had a central role.[395]

283. After the incorporation of Estonia into the Russian empire at the beginning of the eighteenth century (as a result of the Great Northern War), the Lutheran Church preserved its key position in developing schools and organizing religious education. Translated biblical texts remained an important source for Estonians to learn to read and write. For example, at the end of the nineteenth century (during the Russification period[396]), religious education was the only subject which was allowed to be taught in Estonian. This remained the case until the beginning of the twentieth century.

284. At the beginning of the twentieth century, however, religious education had started to run into trouble. This was due to a combination of complex factors, including socio-political ones. As pointed out by Valk, the method of teaching focused on memorizing biblical texts, and whether a student actually understood what he or she read was significantly less important.[397] All school activity was supervised by the Church. No pedagogical preparation was required from supervisors (visitors). This was an increasing source of tension between conservative supervisors and progressive teachers. Secularization and political turbulence at the time also exacerbated the crisis in religious education.[398] By 1917 opinions were polarized, with some calling for abolition of religious education from schools completely and others for the continuation of religious education. Several conferences were held to tackle the crisis of religious education. For example, one of the opinions expressed at the 1st Congress on Education (*Rahvahariduse Kongress*) emphasized that democratic schools needed to be secular (as was the case in France, USA or Helvetia) and that schools needed to be free from church governance.[399] The same

---

394. For a more detailed history of religions in Estonia *see Encyclopaedia Estonica*, 'Culture', 'Religion', www.estonica.org, 1. Apr. 2008.
395. F. Kozyrev & O. Schihalejev, 'Religious Education in Estonia and Russia: Resemblances and Differences', in *Encountering Religious Pluralism in School and Society: A Qualitative Study of Teenage Perspectives in Europe*, ed. T. Knauth et al. (Münster: Waxmann, 2008), 310.
396. The concept of 'Russification' is somewhat confusing. However, it encompasses a series of administrative and cultural reforms, which were intended to unite the Baltic provinces more closely than before with the Russian Empire. T. Raun, *Estonia and Estonians*, 2nd edn (Stanford: Hoover Institution Press, 2001), 59.
397. P. Valk, *Ühest heledast laigust Eesti kooli ajaloos* (Tallinn: Logos, 1997).
398. *Ibid.*, 18.
399. *Kasvatus ja Haridus* 3/4 (1917): 122–128.

year the 2nd Congress on Education adopted a resolution which emphasized freedom of religion or belief in the conduct of religious education. It was emphasized that no child should be forced to take part in religious education if his or her parents objected to it, and argued that older students should be able to decide for themselves whether to attend classes or not. Teachers should not be required to teach religious education and that religious education should be inter-denominational. It was declared that confessional religious education should not be part of the school curriculum. The idea was expressed that the role of the school is not to prepare students for the church but for life. In this regard it was found that supervision of religious education should be conducted by pedagogical institutions and not by the Church.[400]

285. Debates did not end there. Another congress in 1917, organized by leftist movements in Estonia, called for immediate abolition of religious education from schools.[401] As Valk puts it, in the following years there was chaos in religious education. Some schools provided it, some not. The chaos was largely the result of political power struggles and struggles to establish independent statehood at the same time.

286. The Estonian Republic was proclaimed on 24 February 1918. The Transitional Government (*Eesti Ajutine Valitsus*) adopted the ideas expressed by the 2nd Congress on Education held in the previous year. The Government passed a regulation on 21 November 1918, which stated that religious education at schools was voluntary. Neither teachers nor students could be forced to teach or study it, respectively. It further stated that if parents wanted their children to attend religious education, it could be made obligatory for those students. However, in the transition period some practical and legal problems were raised. Another regulation was adopted on 2 December 1918,[402] whose content was specified by the Ministry of Education. It expressed the view that in principle religious education is not obligatory for a school or for the school board/financing body. This meant that if the school board was not prepared to finance it, the parents of those children who are taking religious education classes needed to find the means to take care of the teaching.[403] This attitude, however, seems to have changed the next year. The regulation from 11 January 1919 made it obligatory for schools to maintain all voluntary subjects (including religious education) in the school curriculum. As to the struggle to establish a modern school free from Church supervision, on 26 March 1919 the Lutheran Church sued the Ministry of Education for restricting religious education and for restricting the rights of the clergy at schools. The Estonian Supreme Court decided in favour of the Ministry of Education.[404]

---

400. *Kasvatus* 4 (1917): 209.
401. *Eesti Tööline* [Estonian Worker] 13 Jan. 1918.
402. RT 1918, 5.
403. P. Valk, *Ühest heledast laigust Eesti kooli ajaloos* (Tallinn: Logos 1997), 20.
404. H. Kurm, 'Kooli klerikaliseerimine kodanlikus Eestis', *Eesti Kommunist* 6 (1958): 42; *see also* P. Valk, *Ühest heledast laigust Eesti kooli ajaloos* (Tallinn: Logos 1997), 21.

287. The first Estonian Constitution was adopted in 1920. The Constitution set forth the principle of separation of State and Religion (‘*Riik ja Usk*’ – as different from the formulation of ‘State and Church’). Article 11 of the Constitution stated that there is no State religion.[405] Following the ideas enshrined in the Constitution, the Law on Public Primary Schools, which was adopted by Parliament on 7 May 1920, abolished religious education in primary schools.[406] The same principle was followed in the Law on Public Gymnasiums, which was adopted on 7 December 1922 (the law was superseded by the referendum in 1923, however, and never came into force).[407] There were heated public debates taking place before and after the laws were passed (historical records reveal colourful public debates, quite unusual for the generally reserved and mild tempered Estonians). The intensity of the debates was reflected in Parliamentary discussions.[408] There were accusations made that Parliament did not take into account the views of the majority of the population. This led to a referendum in 1923. However, even before the referendum religious education could still take place at schools provided that the parents or students themselves wanted it, it did not exceed two hours and did not interrupt the curriculum (meaning it needed to take place after the normal school day). At schools where most of the students took religious education classes there was flexibility in the latter requirement. This more flexible attitude was probably related to the fact that the Ministry of Education changed and the new minister was a member of the Christian Party.[409] The legality of this flexibility *strictu sensu* in the light of laws adopted in 1920 and 1922 seem questionable by today’s standards. However, it is clear that legal loopholes were found to satisfy those parents who wanted religious education for their children. In gymnasiums religious education was still a voluntary subject as set out by the Estonian Transitional Government in 1918.

288. The referendum on religious education took place on 17–19 February 1923.[410] It was the first referendum in the history of the independent Estonian Republic. Sixty-six per cent of the voting population participated in the referendum.[411] 71.9% voted for state financed religious education as a voluntary topic in all schools. After the referendum previously adopted laws for primary schools[412] and gymnasiums[413] were amended. From then on religious education was voluntary for students and teachers, but compulsory for schools. After the referendum the debates over religious education calmed down and no significant changes took place until 1940. However, extensive efforts were made to develop the up-to-date curriculum and textbooks.

---

405. RT 1920, 113/114, 243.
406. RT 1920, 75/76, 208.
407. RT 1922, 155/156, 91.
408. *See, e.g.*, P. Valk, *Ühest heledast laigust Eesti kooli ajaloos* (Tallinn: Logos, 1997), 22–28.
409. P. Valk, *Ühest heledast laigust Eesti kooli ajaloos* (Tallinn: Logos, 1997), 26.
410. Riigikogu juhatuse otsus rahvaalgatamise korras esitatud algkooli seaduse muutmise seaduseelnõu, mis Riigikogu poolt 19. detsembril s.a. tagasi lükatud rahvahääletusele panemise kohta, RT I 1923, ½, 23. detsembrist 1922.a.
411. RT I 1923, 35, 36.
412. RT I 1923, 35, 36.
413. RT I 1923, 97/98, 77.

289. To sum up, during the first independence period (1918–1940), Estonia was one of the first countries where a model of non-confessional religious education was introduced. The subject included learning about different world religions. A clear distinction was made between religious education at schools and religious instruction in churches. Nevertheless, as Schihalejev points out, the major content was Christianity with emphasis on moral development and cultural heritage. Bible stories were presented from a non-confessional perspective, which was an attempt to do justice to different denominations.[414] However, the basis of non-confessional religious education was Christianity. This can be seen as justified at the time. Most of the population (ca 78%) belonged to the EELC.[415] The second-largest Church was the Estonian Apostolic Orthodox Church (according to the 1934 census approximately 19% belonged to the latter church).[416] Although secularization of Estonian society was in progress, rural areas were still strongly community oriented, with the Church playing a significant role. Nevertheless, already in the 1930s it was noted that Estonians were becoming relatively less religious; the evidence for this was found in the decline of payments for Church membership.[417]

290. One more fact needs to be mentioned here. In classes where students had the same religious background, the confessional element was allowed to be brought in. In multi-religious schools the grouping of students according to their confession was allowed.[418] As about 86.3% of students were taking religious education classes, the school prayer was introduced again. Some incidents were reported where students who did not take religious education classes were still required to be present at school prayers. This was considered to be against the freedom of religion or belief of students.[419]

291. When the Soviet Union occupied Estonia in 1940, religious education was banned in schools. All forms of religious studies at schools were suppressed and courses of scientific atheism were introduced instead.[420] After regaining independence, in the early 1990s, discussions about religious education started once again. Until rather recently the form and content of religious education was hotly disputed in the media and in academic/educational circles. Although now a compromise

414. O. Schihalejev, *Estonian Young People, Religion and Religious Diversity: Personal Views and the Role of the School* (Tartu: University of Tartu Press, 2009), 42.
415. According to the national census 1934, there were 874,026 Evangelical Lutherans in Estonia of a total population of 1,126,413. Estonian Institute, www.einst.ee/society/Soreligion.htm, 2 Feb. 2000; *See also* Statistical Office of Estonia, *2000 Population and Housing Census: Education. Religion* (Tallinn: Statistical Office, 2002), 17.
416. Riigi Statistika Keskbüroo, *Rahvastiku koostis ja korteriolud: 1 III 1934 rahvaloenduse andmed* (Tallinn: Riigi trükikoda, 1935), Vihik II.
417. Statistical Office of Estonia, *2000 Population and Housing Census: Education. Religion* (Tallinn: Statistical Office, 2002), 17.
418. Haridusministeeriumi ringkirjad (Tallinn: Haridusministeerium, 1932): 79–80.
419. P. Valk, *Ühest heledast laigust Eesti kooli ajaloos* (Tallinn: Logos, 1997), 38–39.
420. O. Schihalejev, 'Meeting Diversity: Students Perspectives in Estonia', in *Encountering Religious Pluralism in School and Society: A Qualitative Study of Teenage Perspectives in Europe*, ed. T. Knauth et al. (Münster: Waxmann, 2008), 248.

seems to have been achieved, it is accurate to say that many aspects of religious education are still unresolved. There are several background factors which seem to influence the debate. The absence of experience, for some fifty years, in providing and receiving religious education in Estonia, due to the Soviet occupation, is probably one of the most important factors. However, the relatively secularised nature of Estonian society and low numbers of affiliation in religious organizations plays a significant role as well.

292. Before returning to the debate over religious education, some information may be useful as to the structure of the school system and the legal framework for the place of religion in education.

293. The Estonian school system consists mainly of public schools (municipal and state schools). The majority of schools are municipal schools. The general education schools are basic schools and gymnasiums. Compulsory school attendance begins when a child reaches the age of seven. Article 9(2) of the Basic Schools and Gymnasiums Act (BSG, *Põhikooli- ja gümnaasiumiseadus)* sets forth that a person who has reached the age of seven years before October 1 in the current year is subject to the duty to attend school. Basic education school is divided into three stages of study: stage I – grades 1-3 (7-10 year olds), stage II – grades 4-6 (10-13 year olds) and III – grades 7-9 (13-16 year olds). After basic school students may attend upper secondary school (gymnasium), a secondary vocational school or enter a profession. Only basic school is compulsory.

294. As to the law on education, Article 37 of the Estonian Constitution creates the basis for the entire school system and states that:

(1) Everyone has the right to education. Education is compulsory for school-aged children to the extent specified by law, and shall be free of charge in state and local government general education schools.
(2) In order to make education accessible, the state and local government shall maintain the requisite number of educational institutions. Other educational institutions, including private schools, may also be established and maintained pursuant to law.
(3) Parents shall have the final decision in the choice of education for their children.
(4) Everyone has the right to receive education in Estonian. The language of instruction in national minority educational institutions shall be chosen by the educational institution.
(5) The provision of education shall be supervised by the State.[421]

295. In addition to the Constitution there are three principal laws that regulate provision of basic and upper secondary education in Estonia. First, the Education

421. RT I 1992, 26, 349; RT I, 15.05.2015, 1 (last amended).

Act (*Haridusseadus*)[422] sets forth the objectives and levels of education. It also determines the competences and responsibilities of the State and local governments in providing education. It also specifies the general division of responsibilities between legislative and executive authorities. Second, the current Basic Schools and Gymnasiums Act was adopted on 9 June 2010 (in force from 1 September 2010).[423] The BGS replaced the previous BGS adopted in 1993.[424] The new BSG introduced a few changes to the school system in Estonia generally. There are many aspects of this law which are still unclear and need to be tested out in practice. It is also likely that some further amendments to the law are needed. Third, the Private Schools Act[425] (PSA, *Erakooliseadus)* regulates the establishment of private educational institutions including basic schools and gymnasiums. The BGS is applied to private schools to the extent the PSA does not regulate them differently.

296. The BGS has delegated certain issues to be regulated at the Governmental level. The Ministry of Education and Research adopted two important regulations on 06 January 2011: the National Curriculum for Basic Schools (*Põhikooli riiklik õppekava*)[426] and National Curriculum for Gymnasiums (*Gümnaasiumi riiklik õppekava*).[427] There is a regulation on home schooling which was adopted by the Ministry of Education and Research (*Koduõppe ja haiglaõppe tingimused ja kord*) on 11.08.2010 (in force 01.09.2010–09.03.2018).[428] In 2018 this regulation was replaced by a new regulation on home schooling.[429] There are also several other regulations, for example, regarding assessment of (exam) papers, provision of school meals, expulsion from a school.

297. Thus, based on the principles enshrined in the Constitution and laws the national curriculum and standards are set by the State. It is the responsibility of the Government to establish the national curriculum for basic schools, the simplified national curriculum for basic schools (for pupils with learning difficulties) and the national curriculum for upper secondary schools (gymnasiums). The national curriculum sets out the goals and objectives of studies, expected learning outcomes, assessment criteria and procedure, and requirements for the learning and teaching environment, organization of teaching and education, graduation from school and school curricula (BGS, Article 15(1)). On the basis of the national curriculum every school adopts its own curriculum (school curriculum) (BGS Article 17(1)). The law is flexible, allowing specificity of a school to be taken into account and provide optional courses (BGS Article 15), provided, of course, that there are resources available for that purpose. The curriculum of a school is established by the head of the school. The curriculum of the school and amendments to it are submitted to the board of trustees, student council and teachers' council for the expression of an

422. RT I 1992, 12, 192; RT I, 16.06.2020, 1 (last amended).
423. RT I 2010, 41, 240; RT I, 16.06.2020, 1 (last amended).
424. RT I 1993, 63, 892; RT 2010, 22, 108 (last amended).
425. RT I 1998, 57, 859; RT I, 19.03.2019, 12 (last amended).
426. RT I 14.01.2011, 1; RT I, 03.03.2021, 9 (last amended).
427. RT I 14.01.2011, 2; RT I, 28.07.2020, 4 (last amended).
428. RT I 2010, 56, 367; RT I, 03.09.2013, 4 (last amended).
429. RT I, 06.03.2018, 1.

opinion before enactment. Information about the curriculum of a school is registered in the education information system's sub-register of curricula and education licences.

298. Home schooling is allowed in accordance with the regulations (*Koduõppe ja haiglaõppe tingimused ja kord*) adopted by the Ministry of Education (on the basis of Article 23(2) of the 2010 BSG). There are two types of home schooling: (1) home schooling resulting from a medical necessity and (2) home schooling resulting from parental wishes. In both cases a parent can apply for home schooling stating relevant reasons. In the first case, the counseling committee makes a recommendation (Regulation, Article 2(1)). The decision itself is made by the head of the school. The school is responsible for arranging the home schooling in the case of the medical necessity. The schooling is publicly funded. In the second type of home schooling the parent needs to state the reasons for home schooling (e.g. religious reasons) and name the person who is going to carry out the teaching (Regulation, Article 5(2)). The law does not specify what kind of reasons should be given. It also does not say the reasons need to be substantial or backed up with evidence. The parent is responsible for managing and financing the home schooling. He or she is also responsible for the quality and results of teaching. The school provides books and other materials needed to cover the school curriculum (Article 6(1)). Home schooling is conducted in cooperation with the relevant school. The emphasis seems to be not on the reasons for home schooling but on the quality of home schooling, which can be assured in cooperation with the school, making sure that individual work plans and obligatory curriculum are followed. There have been no known cases in practice indicating a conflict of interest in this regard yet. The school's teachers' council can terminate the home schooling if during the assessment (arranged by the school twice a year) it appears that the student has significant deficiencies in achieving results specified in his/her individual work plan/curriculum (Regulation, Article 8)[430] .

299. There are also no known cases of school students (or their parents) trying to opt out from, for example, obligatory biology or physical education classes on religious grounds. It is difficult to speculate what the interpretation of the law would be in these cases. As mentioned in the general introduction, Estonia does not consider itself a country of immigration. The social fact is that it is not yet facing many of the challenges related to the growing Muslim communities experienced in other European countries.[431] As regards believers in creationism, no issues have been raised so far.

300. As to religious symbols at school, there have been no publicised incidents of conflict of interests/rights. There is very little socio-political debate going on in this regard. Religious symbols like crucifixes have not been displayed in public schools at least since 1940. As mentioned above, Estonia does not have significant immigration from any countries, including countries with a Muslim population.

430. RT I 2010, 56, 367; RT I, 03.09.2013, 4 (last amended).

431. *See* General Introduction, §1 General Background of the Country above.

There are no rules prohibiting the wearing of religious garb in state schools. This tolerance is perhaps a reaction to Soviet times when all schoolchildren were obliged to wear school uniforms. Both public schools and private schools have the right to establish internal rules of their schools. In today's Estonia, many private schools require school uniforms and so far this requirement has not been disputed. The purpose of the requirement of the uniforms is to promote an atmosphere of unity and equality at the school. There are also no rules prohibiting the wearing of religious garb by teachers, and no reports of any difficulties at this time. It is simply speculative at the moment as to how an Estonian legislature or court would react if someone (e.g., parents) disputed the wearing of religious garb in state schools either by students or by teachers. The ideal may be to teach children to respect differences and bring them up in an atmosphere of mutual respect.

301. There are no known cases of conflict as to opting out for religious holidays and law does not specifically regulate the matter. However, students may be absent from school for well-grounded reasons. It is hard to speculate at the moment as to what the legal solution would be in cases of conflict regarding a student or a teacher taking days off in order to celebrate religious holidays in accordance with their faith.

302. The benediction of schools or school buildings is a quite common practice. There are a couple of reports of school children being forced to participate in services at the beginning of the school year.[432] Generally, the way to solve possible conflicts has been to follow the principle of voluntary participation.

303. Article 2 of the Education Act sets objectives and levels of education, stating *inter alia* that: the fundamental principles of education are based on the recognition of universal and national values, of the individual and of freedom of religion and conscience. Article 3 of the BGS further specifies the framework of fundamental values of general education schools. The values arising from the ethical principles specified in the Constitution of the Republic of Estonia, the Universal Declaration of Human Rights, the Convention on the Rights of the Child and the fundamental documents of the European Union are considered important. The BGS sets forth that the socialization of the new generation is based on the traditions of Estonian culture, common European values, and the recognition of the main achievements of world culture and research. It further notes that people who have acquired general education should be able to integrate into society and contribute to the sustainable social, cultural, economic and ecologic development of Estonian society. Article 2 of both the National Curriculum for Basic Schools and National Curriculum for Gymnasiums adds that general education is based *inter alia* on the fundamental human values such as honour, care, dignity, justice, respect to oneself and others and societal values such as democracy, freedom, respect to mother tongue and culture, patriotism, cultural pluralism, tolerance, economic sustainability, solidarity, rule of law, responsibility and gender equality.

---

432. R. Villems, Speech at the General Assembly of the Estonian Academy of Science (10 Dec. 2008), www.akadeemia.ee/_repository/File/TEGEVUS/ETTEKANDED/RV%2010.12.08.PDF, 1 May 2010.

304. Thus it could be said that the State has broadly defined what sort of values should be taught both in public and in private schools. There is also room for cultural and religious pluralism. Private schools are entitled to keep to their ethos and values within the given framework.

305. As to religious education at general education schools, it is primarily taught in public schools. The Estonian school system consists mainly of public schools (municipal and state schools). The majority of schools are owned by the municipalities. Religious education in public schools is a semi-voluntary, non-confessional (non-denominational) subject. It is intended to be a mix of teaching about religions and ethics. This type of religious education reflects Estonian constitutional principles of neutrality, non-discrimination and freedom of religion and belief. The teachers of religious studies are paid from the state or municipal budget. The teachers of religious studies have to have both theological and pedagogical preparation (there are some exceptions). Confessional religious education is provided for children by Sunday schools and private schools. Religious organizations can set up private educational institutions. Private educational institutions enjoy a greater amount of autonomy regarding their syllabus and admission policies than public schools.

306. As noted above the 2010 BSG introduced a few changes to the school system in Estonia generally.[433] It also introduced changes to providing religious education. Until 1 September 2010, Article 4(4) of the Education Act set forth that the study and teaching of religion in general education schools is voluntary and non-confessional.[434] The Act of Basic Schools and Gymnasiums (BSG) set forth that religious education is compulsory for the school if at least fifteen pupils wish it to be taught.[435] Article 3(4) of this Act also specified that religious education is non-confessional and voluntary.[436] There was no unified curriculum for religious education provided by the State; however, there were guidelines.

307. The new BSG, adopted on 9 June 2010, took effect on 1 September 2010. As to religious education, the above-mentioned provisions in the Education Act and BSG have been removed. The new BSG mentions religious education as one of the voluntary subjects (Article 15(4)). Although schools have relative freedom to provide and design their voluntary courses, the courses on religious education have to follow the State provided syllabus (Article 15(4)). This is a result of the intense debates on religious education which were held from the end of the Soviet occupation in 1991, and it seems to be an attempt to unify and establish control over the content of religious education nationally. There is another change relating to religious education: in gymnasiums (upper secondary schools) depending on the modules the student chooses, religious education may become compulsory once chosen.

---

433. RT I 2010, 41, 240; RT I, 29.06.2014, 109 (last amended)
434. RT I 1992, 12, 192; RT I 2007, 12, 66 (last amended).
435. RT I 1999, 24, 358. In 1999 the Estonian Parliament passed amendments to the then in force BSG. Before the adoption of this provision it was likely that schools just did not provide religious education even if there were pupils who wished to be taught.
436. RT I 1993, 63, 892; RT I 2008, 18, 125 (last amended).

It also is now an obligation of the school to facilitate at least two religious education courses in gymnasium.[437] If at least twelve students wish to be taught an optional course, specified in Article 11(6) of the National Curriculum for Gymnasiums, the school has to provide it.[438] According to Article 17(4) of the BSG, the school may also take into account (accept) that a student takes classes in another school (basic or upper secondary), provided there is an agreement between his or her parents and the school's director. This provision may become relevant as regards religious education, for example, in the case where a student wishes to take confessional religious education in a denominational basic or upper secondary school. However, the implications of this provision are not clear.

308. In 2006–2007 there were about fifty schools, out of a total of 601, teaching a subject related to religion, mostly for a year or two for 7–10-year-old students or a year in upper secondary school (16–19-year-old students). In 2009, of 575[439] basic education or upper secondary schools, forty-seven provided religious education and eighty-four provided related or some alternative subjects to religious education.[440] In the academic year 2013/2014 sixty-five schools provided religious education. In total there were seventy-five schools providing religious education or some alterative religions related subject. It has been exceptional for schools to offer systematic religious education classes in all grades. Students who have chosen such classes normally have an extra lesson at the end of the school day. As a rule, there is no alternative subject to religious education (e.g., ethics) for pupils who do not attend religious studies lessons. Some schools have religious education as a compulsory subject, calling it the 'choice of the school' and terming it religious studies, history of religions, or cultural studies.[441] Although essentials of the compulsory school system are regulated centrally, schools have had relative freedom to develop their own profiles and curriculum within the given framework.

309. There was one case in the 2006 practice of the Chancellor of Justice where he noted a violation of then in force Article 4(4) of the Education Act and Article 3(4) of the Act of Basic Schools and Gymnasiums ('religious education has to be voluntary'). This case concerned a school which provided compulsory religious education in its humanitarian module (in upper secondary school, gymnasium). Once a student had chosen to enrol in the humanitarian module, religious education became obligatory for him or her.[442] The issue was not raised by students or parents, but by a citizen not related to the school and not directly affected by the activities of the school. The Chancellor of Justice has the right to initiate verification procedures on his own initiative with regard to the activities of agencies exercising public functions if, based on previously available information, there is reason to

437. RT I 14.01.2011, 2; RT I, 28.07.2020, 4 (last amended).
438. RT I 14.01.2011, 2; RT I, 28.07.2020, 4 (last amended).
439. Haridus- ja Teadusministeerium, www.hm.ee, 24 Jun. 2010.
440. Interview with Ms Kristel Vahter from Ministry of Education and Research, 22 Jun. 2010.
441. O. Schihalejev, 'Dialogue in Religious Education Lessons – Possibilities and Hindrances in the Estonian Context', *British Journal of Religious Education* 31, no. 3 (2009): 280.
442. *Õiguskantsleri 2006. aasta tegevuse ülevaade* (Tallinn, 2007), 102, Chancellor of Justice, www.oiguskantsler.ee, 1 May 2010.

believe that the respective agency may have violated the constitutional rights or freedoms of persons. In this capacity and in response to the letter from the citizen, the Chancellor of Justice found that the school was violating the law. In response to his decision, students protested by gathering signatures in support of compulsory religious education. Currently, religious education is voluntary in this particular school. However, most students have chosen to attend it.[443] As noted above, according to the changes in law since 2010, in gymnasiums depending on the modules the student chooses religious education may become compulsory once chosen. It was also noted that the law leaves room for school autonomy. Some schools have religious education as a compulsory subject, calling it the 'choice of the school'. Many aspects of the new law still need to be clarified.

310. Unlike other countries with non-confessional models of religious education, in Estonia religious education is, in principle, an elective, not a required course (however, this depends on the school or modules chosen in gymnasium). There have been debates to re-organize voluntary religious education into compulsory education. However, these debates are still ongoing. One of the concerns opposing the reorganization goes back to some negative experiences from the first days of religious education in state schools after regaining independence. When schools became open to religious education, many eager people without pedagogical experience and professional skills rushed to teach it. Sometimes religious education turned into confessional instruction in schools.[444] The lack of an adequate number of teachers with sufficient professional and pedagogical preparation to communicate this subject is acute even today. There was also a lack of adequate course materials for non-confessional religious education. The first textbooks and handbook for teachers were translated from Finnish. In basic education school they introduced Bible stories and were generally meant for students from a Christian background. In upper secondary schools (gymnasiums) world religions, church history, dogma and bible studies were addressed. The recommended text on didactics of religious education was also more suitable for confessional religious education. However, adequate materials provided by Estonian authors have emerged gradually.[445]

311. As to the lack of qualified teachers and adequate materials, the situation at the beginning of the 1990s was to great extent similar to the situation at the beginning of the 1920s. However, there were, and still are great differences as well. Estonia today is one of the least religious countries in Europe (depending on how religiosity is measured). For example, according to the Euro barometer survey ('Social Values Science and Technology') carried out in 2005, Estonia was shown to be the most sceptical country in Europe in regard to belief in the existence of

443. O. Schihalejev, *Estonian Young People, Religion and Religious Diversity: Personal Views and the Role of the School* (Tartu: Tartu University Press, 2009), 51.
444. P. Valk, *Development of the Status of Religious Education in Estonian School. European and Local Perspectives*, Paper given at the Conference on Law, Religion and Democratic Society (Estonia: University of Tartu, 1999). Conference materials are available at the University of Tartu Faculty of Law Chair of Public International Law and EC Law.
445. O. Schihalejev, *Estonian Young People, Religion and Religious Diversity: Personal Views and the Role of the School* (Tartu: Tartu University Press, 2009), 50.

God. Less than one out of five declared any belief in God (approximately 16%). This probably shows a relative coolness towards traditional religions. However, more than 54% believed in a non-traditional concept of 'some sort of spirit or life force'.[446] As to students' attitudes, one of the surveys conducted by Estonian researches showed that religion was valued as the least important subject and readiness for globalization the next lowest.[447] Some fifty years of Soviet occupation has also affected attitudes towards religious education. It should not be overlooked that there is a lack of experience in terms of both teaching and receiving religious education, which probably predisposes participators in the debate to take a negative view of religious education (e.g., by parents). Some research conducted by Estonian academics shows that students who have taken religious education classes feel positive about it even if the subject was compulsory for them.[448]

312. Among opponents of compulsory religious education the major concern has been that it could turn into promotion of one brand of religion – Christianity. There has also been a concern that teachers of religious education have a mostly Christian background, and thus cannot deliver instruction in the subject objectively. These concerns are very similar to those expressed in the 1920s and thus cannot be completely attributed to Soviet propaganda during the fifty years of occupation. It also needs to be noted that some proponents of compulsory religious education, including churches, have considered it to be necessary to have an emphasis on Christian religion considering the cultural background of the country. In the context of compulsory religious education this has been seen as problematic. The major concern has been the protection of freedom of religion or belief of students and parents, both non-believers and non-Christians. These concerns also seem to relate to rather controversial attempts to re-build national identity after the occupation. Strong political/governmental favouritism of traditional religions has added an extra dimension to this debate.

313. In 2001, representatives of non-Christian religions[449] formed an informal body called the Roundtable of Religious Associations, as a reaction to the proposal to make religious education compulsory in State schools.[450] They criticized the draft

446. European Commission, 'Special Eurobarometer: Social values, Science and Technology' (2005), 11.

447. I. Rüütel & E.-M. Tiit, 'Eesti kooliõpilaste väärtushinnanguist ja huvialadest' ('Estonian Students Values and Hobbies'), *Akadeemia* 11 (2005): 2401–2442.

448. *See, e.g.*, K. Pärkson, *Religiooniõpetus gümnaasiumiõpilaste isikliku arengu toetajana Tartu Tamme Gümnaasiumi õpilaste nägemuse põhjal* [Religious Education as a Facilitator of Personal Development According to the Students from Tartu Tamme Gymnasium (Tartu: Tartu Ülikool, 2006); A. Saar, *Religiooniõpetuse kvalitatiivuuringu tulemuste esitluse materjale [Results of the Qualitative Research about Religious Education in Upper Secondary Schools*] (Tallinn: SaarPoll, 2006); O. Schihalejev, 'Meeting Diversity – Students' Perspectives in Estonia', in *Encountering Religious Pluralism in School and Society – A Qualitative Study of Teenage Perspectives in Europe*, ed. T. Knauth et al. (Münster: Waxmann Vwerlag GmbH, 2008), 247–278.

449. The Taara and Earth believers, the Bahá'i Congregation, local branch of the ISKCON, two Buddhist congregations, the Jewish Organizations and the Estonian Islamic Congregation.

450. T. Vakker & P. Rohtmets, 'Estonia: Relations between Christian and Non-Christian Religious Organizations and the State of Religious Freedom', *Religion, State & Society* 36, no. 1 (2008): 50–51.

curriculum as biased and Christianity centric. In his 2003 report the Chancellor of Justice expressed the opinion that the State does not have to guarantee absolutely equal presentation of world religions in the curriculum. He stated that it is justified to include Christianity in the curriculum because of the cultural and historic background of Estonia. But he also pointed out that presentation of Christianity should not become the prevailing subject in the curriculum. He warned that the majority of qualified teachers are of Christian background and this can offset the balance. He also emphasized that compulsory religious education would be possible only if the State guarantees a balanced representation of world religions.[451] Concerns about compulsory religious education have also been expressed by many leading writers, actors and columnists, whose opinions matter and influence the public debate.[452]

314. As a reaction to new proposals and debate in 2008, the President of the Estonian Academy of Science expressed his opinion at the general meeting of the academy that religious education should be voluntary in upper secondary schools and should not be allowed in basic school at all. He expressed the concern that children at that age are not sufficiently protected from the possibility that non-confessional religious education turns into confessional instruction. He also expressed the view that introducing religions within history classes is sufficient. Elaborating his argument further, he expressed the view that teaching about religions has to be contextual, meaning it should be taught in the context of history and society. Placing teaching about religions outside an historical context is, in his view, a gross methodological mistake.[453]

315. The idea that religion can be sufficiently covered within other disciplines, such as history and arts, has been held by many in the academic and educational community. The drawback to this idea is that those subjects are already overloaded and teachers may not be sufficiently qualified to talk about religions, so that what may theoretically be a good idea may not necessarily be good in practice. However, another point was made by the President of the Estonian Academy of Science, which reflects the broader debate as to the substance of religious education: he expressed his concern that the proposed curriculum and explanatory note to it emphasized that moral and ethical behaviour stems from religion (and in an Estonian context from the Old and New Testaments); observing that the history of Christianity and other religions shows that a connection between ethics and actual behaviour has not always been well established.[454] Teaching ethics as stemming solely from religion has thus been seen as problematic.

451. *Õiguskantsleri 2003–2004. aasta tegevuse ülevaade* (Tallinn, 2004), 169. Chancellor of Justice, www.oiguskantsler.ee, 1 May 2010.

452. *See, e.g.*, A. Kivirähk, 'Majamaniakind ja usundiopetus' [House-maniacs and Religious Education], *Äríleht*, 4 Nov. 2006.

453. R. Villems, Speech at the General Assembly of the Estonian Academy of Science (10 Dec. 2008), www.akadeemia.ee/_repository/File/TEGEVUS/ETTEKANDED/RV%2010.12.08.PDF, 1 May 2010.

454. R. Villems, Speech at the General Assembly of the Estonian Academy of Science (10 Dec. 2008), www.akadeemia.ee/_repository/File/TEGEVUS/ETTEKANDED/RV%2010.12.08.PDF, 1 May 2010.

316. To summarize the debate, there is some agreement as to the need to teach students about religions. However, there are different opinions as to how religious education should be taught. As shown above, views vary regarding the age at which religion needs to be introduced in schools and by whom it needs to be taught. There are also some additional practical and broader structural problems which relate to the school curriculum and teaching methods as a whole. According to some estimations the curriculum is generally overloaded. It is also fact oriented, leaving little time for students to develop discussion skills and form their own opinion. As the curriculum is overloaded, non-confessional religious education is often pushed to the fringe of the school day. Although reforming the educational system in Estonia has been slowly moving from a teacher-centred to a student-centred approach, the reform is still in progress. Regarding religious education specifically, the major concern has been its content and purpose. Concerns have been expressed as to how to strike a balance between Christianity and other world views. This has fuelled the debate about obligatory religious education.

317. As religious education has been a voluntary subject, for a long time there had only been guidelines as to how it should be conducted. Since 2010, as noted above, although schools have relative freedom to provide and design their voluntary courses, the courses on religious education have to follow the State provided syllabus (BSG, Article 15(4)). It was also mentioned that the Ministry of Education and Research has adopted two important regulations the National Curriculum for Basic Schools (*Põhikooli riiklik õppekava*) and National Curriculum for Gymnasiums (*Gümnaasiumi riiklik õppekava*).

318. The model syllabus for religious education adopted by the Ministry of Education seems to have grappled with some of the concerns expressed in previous debates. However, it remains to be seen whether this syllabus is convincing enough to pave the way for compulsory religious education at all school levels and in all schools. It also needs to be seen how it will work out in practice.

319. The model syllabus seems to be a mix of learning about religions and ethics (broadly defined). The aim is to give a non-confessional overview of world religions and to help students to understand the impact of different religions in world culture, and most importantly, to prepare them for life in a pluralistic and multicultural world. Not only are religious worldviews covered, but also non-religious views. Topics such as secularization and the relationship between science and religion are also included. The syllabus seems to be aimed at teaching into tolerance. It is intended to develop religious literacy and readiness for dialogue by introducing different world religions/views. An interesting aspect is that it encourages students' abilities to recognize and understand religious discrimination and analyse both positive and problematic religious manifestation in context. Discussions are also held about existential questions. There are obviously differences in methods of teaching and learning according to the age of students.

320. Both the basic school and upper secondary school's syllabus emphasize that religious education is founded on the UN Declaration of Human Rights. Religious education is a precondition for protection of freedom of religion or belief. The aim of religious education is to provide knowledge about religion in order to help students understand the world, its culture and the role of the religious dimension in human life. It also emphasizes the importance of learning about local religions and cultural heritage. An important aim of religious education is to support pupils' moral development and special attention must be paid to the problems of pupils' everyday life and their questions. The syllabus seems to take into account some of the Toledo Guiding Principles on Teaching about Religions and Beliefs in Public Schools adopted by the OSCE Office of Democratic Institutions and Human Rights in 2007.[455]

321. Thus, there is a strong emphasis on learning how to navigate in a multi-religious world, while remaining open-minded and critical at the same time. Dialogue and respect seem to be the keywords which characterize both the curriculum of basic schools and gymnasiums. As to the methods of teaching, there seems to be a strong emphasis on a student-centred approach. All in all it seems to be a rather convincing syllabus, which should satisfy people from various belief backgrounds. However, it is rather ambitious and it needs to be seen how it will work in practice. Ideally individual failures should not hinder religious education as such again, especially taking into account that education is the key to the eradication of many problems related to religion.

455. Toledo Guiding Principles on Teaching about Religions and Beliefs in Public Schools (Warsaw: OSCE 2007).

Chapter 2. Religious Schools

322. Confessional religious education is provided for children by Sunday and Bible schools operated by religious organizations. Additionally, religious organizations can set up private educational institutions. The Private Schools Act (*Erakooliseadus*) regulates the establishment of private educational institutions at all school levels (pre-school, basic, secondary, vocational and higher education).[456] These private schools need to obtain a license from the Ministry of Education and Research (§5(1)). Sunday or Bible schools run by churches and congregations do not need the license.

323. The license is issued for a certain period of time, for up to five years (PSA, §5(6)). Private schools have some access to public funding. The license is necessary in order to apply for this funding and projects financed by the State or municipal government.[457]

324. As noted above, according to the Estonian Constitution provision of education is supervised by the State. However, private schools have relative freedom as regards curriculum, ethos and admissions. Private educational institutions, when providing state-licensed/state-supervised basic or upper secondary education, have to follow the standards set in the National Curriculum for Basic Schools or Gymnasiums. The National Curriculum applies to all schools irrespective of their legal status (public or private), if specific laws do not provide different regulation (for example, the PSA). The manager of a private school approves the school curriculum. According to the amendments applicable from 1 September 2010, Article 11(5) of the PSA explicitly sets forth that it is allowed to provide confessional religious education in private educational institutions (previously there was no explicit mentioning of this, although it was not prohibited either).[458] This is a general provision which applies to all private schools, not just confessional ones. The PSA further states that confessional religious education is voluntary.

325. The conditions for the admission of students are determined by the school. Admission to a basic school, upper secondary school, vocational educational institution and an institution of professional higher education is subject to the admission conditions established by law for state and municipal educational institutions or universities in public law of the same type. However, the board of a private school has the right to establish additional requirements (PSA, §12). Many private schools have admission tests. Although the law is not explicit about it, private schools can (are allowed) to discriminate on religious grounds. For example, Tartu Catholic School gives priority to members of the Tartu catholic congregation[459] and the Jewish School in Tallinn gives priority to students who are loyal to Jewish traditions,

456. RT I 1998, 57, 859; RT I, 19.03.2019, 12 (last amended).
457. *See* Part VII, Ch. 2 above.
458. This provision was included by the new BSG which amended several paragraphs of the PSA (*see* Art. 105 of the BSG).
459. Tartu Katoliku Harisuskeskus, http://www.katoliku.edu.ee/node/33, 1 Sep. 2014.

history and learning Hebrew.[460] There are no cases contesting these arrangements; as there are, for example, in the United Kingdom[461] and in the Netherlands.[462] The organization of studies is based on the curriculum and the rules established by the board of the private school (§13).

326. In law there is no real difference in control over public and private basic or upper secondary schools. One can differentiate between *ex ante* and *ex post facto* control over the quality of schools. As to the *ex ante* control, for obtaining an education licence both municipal and private schools need to submit certain documents, for example, the school curriculum, a certificate of the owner of the school regarding the existence of teachers complying with the qualification requirements (BGS, Article 63). The Minister of Education and Research does not issue the licence if the information or documents specified in the BGS have not been appended to the application or if these do not comply with the requirements established by legislation and the material base of teaching and learning does not correspond to the needs arising from the school curriculum. The PSA also sets forth minimum capital requirements for the owners of private schools.

327. When the school is already operational, the Ministry of Education and Research or, at the request of the Minister of Education and Research, the governor of the county of location exercises state supervision over teaching and education carried out by schools. The functions of officials exercising state supervision are as follows: (1) to inspect the adherence to the requirements arising from the legislation regulating teaching and education; (2) to analyse problems in the implementation of the legislation regulating teaching and education. The BGS delegates details of the supervision to be worked out at the Ministerial level. These details are reviewed every year. The supervision methodology is specified in the regulation. Both 'inputs' of schooling (such as staff qualifications, curriculum followed, resources) and results of external examinations, statistics etc. are taken into account in the assessment of the school (Article 4).

328. Not many religious organizations have established schools in accordance with the Private Schools Act. Currently there is a small number of registered kindergartens (pre-schools), one, for example, run by Tallinn Toompea Kaarli Congregation of the EELC and another run by the Catholic Educational Centre in Tartu. There are also three basic schools run by the Word of Life (*Elusõna*) Tartu Congregation,[463] by the Society of Orthodox Education called 'Resurrection' and by the Catholic community in Tartu. There is one gymnasium – Tallinn Jewish School (Tallinna Juudi Kool). There are also three separate professional higher education

---

460. Tallinna Juudi Kool, http://www.jkool.tln.edu.ee/JKOOL/images/stories/content/files/vastuvotukord.pdf, 1 Sep. 2014.
461. *See, e.g.*, controversial case about admission policy of the *Jewish Free School in the UK Supreme Court. R (on the application of E) (Respondent) v. The Governing Body of JFS and the Admissions Appeal Panel of JFS and others (Appellants)* [2009] UKSC 15.
462. Netherlands: HR 22 Jan. 1988, NJ 1988, 891. *See also* N. Doe, *Law and Religion in Europe* (Oxford: Oxford University Press, 2011), 202.
463. *Tartu Elusõna Kogusus* is a sister congregation of the Uppsala *Livets Ord.*

institutions (*rakenduskõrgkool*) run by the Estonian Methodist Church, the Union of Free Evangelical and Baptist Churches of Estonia and by the non-profit organization Tartu Academy of Theology. The Estonian Evangelical Lutheran Church has one university in Tallinn (Institute of Theology).[464]

329. The Tartu Academy of Theology grew out of the courses provided for religious education teachers at the beginning of the 1990s. The academy has an ecumenical ethos. It was established by the EELC, Orthodox Church of Estonia, Estonian Methodist Church and Union of Free Evangelical and Baptist Churches of Estonia. The academy offers among other courses BA or MA degree studies for teachers of religion and ethics. On 1 July 2013, the Academy joined the EELC Institute of Theology as one of its departments.

330. The Institute of Theology of the EELC is an educational centre for the entire church: for preparing clergy, other church workers, lay people, church musicians, etc., for various types of work within congregations. The institute also trains teachers of religious education in public schools, as well as military, prison and hospital chaplains and people who are to work in the mass media. However, the institute is open for everyone having an interest in humanistic education in the field of theology or education or anyone who would like to learn more about the interaction of Christianity and Western culture and society.[465] There was an interesting development in January 2014. The Institute of Theology of the EELC and the St. Platon Seminary of the Estonian Apostolic Orthodox Church signed a cooperation memorandum which envisaged opening the Chair of Orthodoxy at the EELC institute. The chair was opened in the autumn of 2014. There seems to be a general trend to consolidate training of clergy in Estonia. The trend is a result of limited financial and human resources and the need to meet the standards set by the state for higher or professional education institutions.

331. As to theology at public universities, the Faculty of Theology has existed at the University of Tartu since 1632, although it was abolished by Soviet authorities in 1940. In 1941, German occupation forces did not allow the reopening of the faculty; however, they granted permission to form a Theological Examination Commission at the Consistory, thus providing an opportunity for students to complete their theology degrees. After World War II, theological education continued, and the Examination Commission was converted into the Theological Institute of the EELC, which operates to this day as described above. In 1991, the Faculty of Theology was reopened at the University of Tartu. Since 1991 the Faculty has been non-denominational but evangelical. The Faculty of Theology as part of a public university is fully funded from the state budget. The activities of the faculty include theology and religious studies (religious anthropology), with theology traditionally

---

464. Eesti Hariduse Infosüsteem [Estonian Education Information System], 'Koolid', www.ehis.ee/, 1 May 2010.
465. Estonian Evangelical Lutheran Church, Institute of Theology, http://ui.eelk.ee/english.php, 1 May 2010.

having a greater emphasis on protestant theology. In the theology Master's programme one can also specialize in the field of religious pedagogy. The graduates can teach religious education classes in general education schools, and many also serve in the Estonian defence forces as chaplains.

332. The Faculty of Theology offers a higher theological education, but does not automatically authorize the graduate to serve in the church. The faculty only gives a theoretical preparation for practical work as a minister. Ministerial qualification implies confessional studies in a relevant educational institution. In the case of the Evangelical Lutheran Church this situation is solved in cooperation with the Theological Institute of the Evangelical Lutheran Church. Graduates of the Faculty of Theology can continue their confessional studies in the pastoral seminary of the Theological Institute of the Evangelical Lutheran Church. There is also a cooperation agreement with another private higher education institution providing confessional studies: the Theological Seminary of the Union of Free Evangelical and Baptist Churches of Estonia.[466]

466. University of Tartu, Faculty of Theology, www.us.ut.ee, 1 May 2014.

Part X. Matrimonial and Family Law

Chapter 1. Legal Position of Religious Marriage

333. Historically, with minor exceptions, Lutheran and Orthodox churches have registered births, death and marriages in Estonia. Before relevant laws were adopted at the beginning of the first independence period, there was no unified system or common conditions for marriage established by the State.[467] Also until 1926, laws adopted during the Tsarist times existed in parallel with changes adopted by the Estonian Republic.

334. The 1920 Constitution set forth the principle of separation of State and Religion. Although civil marriage was also available, churches still played the major role in registration of religious marriages. Thus, marriages were conducted on a confessional basis and tradition played a great role. However, the low numbers of civil marriages may have been due also to the fact that for many it was not possible to travel to bigger cities (Tallinn, Tartu, Narva and Pärnu) where civil marriages were performed.

335. Churches were also allocated some public funding for keeping the marriage register.[468] Although the debates over religious marriage were not as furious as those regarding religious education, there was an increasing feeling that the practice of religious marriage did not completely comply with the constitutional principle of separation of state and religion. More importantly, however, the need for some unification of the system was recognized. It was felt that registration of marriages was a responsibility of the State[469] and also important in order to keep adequate up-to-date data on family matters. Early drafts of new laws prescribed centralization of the registration of marriages (and also annulment and divorce), and excluded clerics from the possibility of registering marriages.[470] Later the idea of

467. K. Kask, *Kirikliku abielu institutsioon Eestis: aastate 1920–1940 ning 1991–2002 võrdlev analüüs* [Institution of Religious Marriage in Estonia: A Comparative Analysis of 1920–1940 and 1991–2002] (Tartu: Tartu Ülikool, 2002).
468. For example, Estonian Transitional Government allocated some funds to the Lutheran Church in 1919.
469. J. Lõo, 'Perekonnaseisu ja abielu seaduse eelnõud', *Õigus* 2 (1922): 41.
470. *See, e.g.*, II Riigikogu IX istungjärk. Protokollid 253-302 (Tallinn: Riigi Trükikoda): 237–238.

radical centralization and exclusion of clergy was dropped as it was too expensive and impractical for the recently proclaimed Republic.[471]

336. However, one aspect of the law was debated. There were different opinions as to whether the clergy had to register marriages of people from different confessions or non-believers. Family Law adopted on 11 November 1925 (entered into force 1 July 1926)[472] required clergy to register marriages despite religious affiliation. The law delegated the rights of the civil registrar to a clergyman. The argument was that as it was voluntary for the clergy to accept the duties of the civil registrar, religious affiliation in performance of these duties was not relevant. The guidelines adopted by the Ministry of Internal Affairs also suggested that civil registration should be performed before the religious ceremony.[473] After a while the new situation was accepted by the clergy. The obligation to register anyone, not just members of their Church, was seen as necessary as it provided correct and up-to-date statistics about changes in personal status that the previous system was not able to ensure.

337. In 1929, Parliament also adopted a law which regulated social guarantees of clergy who conducted civil marriages.[474] This law set forth the establishment of the state pension fund. Even clergymen who performed marriages before the 1926 Family Law were entitled to allocations from this fund.

338. The right to register marriages with civil validity was annulled in July 1940.[475] This was a result of the Soviet occupation of the Estonian territory in June 1940. On 28 September 1940 the Law on Pension Funds was annulled. From then onwards clergy and their family members were left without any social security.

339. Interestingly, during the occupation period religious marriage was not legally (specifically) regulated at all. Paradoxically it could be argued that the attitude was more liberal than in Holland or Germany where civil registration had to take place before religious ceremony. However, the social and political reality was quite different. Although religious marriages were taking place, they did not have any legal status. Religious ceremonies were also condemned/discouraged through the use of negative pressure (such as expulsion from university) for people who decided to marry in the church (the parents of the current author were married in church, but luckily there were no negative results).

340. After Estonia regained independence, the issue of granting authorization was discussed several times. At the beginning of the 1990s neither society nor the

471. II Riigikogu IX istungjärk. Protokollid 253–302, Protokoll No. 257 (Tallinn: Riigi Trükikoda): 238.
472. RT I 1925, 191/192, 110.
473. RT 1926, 48.
474. RT 1929, 30, 217.
475. RT 1940, 88, 853.

Church were ready for change. The topic was brought up again in 2000, when several proposals to change the law were put forward. Finally, in May 2001, the Estonian Parliament passed amendments to the then in force Family Law (*Perekonnaseadus*).[476] The amendments came into force in December 2001. A new Family Law was adopted in November 2009.[477] The 1994 Family Law was replaced by new Family Law on 1 July 2010, when it came into force. In line with the new Family Law, specific regulation for authorization of clergy is also regulated by the second chapter of the Vital Statistics Registration Act (*Perekonnaseisutoimingute seadus*).[478] This law also came into force on 1 July 2010. These legal acts did not change the status of religious marriages. In accordance with the law, since 2001, a clergyman who has received authorization from the Minister of Regional Affairs is entitled to perform civil marriages. Thus, the State has not recognized the concept of religious marriage per se but, rather, has established the possibility of delegating the obligations of the registry office to a clergyman of a church, congregation or association of congregations. However, this has been considered more as a delegated right rather than an obligation, and thus clergy with this right do not get a salary from the State to conduct marriages.

341. In contrast with the 1926 law, under current Family Law an authorized minister can refuse to perform a marriage if those being married oppose the conditions set for marriages by the confessions of the church, congregation or association of congregations (§6 Family Law). Thus the minister has a right, but not an obligation to refuse registration according to his or her own religious affiliation. For example, the minister may need to use his or her right to refuse to marry when one of the intended spouses has been married under church law, but later divorced according to civil law. The new marriage may not be acceptable according to religious rules. In an Estonian context, this would mostly apply to Orthodox and Roman Catholic priests.

342. The authorized minister has the right to conduct civil marriage (§7(1)[1] Family Law). In conducting the civil marriage, the minister has to follow the law as to the eligibility of persons to marry. He or she also issues marriage certificates. The latter is regulated by the Vital Statistics Registration Act (*Perekonnaseisutoimingute seadus*).[479] Clergy has not been delegated the right to divorce or register births or deaths according to the law.

343. The Minister of Regional Affairs may authorize clergy to perform civil marriages only if they have successfully taken an exam organized by the Ministry of Internal Affairs in conjunction with the registry offices (§4 Vital Statistics Registration Act). There is training organized prior to the exam. Participation in the training is not generally an obligatory precondition for taking the exam. However,

476. RT I 1994, 75, 1326.
477. RT I 2009, 60, 395; RT I, 27.10.2020, 1 (last amended).
478. RT I 2009, 30, 177; RT I, 18.12.2019, 3 (last amended).
479. *RT I 2009, 30, 177*; RT I, 31.12.2015, 31 (last amended).

it is obligatory for clergy (§17 (5) Vital Statistics Registration Act).[480] The Minister of Regional Affairs may refuse to authorize clergymen only on very limited grounds. Thus, the discretion of the Ministry has been reduced to a minimum. Only churches, congregations or associations of congregations registered under the 2002 Churches and Congregations Act may apply for authorization to perform civil marriages. The Minister of Regional Affairs may declare such authorization void if, *inter alia*, a minister does not perform civil marriages in accordance with the law. The Minister may also declare the authorization to perform civil marriages void on the recommendation of a church, congregation or association of congregations (§20 Vital Statistics Registration Act).

344. In contrast to practice during the first independence period, current law does not specify in which order civil and religious ceremonies have to take place. The problem is that the moment at which a marriage begins can be regarded differently by religious or civil authorities. So far there have been no known cases in practice where the beginning of a marriage has been contested.

345. The 2010 Family law introduced some changes as to when by law the marriage is considered contracted. According to the 1994 law, prospective spouses contracted marriage with both being present in person at the same time. A marriage was contracted when the marriage registration was signed by the prospective spouses (§1(5) 1994 Family Law). According to the current law after the authorized person has received the 'yes' word to his or her question as to whether both parties involved want to get married he or she proclaims them married according to the law. Thus the 'yes' word, and proclamation of marriage will be legally important. This change in law has been influenced by religious organizations. Already before the adoption of changes to the Family Law in 2001, a similar change was proposed, but was disregarded at that time.[481]

346. The 2010 law introduced a few controversial changes/clarifications as to the requirements for a clergyman performing civil marriage. The clergyman has to be at least 21 years old, he or she has to have at least a secondary education, and he or she needs to be fluent in spoken and written Estonian (§17, Vital Statistics Registration Act). A clergyman has to be a citizen of Estonia, EU, European Economic Area or Switzerland. These requirements partly stem from the Civil Service Act (§14, *Avaliku teenistuse seadus*).[482] The requirements of citizenship or fluency in Estonian may prove to be difficult for some to comply with, especially for priests of

480. Detailed rules about the training and exam are set forth in the governmental regulation, *Perekonnaseisuametniku koolituse ja eksami läbiviimise kord ja perekonnaseisuametniku tunnistuse vorm*, Government Regulation 25 Feb. 2010 no. 4 (in force 14 Mar. 2010), RTL 2010, 11, 201; RT I, 24.01.2014, 1 (last amended).

481. K. Kask, *Kirikliku abielu institutsioon Eestis: aastate 1920–1940 ning 1991–2002 võrdlev analüüs* [Institution of Religious Marriage in Estonia: A comparative analysis of 1920–1940 and 1991–2002] (Tartu: Tartu Ülikool, 2002), 61.

482. RT I, 06.07.2012, 1; RT I, 18.02.2014, 1 (last amended). The current Civil Service Act came into force on 1 Apr. 2013. It replaced the earlier Civil Service Act (RT I 1995, 16, 228).

the Estonian Orthodox Church of Moscow Patriarchate.[483] However, it should be noted that to date no applications for authorization have been received from this church.[484] The reasons for this, however, may not be the named requirements for the clergyman. The Estonian Orthodox Church of Moscow Patriarchate has also indicated unwillingness to be part of a system, in which divorce is allowed by law.[485] The new law also requires clergy to introduce options about property relationships between spouses (e.g., about property contract (*abieluvaraleping*). This new requirement has generally not been looked upon favourably by clergy.

347. There have been no court cases or incidents related to registration of marriages by clergy. On 3 November 2020, there were 112 persons with the right to conduct religious marriages with civil validity.[486]

483. *See also* General Introduction, §2 Social Facts about Religion above.
484. Interview with Mr Ilmo Au, the Head of the Religious Affairs Department of the Ministry of Internal Affairs, 22 Jun. 2010.
485. Interview with Mr Ringo Ringvee, the Advisor of the Religious Affairs Department of the Ministry of Internal Affairs, 22 Jun. 2010.
486. The information is obtained from the Ministry of Internal Affairs. Siseministeerium, https://www.siseministeerium.ee/et/tegevusvaldkonnad/usulised-uhendused-ja-represseeritud/vaimulik-solmib-abielu, 31 Mar. 2021.

Chapter 2. Legal Position of Religious Family Law

348. In Estonian Family Law there are currently no exemptions which recognize religious family law in Estonia. Changes in family status (such as marriage, divorce, heritage, subsistence) need to be conducted according to the civil law to be legally recognized. However, application of religious family law as such is not prohibited either. There is no information available as to whether parties resort to religious family law, or to what extent they do so. From limited information available it can be pointed out that the Estonian version of a Muslim journal Iqra has made readers aware of the opportunities to solve family issues without the interference of state authorities. Allegedly in 2012 twelve marriage contracts (nikah) were signed under the supervision of an imam. Inheritance can be apportioned according to Islamic regulations provided it is accepted by all parties involved.[487] In the case of legal disputes, civil law applies in Estonia. In addition, laws applicable to all may set certain limits to use of religious law. There have been no known cases of conflict of interests/rights in this regard.

349. However, Estonian law allows some exceptions in a specific case where a legal relationship falls under private international law. The Private International Law Act[488] (*Rahvusvahelise eraõiguse seadus*) regulates legal relationships which are connected with the law of more than one state. For example, a marriage contracted in a foreign state is deemed to be valid in Estonia if it is contracted pursuant to the procedure for contraction of marriage provided by the law of the state where the marriage is contracted, and the material prerequisites (such as age, consent) of the marriage are in compliance with the laws of the states of residence of both spouses (§55 of the Private International Law Act). A previous marriage of a spouse does not hinder the contraction of a new marriage in Estonia, if the previous marriage has been terminated on the basis of a decision made or recognized in Estonia, even if such a decision is not in accordance with the law of the state of residence of the prospective spouse (§56(3) of the Private International Law Act).

350. Although religious family law may be recognized in Estonia (in cases where religious family law is recognized by the relevant State), there is one general restriction. The Private International Law Act sets forth that a foreign law should not be applied if the result of such application would be in obvious conflict with the essential principles of Estonian law (public order). In such cases Estonian law applies (§7). For example, this would most certainly be true in cases involving child or forced marriage or polygamy. Where gender equality is at issue, it is possible that courts may consider Estonian law to take precedence, for example when ruling on subsistence, custody or inheritance. However, at the moment this is only speculative as there is no case law to rely on.

487. R. Ringvee, 'Estonia' in *Yearbook of Muslims in Europe* Vol. 5., ed. J.S. Nielsen et al. Leiden: Koninklijke Brill NV, 201.
488. RT I 2002, 35, 217; RT I, 26.06.2017, 1 (last amended).

351. Furthermore, as discussed above, Estonia is not a country of extensive immigration.[489] Currently immigration is discouraged although all forms of immigration are possible, such as family reunification, immigration for work and study purposes, asylum and protection from inhuman treatment. Estonia has several acts that regulate immigration. The main legal provisions regulating the field are contained in the State Borders Act (*Riigipiiri seadus*),[490] Aliens Act (*Välismaalaste seadus*),[491] Act Granting International Protection for Aliens (*Välismaalastele rahvusvahelise kaitse andmise seadus*)[492] and Obligation to Leave and Prohibition of Entry Act (*Väljasõidukohustuse ja sissesõidukeelu seadus*).[493] Other acts relevant in this field are the Citizen of EU Act (*Euroopa Liidu kodanku seadus*),[494] and Citizenship Act (*Kodakondsuse seadus*).[495] Additionally there are several government regulations that deal with residence permit issues.

352. Family unity is generally respected in Estonia by law. The Council Directive 2003/86/EC on family reunification was transformed to the Aliens Act. This act regulates the family reunification of Estonian citizens and foreigners living legally in Estonia. The family reunification of a refugee or a person in need of other international protection is regulated by the Act Granting International Protection for an Alien. Family reunification of European Citizens is regulated by the Citizens of the EU Act. The applicable rules depend mostly on the status of the sponsor who applies for family reunification.

353. Polygamy is not recognized in Estonia. As regards children, it is possible to invite all the children of a sponsor to cohabit, including the children of a second or third wife, but not the wives themselves. The husband has to choose which wife he wants to join him in Estonia. Only official marriage is recognized and partners who are not officially married cannot benefit from family reunification. In family reunification cases, immigration officials check that there are no marriages of convenience. Both partners are questioned, and their neighbours can also be interviewed. An alien who applies for family reunification must have lived in Estonia for at least two years (§137 of the Aliens Act).

354. A family member can obtain a temporary residence permit for the purpose of settling with his or her spouse. Spouses have to share close economic ties and must have a psychological relationship. The family has to be stable and the marriage not fictitious. In these cases a residence permit for the purpose of family reunification can be justified. In order to benefit from family reunification, the spouse has to reside permanently in Estonia. The permanent residence requirement does not

489. *See* General Introduction, §1 General Background of the Country above.
490. RT I 1994, 54, 902; RT I, 08.07.2020, 1 (last amended).
491. RT I 2010, 3, 4; RT I, 10.07.2020, 4 (last amended). The Aliens Act came into force 1 Oct. 2010 and replaced the 1999 Aliens Act (RT I 1999, 44, 637). The new law does not differ from the previous law substantially (except paragraph numbers).
492. RT I 2006, 2, 3; RT I, 17.06.2020, 1 (last amended).
493. RT I 1998, 98/99, 1575; RT I, 17.06.2020, 1 (last amended).
494. RT I 2006, 26, 191; RT I, 19.03.2019, 9 (last amended).
495. RT I 1995, 83, 1442; RT I, 03.12.2020, 1 (last amended).

apply to the Estonian citizen who wants to invite his or her spouse in order to settle together in Estonia. Similar rules apply to descendent relatives. In some cases the ascendant relatives can also join the sponsor.

355. According to information from the Population Department, the Department of Gender Equality Commissioner and Department of Religious Affairs of the Ministry of Internal Affairs, there are no statistics about forced marriages.[496] As the Population Department records only registered marriages, they do not have any information on other forms of marriage. The Citizenship and Migration Board does not have relevant statistics either.[497] There is also no debate in society or media coverage as regards these issues. The Estonian Women's Associations Round Table does not have any information on forced marriages.[498] One of the possible conclusions is that the Estonian population is still fairly homogeneous as regards traditions concerning marriage. Estonia has not yet become a destination for extensive new immigration. However, info provided by the above-mentioned institutions also appears to be based on a narrow, culture-specific definition of forced marriage; a broader definition might reveal cases of this practice in Estonia or the broader Western/Eastern European society. There are currently no studies or statistics available: gender studies in Estonia have focused more on equal pay for men and women, homosexuality and on domestic violence.

356. As regards forced marriage among asylum seekers, refugees and their family members, Estonia has no recorded information. As there are very few asylum applicants, the problem of forced marriages has not yet emerged in society, or at least is not known by officials dealing with asylum applications.[499]

496. M. Kiviorg communication/interview with Mr Ringo Ringvee, Ministry of Internal Affairs (7 Jan. 2008 at 08:54).
497. Now renamed as Police and Border Guard Board. Communication Registered in the Citizenship and Migration Board: M. Kiviorg, Information Request No 15.6-06/11710-1, Anneli Viks, Reply No 15.6-06/11710-1.
498. Estonian Women's Associations Round Table, www.enu.ee, 1 May 2010; M. Kiviorg, communication/ interview with Mrs. Ilvi Jõe (6 Mar. 2008 at 14:31:01).
499. M. Kiviorg & L. Roots, 'Immigration, Asylum and Religion Estonia', in *Immigration, Asylum and Religion in Europe*, ed. A. Motilla (Leuven: Peeters, 2012).

Part XI. Religion and Culture

Chapter 1. Religion and Art

357. Freedom of artistic expression is constitutionally protected in Estonia. There have been some incidences involving artwork (broadly defined) that has caused major public debate or uproar.[500] To some degree debates over building a Mosque in Tallinn can be seen in this context as the design of the building was seen by some as architecturally unsuitable in Tallinn city centre.[501]

358. Because of historical reasons and its geographical location, Estonia has been influenced throughout the centuries by a large variety of cultures. 'Bearers of different cultures arrived here at different times and for different reasons – either as colonizers or peaceful merchants and workers.'[502]

359. Treier summarizes some of the more distinct influences. She points out that the material culture in the middle ages was dominated by Baltic-German influence. This is evident in the old town of Tallinn, late medieval churches with their laconic style and the manor houses scattered all over Estonia together with the art heritage that they contain. Two prominent fifteenth-century painters, known throughout Europe, are associated with Tallinn: Bernt Notke (1430/40–1509) whose *Dance of Death* (1463 or 1466) is located in the St Nicholas Church in Tallinn, and Michel Sittow (1469–1525) whose clients included several crowned heads, such as Isabel I (Castilia), Christian II (Denmark), Fernando II (Spain) and Carlos I (later the German-Roman Kaiser Carl I).[503]

360. Old Believers[504] who settled in Eastern Estonia by Lake Peipsi in the seventeenth century have created an independent school of icon painting and are still

500. A. Põld, 'ERM-i skandaalne eksponaat külvab pettumust: kuhu jääb austus naiste ja usklike vastu? Mis siis, kui sinimustvalge mänguasi pannakse virtuaalselt põlema?', *Delfi*, 2 Oct. 2016, https://www.delfi.ee/artikkel/75784189/erm-i-skandaalne-eksponaat-kulvab-pettumust-kuhu-jaab-austus-naiste-ja-usklike-vastu-mis-siis-kui-sinimustvalge-manguasi-pannakse-virtuaalselt-polema, 1 Apr. 2021; P. Rajalo, Holokausti näitusele päitsete pähe panemine kurvastas Eesti kultuuriinimesi, *ERR*, 15 Feb. 2015.
501. *See also* the debates about building the Mosque, Part V, Ch. 2: Political Influence in Religion.
502. H. Treier, 'At the Crossroads of Cultures', in *Estonica: Encycopeadia about Estonia*, www.estonica.org/ en/Culture/Art/At_the_crossroads_of_cultures, 1 Jul. 2010.
503. *Ibid.*
504. For more information about the Old Believers *see* General Introduction, §2 Social Facts about Religion above.

developing it today. The south-eastern part of Estonia is inhabited by the Setu people who combine elements of both Russian and Estonian culture.[505] Scandinavian cultures have also influenced culture and art in Estonia. The heritage of coastal Swedes has survived in Western Estonia and on the islands (a much-valued sight is the seventeenth century wooden church on Ruhnu Island). Finnish culture has left a lasting imprint on Estonian urban architecture.[506]

361. During and after the national awakening period[507] in the late nineteenth and early twentieth century, some artists of Estonian origin developed into professionals not in Estonia, but by studying at various art schools in St. Petersburg, Pensa, Düsseldorf, Munich, Paris and other big cities:

> It is natural that Estonian professional art being a relatively young phenomenon has gone through a 'German period' (expressionism during World War I), a 'French period' (post-impressionism of the 1930s, represented mainly by the Tartu Pallas school which was both a teaching establishment and an artistic style), and the forced 'Russian period' (socialist realism of the 1940s and 1950s). As a reaction to the latter, the younger generation greatly encouraged the triumphal breakthrough of an 'American period' (pop art) in the late 1960s. 21st century Estonian figurative art, on the other hand, exhibits clear English influences.[508]

362. Religion has been a source of inspiration for many artists and writers. Today, however, only a few have linked their works directly to Christian beliefs in Estonia. This fact has been pointed out by the Archbishop of the EELC (A. Põder) himself. He observes that not many writers, poets or artists today inspire to search for eternity or God. Most of the literature is secular. He further observes that this tendency was already noticeable at the beginning of the twentieth century and was further fuelled by atheistic imperative during the Soviet occupation.[509]

363. However, some artists like Jüri Arrak, Mati Karmen, Uno Roosvalt and Eva Jänes can be mentioned as having been inspired by Christian beliefs. Likewise, in the field of performing art Jaan Tooming and Lembit Peterson can be put forward. Religious influence is probably most 'visible' in music. Internationally recognized composers like Arvo Pärt and Erki-Sven Tüür are known for their religiously inspired music.

---

505. H. Treier, 'At the Crossroads of Cultures', in *Estonica: Encycopeadia about Estonia,* www.estonica.org/ en/Culture/Art/At_the_crossroads_of_cultures, 1 Jul. 2010.
506. *Ibid.*
507. *See* General Introduction, §3 Historical Background above.
508. H. Treier, 'Identety and Art', in *Estonica: Encycopeadia about Estonia*, www.estonica.org/en/ Culture/Art/At_the_crossroads_of_cultures, 1 Jul. 2010.
509. A. Põder, 'Tulevikupeegeldusi kirikust', Paper given at the Scientific Conference: The Estonian Evangelical Lutheran Church on the Way to Tomorrow [Teaduskonverents Eesti Evangeelne Luterlik Kirik – teel homsesse] (Tartu, 2007).

364. While Christian beliefs do not inspire works of the majority of artists or writers, it is probably wrong to say that religion broadly speaking has a marginal role in the art world of Estonia. Throughout this monograph it has been hinted that questions about identity are poignant in Estonia. This search for and perhaps redefinition of one's identity and spirituality has inspired artists to look into history, folk art and beliefs, and one's place and role in the world. While Christian beliefs do not dominate this search they have their place and role in this. Treier, discussing the connection between art and identity, has quite interestingly captured the complexity of the matter stating that:

> The understanding of our identity in Estonia largely relies on our belonging to the Finno-Ugric peoples. It is a multi-faceted complex of ideas and understandings that primarily derives from language, the frame of mind of forest people, but also religious tradition, the geographical location in northern Europe, a damp and cool climate, long summer days and long winter nights, and many other things.[510]

365. Estonian national identity has been a prominent theme since the middle of the nineteenth century when it coincided with the national awakening, and it is still a source of inspiration after fifty years of Soviet occupation, relevant for many in the search for one's place and role in the world today.

510. H. Treier, 'Identety and Art', in *Estonica: Encycopeadia about Estonia,* www.estonica.org/en/Culture/Art/At_the_crossroads_of_cultures, 1 Jul. 2010.

Chapter 2. Religion and Media

366. As to religion and the media, freedom of expression is protected primarily by Articles 44 (freedom of information[511]), 45 (freedom of expression) and 46 (freedom of petition[512]) of the Estonian Constitution. The religious organizations' right to receive and impart information is regulated by law. The Media Services Act (*Meediateenuste seadus*) establishes general provisions for public and private broadcasting organizations.[513] The broadcasting organizations have a right to freely decide upon the content of their programmes within the limits of the law and their broadcasting permits (the permits are required only from private broadcasting organizations).

367. Currently there are multitude private broadcasting organizations. There are four organizations which have a Christian ethos – the non-profit organization Radio 7 (*MTÜ Raadio 7*)[514] and three interlinked organizations under the common name – Family Radio (*Pereraadio*), which provide programmes both in Estonian and in Russian.[515]

368. There are no religious television broadcasting organizations. There is a non-profit organization Estonian Christian Television (*Eesti Kristlik Televisioon*)[516] which produces programmes for different broadcasting organizations including public broadcasting. Four church denominations are represented on its Board: the EELC, the Union of Evangelical Christian and Baptist Churches of Estonia, the United Methodist Church in Estonia, and the Estonian Christian Pentecostal Church.

369. There is one public broadcasting organization – Estonian Public Broadcasting (*Eesti Rahvusringhääling, ERR*). Pursuant to the Estonian Public Broadcasting Act (*Eesti Rahvusringhäälingu seadus*),[517] passed by the Estonian Parliament on 18 January 2007, the two public service broadcasting organizations – Estonian Radio (*Eesti Raadio – ER*) and Estonian Television (*Eesti Televisioon – ETV*) – were merged as of 01 June 2007, whereby a new legal person in public law – the Estonian Public Broadcasting, the legal successor of *ER* and *ETV*, with the generally recognized abbreviation in Estonian being *ERR*, was founded. The Estonian Public Broadcasting Act regulates *ERR*'s actions as *lex specialis* in relation to the Media Services Act.

---

511. 'Everyone has the right to freely obtain information disseminated for public use.'
512. 'Everyone has the right to address state agencies, local governments, and their officials with memoranda and petitions. The procedure for responding shall be provided by law.'
513. RT I, 06.01.2011, 1; RT I, 12.12.2018, 3 (last amended). The Media Services Act replaced the Broadcasting Act (*Ringhäälinguseadus*) on 16 Jan. 2011.
514. Raadio 7, www.raadio7.ee/, 1 May 2010.
515. Tartu Pereraadio Ühing, http://www.pereraadio.ee/uus/, 1 Apr. 2021.
516. Estonian Christian Television, www.ektv.ee/eng.index.php, 1 Aug. 2014.
517. RT I 2007, 10, 46; RT I, 29.06.2014, 109 (last amended).

370. The Public Broadcasting Council is the highest management body of the *ERR* and consists of nine members.[518] On the proposal of the Cultural Affairs Committee of the Parliament, the Parliament appoints five parliament members to the Council on the basis of the principle of political balance and four members among recognized specialist in fields relating to the performance of public broadcasting functions. Currently there are no representatives from religious organizations in the Council.[519]

371. However, Estonian Public Broadcasting (and previously both *ETV* and *ER*) has long-established cooperation with the Estonian Council of Churches. The *EER* has an agreement with the Estonian Council of Churches regarding programmes on religious issues. On public holidays and Christian holidays the *ETV* broadcasts religious services. There are also several television programmes where religious issues are discussed (e.g., '*Ajalik ja Ajatu*'). The *ETV* also broadcasts 'Church Chronicles' ('*Kirikuelu Kroonika*'). There are everyday prayer mornings on Estonian Radio (*ER*) and service broadcasting on Sundays. The Estonian Council of Churches decides upon the air-time that is given to members of the Council and the content of programmes, while the financing of programmes comes mainly from religious organizations (including some international ones). The Estonian Council of Churches has also used its yearly allocations from the State budget for support. The domination of Christian Churches in the Estonian public media has been criticized.[520]

372. Currently, anyone may freely publish newspapers, periodicals or books. The Penal Code prohibits the printing of certain materials, such as war propaganda and the incitement of racial or religious hatred. Many religious organizations have their own newspapers. In 1991, a non-profit-making organization was established – the Estonian Press Council (*Avaliku Sõna Nõukogu*) – which since 1997 has been a joint organization of the Newspaper Association, the Association of Broadcasters, the Journalists' Union, the Union of Media Educators and the Consumers' Union. Later, also the Network of Estonian Non-profit Organizations, the Estonian Council of Churches and an NGO called Media Watch became members of the non-profit organization. According to the Estonian Press Council the first two of the three subsequent joiners have since discontinued their membership in the NGO.[521] Every member organization nominates one to three members to the Press Council. The aims of the Press Council are: to protect press freedom; to examine complaints about print media (and broadcasting) from the aspect of media ethics; to support the development of journalists' professional skills (including ethics); and adherence to the good tradition of journalism. This is to assure that all media (including religious media) adheres to professional standards of the Estonian Press Council. There have been no major complaints about the activities of religious media.

518. Estonian Public Broadcasting, www.err.ee/default-en.aspx?s=31, 1 May 2010.
519. RT III 2010, 25, 31.
520. E. Liiv, 'Usuvabadusest Eesti moodi ehk elame luterlik-kristlikus riigis' [Freedom of Religion in Estonian Style: We Live in a Christian-Lutheran State], *Kultuur ja Elu*, 17 Mar. 2002.
521. Estonian Press Council, www.asn.org.ee/english/index.html, 1 May 2010.

Chapter 3. Religion and Civil Society

373. The relationship between religion and civil society was to a certain extent addressed in Part V (Religion and Politics) above. Some further points can be added here. Ringvee has observed that religion is not perceived as a problem in Estonia as long as it remains in the private sphere.[522] This does not mean that religion should not be active in the public sphere at all. However, Estonian society seems to be very sensitive to forceful expressions of religion, especially when it is favoured by the State.

374. Thus, participation of religion in civil society is not considered as a problem per se. This is not just reflected in the democratic process, but also in acknowledgement of the contribution religious organizations make for the public good (crime prevention, social services, etc.). Favouritism of Christian churches (especially the EELC and other churches belonging to the Estonian Council of Churches) by the State has been criticized. However, Christian communities generally have been more active and capable of initiating and applying socially relevant projects. Considering the latter, it is only logical that cooperation with the State follows.

375. When discussing the 1993 and 2002 Churches and Congregations Acts in Part I above, the generally individualist mentality of Estonians was pointed out. However, this mentality seems to be changing. This change has been most visible in the last few years. There has been an increase in social and communal activity. It is not just the independence and economic well-being that interests people, but also charitable and other communally relevant projects (such as, e.g., protection of the environment). It is right to say that churches (and other religious communities) do not have a leading role in this communal activity. However, they are active participants and their presence reminds one that there are higher values which need to be protected. The religious communities have also been contributing to the integration and cooperation of segments of Estonian society.

376. The radical economic reforms since the beginning of the 1990s have been good for the economy. However, many have not been able to cope with these radical changes. The State has not been interested or wealthy enough to deal with social problems of many. One could speculate that this has been one of the triggers which has contributed to the increase in communal activity at least in the area of social care.

522. R. Ringvee, 'Sallivus ja religioon Eestis' [Tolerance and Religion in Estonia], *Virumaa Teataja*, 19 Sep. 2007.

Chapter 4. Religion and Public Debate

377. Two major areas of academic/public debate can be detected in Estonia regarding religion:

(1) the role of major churches in Estonia and;
(2) equal treatment of religions.

In this regard there seem to be at least two different or even opposing views on how Estonia should be modelling its relationship between State and religion. The first one recognizes the historical contribution of Christian churches in shaping Estonian culture, values and identity; however, it takes into account the diversity of beliefs (past and present), and the fact that Estonia is one of the most secularised countries in Europe. This view places the emphasis on individual and collective freedom of religion or belief and sees the privileged position of churches as debatable in Estonian society. However, cooperation between religious organizations (not just Christian churches) and the State on mutual fields of interests is recognized and appreciated. The second view is based on the historical importance of Christian churches in Estonia, as such the more active role and privileged position of churches is seen as necessary to shape Estonian statehood and perhaps its post- Soviet identity. The latter view is not so dominant in academic circles (or in public debate generally), but rather reflects policy choices and strong symbolic gestures by key political figures in support of major churches.

378. These two contradicting views were most visible in the quarrel over the liberty statue, which was erected in 2009 to commemorate the Estonian War of Liberation against Bolshevik Russia and *Baltiche Landeswehr* (1918–1920).[523] A prominent, major feature of the liberty statue is a cross, which triggered heated debate over its symbolic meaning and value in contemporary Estonian society. The religious dimension of the debate was fuelled by the fact that the head of the selection commission (established with the decision of the Estonian Government to select the project and design submitted on public competition) was the Archbishop of the EELC. It was argued that his nomination as a leader of the commission did not guarantee impartiality as regards different world views represented in Estonia.[524] At the time even the Estonian President mentioned in his interview with a major newspaper that unfortunately the Estonian public had not received a clear answer (from the commission) as to what the statue symbolized in order to assess the proposed idea for the design of the statue.[525]

---

523. *See* General Introduction, §3 Historical Background.
524. *See, e.g.*, 'Avalik pöördumine', www.vabadusesammas.co.ee/, 1 May 2010; M. Kala, 'Riik ja kirik – koos või lahus?', *Postimees*, 11 Sep. 2007.
525. President Ilvese intervjuu ajalehele Postimees 1 Sep. 2007, www.president.ee/et/meedia/intervjuud.php?gid=102298, 1 May 2010.

379. At the beginning of the statue design debates there were two competing ideas: (1) the liberty statue had to symbolize Estonian liberty/independence generally; or (2) it should specifically commemorate the Estonian War of Liberation. On 23 March 2005 the first idea gathered thirty votes and the second idea fifty votes in the Parliament.[526] In 2006 competition began for the design of the statue. The selection committee's winning design provoked heated debates from the very beginning. There were accusations that the State was forcing its ideas on the people, that the State did not take into account the opinion of the artistic community, and that its costs were (are) enormous. The story of the liberty statue actually goes back as far as the first independence period, because of the extensive public debates then the planned statue never materialized. The discussions lasted for the entire first independence period and were eventually stopped by the Soviet occupation in 1940. The debate did not seem to have a religious dimension and none of designs discussed had a cross as a main feature. Criticisms of some designs were in regard to their grandiosity. For instance, in the beginning of the 1930s, the architect Ostrat criticized the grand designs as indicating a lack of culture. Finally, a pompous design was imposed by the authoritarian regime in 1937. This last project was supposed to be finished by the 25th anniversary of the Estonian Republic in 1943.[527] Although the current statue is not comparable to the one approved in 1937, its appearance is rather controversial.

380. As to the religious dimension of the current debate, it has been explained now that the cross symbolizes the Liberty Cross (*Vabaduse Rist* – a high State honour meant to be given for exceptional bravery). It was established during the first independence period, but has never been awarded to anybody. Now situated at the top of the statue it is symbolically given to the Estonian people. However, the meaning of the cross still creates debates.

381. Since its erection the liberty statue has already gone through major refurbishments due to construction problems and for a while was in a rather miserable condition. It is justified to say that whatever it symbolizes, it does not symbolize the unity of Estonian society. It seems that the quarrels over its meaning and design created a negative aura around it (metaphorically speaking), which is now reflected in its care and physical appearance. Perhaps some sort of consensus should have been reached in society before the statue was erected.

382. Professor Lauristin has quite rightly pointed out that in debates over the liberty statue people have started to pay attention to questions which have not been seriously discussed before (Lauristin also suggests that digitalization of Estonian society has contributed to active public debate and e-democracy).[528] She points out that the debate is essentially about values: the importance of past and present, the relationships between aesthetics and ethics, nationalism and international openness,

---

526. Riigikogu, www.riigikogu.ee, 1 May 2010.
527. A. Lõhmus, 'Vabadusmonumendi ajalugu: verine kaklus kunstimaitse üle', Vabaduse monument, www.vabadusemonument.ee/index.php?id=10390, 1 May 2010.
528. M. Lauristin, 'Vabadussammas ja (e-)demokraatia', *Postimees*, 14 Mar. 2008.

the importance or non-importance of art and culture and democratic debate, and the role of Christianity in Estonian development.[529] She rightly suggests that the debate is not just about the statue, but about what sort of message it gives to the world and the Estonian people, it is a debate over Estonian identity and values. She further explains that understanding of one's identity and liberty is a matter of cultural maturity and self-understanding. She criticizes the point of view of the Ministry of Defence, that the debate is reflecting a conflict between different world views. Different opinions about the meaning of the statue, in her view, rather reflect the opposition of traditionalist and (post-) modern views, which are present in all post-communist societies.[530]

383. As to other debates, as already elaborated above, religious education is a sensitive and long debated topic in Estonia (the past and present debates over religious education in Estonia were discussed in Part IX above). However, as discussed above, the compromise over the curriculum of religious education seems to have taken the edge off the public debate and the media is now relatively quiet on this issue. The debates over political involvement of religion were discussed in Part V. Debate over financing of religious communities and also religious marriages were addressed under specific headlines above. It can be said that for a long time abortion, euthanasia and homosexuality created only mild debate in Estonia. However, the 2016 law on co-habitation (*Kooseluseadus*) has generated extensive and rather furious public debate.[531] The law made registration of civil partnership possible for (all) couples who for some reason don't want to or can't marry but still need legal guarantees for their partnership. Most young Estonians prefer not to get married. It has been felt that this social fact needs regulating to give co-habiting partners and their children some legal certainty and guarantees. This law is gender neutral. The latter fact has generated extensive debate as it also facilitates same-sex couples to legalize their co-habitation. Religious organizations have expressed their opposition to the law.[532] Opponents of the law also fear that the co-habitation law paves the way to same-sex marriage. As a result there was an attempt to have a referendum in spring 2021 to amend the Estonian Constitution to clearly state that marriage can only be concluded between a man and a woman (currently the relevant paragraph in the Constitution is gender neutral). This attempt was led by the far-right party – *EKRE*.[533] The opposition to this law and the attempt to have a referendum have also been attributed to intolerant attitudes in Estonian society generally. Some statistics paint a rather worrying picture of Estonia not being a very tolerant country regarding minorities. For example, the 2011 OSCD survey indicated that Estonia is one of the least tolerant regarding minorities. Some have also attributed opposition to the

529. *Ibid.*
530. *Ibid.*
531. RT I, 16.10.2014, 1.
532. Rooma-Katoliku Kirik, 'Kristlik eetika ja moraal. Abielust, kooselust ja perekonnast' (3 Dec. 2020), https://www.katoliku.ee/index.php/et/katoliku-kirik/kristlik-eetika-ja-moraal/472-abielust-kooselust-ja-perekonnast, 1 Apr. 2021; M. Pärli, 'Viilma:Pärast rahvahääletust võib kooseluseaduse rakendusaktid vastu võtta', *ERR*, 7 Oct. 2020.
533. K. Meiel, 'Kaja Kallas: abielureferendum on EKRE provokatsioon, milles ei peaks osalema', *ERR*, 1 Sep. 2020.

law to being in the sphere of post-Soviet and Russian influence with its intolerance towards homosexuality and discriminative practices.[534] However, in spring 2021 the law to carry out the referendum failed in the Parliament by 26 to 49 votes and was taken off the table.[535]

384. Openness of Estonian society to the possible influx of Muslim communities to Estonia has been a topic in public debates. The concerns have been expressed as to the capacity of Estonia to welcome new arrivals, because of its small population and already existing large Russian-speaking minority. Estonia has been applying conservative politics to immigration issues (immigration issues were discussed in General Introduction, §1 General Background of the Country).[536] Lately, all the debates have been pushed away by concerns and debates over COVID-19 and over proportionality of restrictions imposed, including on religious communities.[537]

534. S. Kiin, 'Opposition to Civil Partnership Bill Is a Vestige of Authoritarian, Eastern Mindsets' *ERR* 27 Jun. 2014, available at http://news.err.ee/v/opinion/71fc7bcc-41eb-4d2e-8b19-4ca84e36c0ad, 1 Aug. 2014.
535. U. Jaagant, 'Abielureferendumi plaan kukkus riigikogus läbi' *Äripäev*, 13 Jan. 2021.
536. P. Pullerits, 'Eesti sõnum võõrastele: te ei ole siia teretulnud!', *Postimees*, 16 Oct. 2009.
537. P. Rohtments, M. Kiviorg, 'Usuvabadus – inimõigus või võluvõtmeke', ERR, 23 Dec. 2020, https://www.err.ee/1216816/priit-rohtmets-ja-merilin-kiviorg-usuvabadus-inimoigus-voi-voluvotmeke, 1 Apr. 2021; M. Kiviorg & P. Margna, 'COVID-19 in Estonia: A Year in Review', *Verfassungsblog: On Matters Consitutional*, 1 Mar. 2021, https://verfassungsblog.de/covid-19-in-estonia-a-year-in-review/, 1 Apr. 2021.

Part XII. Conclusion

385. As emphasized above, when the 1992 Constitution was created there were hardly any debates over the text or meaning of Article 40 of the Estonian Constitution. At the time other issues were considered more important. This kind of neglect in constitutional thinking has affected State and religious communities up to this date. However, the relationship between State and religion has been gradually evolving through the heated debates over co-habitation law, religious education, preferential treatment of Christian communities, financial support and property matters. Most importantly, however, this relationship has evolved through public debates over Estonian values and identity. As to the legal framework, there is also limited but emerging case law to provide some clarification on matters of religion or belief. The future of the State and religion relationship, however, remains to be seen.

Selected Bibliography

Books in English

Kiviorg, M. (edited). *Securitisaton of Religious Freedom: Religion and Limits of State Control.* Editorial Comares, 2020.

Misiunas, R.J. & R. Taagepera. *The Baltic States: Years of Dependence, 1940–1990.* Expanded and updated edn. Berkeley: University of California Press, 1993.

Narits, R. & K. Merusk. 'The Constitution of the Republic of Estonia'. In *International Encyclopaedia of Laws: Constitutional Law*, edited by A. Alen. London: Kluwer Law International, 1998.

Narits, R. 'About the Principles of the Constitution of the Republic of Estonia from the Perspective of Independent Statehood in Estonia'. *Juridica International* XVI (2009): 56–64.

Raun, T. *Estonia and Estonians.* 2nd edn. Stanford: Hoover Institution Press, 2001.

Schihalejev, O. *Estonian Young People, Religion and Religious Diversity: Personal Views and the Role of the School.* Tartu: University of Tartu Press, 2009.

Smith, D. J. *Estonian Independence and European Integration.* London: Routledge, 2001.

Vallikivi, H. 'Status of International Law in the Estonian Legal System under the 1992 Constitution'. *Iuridica International* VI (2001): 222–232.

Articles in English

Ernits, M. 'Holders and Addressees of Basic Rights in the Constitution of the Republic of Estonia'. *Juridica International* IV (1999): 11–34.

Huang, M. 'Estonia'. In *Eastern Europe: an Introduction to the People, Lands and Culture,* edited by R. Frucht. California: ABC CLIO, 2005.

Ketola, M. 'Some Aspects of the Nationality Question in the Lutheran Church of Estonia, 1918-39'. *Religion, State and Society* 27, no. 2. Oxford: Keston Institute, 1999, 239–243.

Kilp, A. 'Secularization of Society after Communism: Ten Catholic-Protestant Societies'. In *Religion and Politics in Multicultural Europe,* edited by A. Saumets & A. Kilp. Tartu: Tartu University Press, 2009.

Kiviorg, M. 'The Legal Status of Old and New Religious Minorities in Estonia'. In *The legal status of old and new religious minorities in the European Union*, edited by M. Ventura, Granada: Comares, 2021.

Selected Bibliography

Kiviorg, M. 'Religious Freedom and Security in Eastern Europe and Central Asia. In *Staat – Religion – Recht. Essays in honour of Gerhard Robbers*, edited by K. von der Decken and A. Günzel, Nomos Verlag, 2020.

Kiviorg, M. 'Church and State in Estonia'. In *Church and State in the European Union*, edited by G. Robbers. Nomos Verlagsgesellschaft, 2019.

Kiviorg, M. Religious Assistance in Public Institutions: Estonia. In *Religious Assistance in Public Institutions*, edited by R. Balodis, M. Rodríguez Blanco. Comares, 2018.

Kiviorg, M. Estonia. In Human Rights, Religious Freedom and Faces of Faith, edited by G. Gunner, P. Slotte, E. Kitanović. Geneva: Globethics, 2019.

Kiviorg, M. 'Dangers of the Changing Narrative of Human Rights - Why Democracy and Security need Religious Freedom'. In *Research Handbook on Law and Religion*, edited by Rex Ahdar. Edward Elgar Publishing, 2018.

Kiviorg, M. 'Accommodation of Religious Rules in Estonian Law and Practice'. In *Religious Rules, State Law, and Normative Pluralism - A Comparative Overview*, In R. Bottoni, R. Cristofori, S. Ferrari. Springer International Publishing. (Ius Comparatum - Global Studies in Comparative Law), 2016.

Kiviorg, M. (2016). 'Law and Religion at the Workplace: Case of Estonia'. In *Law and Religion in the Workplace*, edited by M. RodRíguez Blanco. Editorial Comares, 2016.

Kiviorg, M. 'The Emergence of Religious Parallel Jurisdictions in Estonia'. In Religious Adjudication and the State, edited by R. Potz and W. Wieshaider. Granada: Editorial Comares, 2015.

Kiviorg, M. 'Religion and the Secular State in Estonia'. In *Religion and the Secular State,* edited by Donlu D. Thayer. Universitad Complutense Madrid: Universidad Complutense Madrid, 2015.

Kiviorg, M. 'The Mutual Roles of Religion and State in Estonia'. In *The Mutual Roles of Religion and State in Europe*, edited by B. Schanda. Trier: University of Trier, 2014.

Kiviorg, M. 'Religion and Discrimination Law in Estonia'. In *Religion and Discrimination Law in the European Union,* edited by M. Hill QC. Trier: University of Trier, 2012.

Kiviorg, M. 'Religious Education in Estonia'. In *The Routledge International Handbook of Religious Education*, edited by D.H. Davis & E. Miroshnikova. New York: Routledge, 2013.

Kiviorg, M. 'Religion and Criminal Law in Estonia'. In *Religion and Criminal Law*, edited by M. Kotiranta and Norman Doe. Leuven: Peeters, 2013.

Kiviorg, M. 'Distinctive Religious Character'. In *Finding the Right Balance: Comparative Studies on Freedom, Autonomy and Accountability in Education*, edited by J. de Groof and C. L. Glenn. The Netherlands: Wolf Legal Publishers, 2012.

Kiviorg, M. 'The Application of the Freedom of Religion Principles of the European Convention on Human Rights in Estonia'. In *Religious Freedom in the European Union*, edited by A. Emilianides. Leuven: Peeters, 2011.

Kiviorg, M. 'Financing of Religious Communities in Estonia'. In *Financing of Religious Communities*, edited by B. Basdevant-Gaudemet, S. Berlingo. Leuven: Peeters, 2009.

Kiviorg, M. 'Law, Religion and Politics'. *Rechtstheorie. Zeitschrift für Logik, Methodenlehre, Kybernetik und Soziologie des Rechts.* Berlin: Duncker-Humblot, 2001.

Kiviorg, M. 'Religious Entities as Legal Persons – Estonia'. In *Churches and Other Religious Organisations as Legal Persons,* edited by L. Friedner. Leuven: Peeters, 2007.

Kiviorg, M. 'State and Church in Estonia'. In *State and Church in the European Union.* 2nd edn, edited by G. Robbers. Baden-Baden: Nomos, 2005.

Kozyrev, F. & Schihalejev, O. 'Religious Education in Estonia and Russia: Resemblances and Differences'. In *Encountering Religious Pluralism in School and Society: a Qualitative Study of Teenage Perspectives in Europe,* edited by T. Knauth, et al. Münster: Waxmann, 2008.

Muda, M. 'Regulation of Gender Equality as a Fundamental Right in Estonia'. *Juridica International* VII (2002): 106–116.

Ringvee, R. Estonia: Regulating Religion in Prisons Since the 1990s. In Religion and Prison: An Overview of Contemporary Europe, edited by J. Martínez-Ariño, A.-L. Zwilling. Cham: Springer (Boundaries of Religious Freedom: Regulating Religion in Diverse Societies; 7), 2020.

Ringvee, R. 'Estonia. The Debate on the Role of Religion in a Deeply Secular State'. In *Religion and Secularism in the European Union. State of Affairs and Current Debates,* edited by J. Nelis, C. Sägesser, J.-P. Schreiber. Peter Lang (Dynamiques citoyennes en Europe / Citizenship Dynamics in Europe; 8), 2019.

Ringvee, R. 'Religion: Not Declining but Changing. What do the Population Censuses and Surveys Say about Religion in Estonia?' In *Religion* 44 (3), 2014.

Ringvee, R. 'Estonia'. In *Yearbook of Muslims in Europe* Vol. 5, edited by J.S. Nielsen et al. Leiden: Koninklijke Brill NV, 2013.

Ringvee, R. 'Islam in Estonia'. In *Islam v. Európe.* Bratislava: Centrom pre európsku politiku, 2005.

Ringvee, R. 'Religious Freedom and Legislation in Post-Soviet Estonia'. *BYU L. Rev.* (2001): 631–642.

Ringvee, R. 'Satanism in Estonia'. In *Contemporary Religious Satanism: A Critical Anthology,* edited by J. Aagaard Petersen. Surrey: Ashgate, 2008.

Ringvee, R. 'State, Religion and the Legal Framework in Estonia'. *Religion, State and Society* 32, no. 2 (2008): 181–195.

Rohtmets, P. 'Church and State relations in Estonia during the period of transition from the Russian to the Estonian legal system, 1918-1925'. In *Aatteiden ja herätysten virrassa. Jouko Talosen juhlakirja*, edited by T. Kapanen, N. Lamminparras. Helsingi: Suomen Kirkkohistoriallinen Seura (Suomen kirkkohistoriallisen seuran toimituksia), 2019.

Rohtmets, P., Pekko, I.,Altnurme, R. 'The Lutheran church in Estonian society: the impact of secularization and religious change'. In *Old religion, new spirituality: implications of secularization and individualization in Estonia*, edited by R. Altnurme. Leiden: Brill (International Studies in Sociology and Social Anthropology) 2021.

Roosma, P. 'Protection of Fundamental Rights and Freedoms in Estonian Constitutional Jurisprudence'. *Juridica International* IV (1999): 35–44.

Sillaste, K. 'Conquest and Survival: An Outline of Estonian History'. *World Affairs* 157, no. 3 (1995).

Vakker, T. & Rohtmets, P. 'Estonia: Relations between Christian and Non- Christian Religious Organizations and the State of Religious Freedom'. *Religion, State & Society* 36, no. 1 (2008): 45–53.

Valk, P. 'Development of the Status of Religious Education in Estonian School. European and Local Perspectives'. Conference on Law, Religion and Democratic Society. Estonia: University of Tartu, 1999.

Books in Estonian

Altnurme, L. (ed.). *Mitut usku Eesti II. Valik usundiloolisi uurimusi: kristluse eri.* Tartu: TÜ Kirjastus, 2007.

Eesti Vabariigi Põhiseadus: Kommenteeritud väljaanne [Commentaries of the Estonian Constitution], 3 täiendatud trükk. Tallinn: Juura, 2012.

Henriku Liivimaa kroonika (Heinrici Chronicon Livoniae), edited by E. Tarvel. Tallinn: Eesti Raamat, 1982.

Kiviorg, M. *Religiooni puudutavate õigusaktide analüüs* (Analysis of the Laws Regulating Religion). Tallinn: Siseministeerium, 2012.

Liiman, R. *Usklikkus muutuvas Eesti Ühiskonnas.* Tartu: Tartu Ülikooli Kirjastus, 2001.

Maruste, R. *Konstitutsionalism ning põhiõiguste ja –vabaduste kaitse.* Tallinn: Juura 2004.

Rohtmets, P. *Eesti usuelu 100. aastat. Rahvakirikust uue vaimsuseni.* Tartu: Post Factum, 2019.

Salo, V. *Riik ja kirik.* Tartu: Maarjamaa, 2000.

Valk, P. *Ühest heledast laigust Eesti kooli ajaloos.* Tallinn: Logos, 1997.

Articles in Estonian

Alexy, R. 'Põhiõigused Eesti põhiseaduses'. *Iuridica,* Eriväljaanne (2001): 5–98.

Arrak, J. 'Kunstist ja vaimsusest'. *Kristlik kasvatus* 3 (2002): 6–7.

Karro, K. 'Rahvuslikud narratiivid ja religioon'. In *Mitut usku Eesti II. Valik usundiloolisi uurimusi: kristluse eri,* edited by L. Altnurme. Tartu: TÜ Kirjastus 2007.

Khair Al-Din, R. 'Eesti Euroopa Liiduga ühinemise protsess: Moslemi vähemuse õiguste kaitse islami õiguse seisukohast'. *Akadeemia* 12 (2000): 2616–2628.

Kilemit, L. & U. Nõmmik. 'Eesti elanike suhtumisest religiooni'. In *Mitut usku Eesti II. Valik usundiloolisi uurimusi: kristluse eri,* edited by L. Altnurme. Tartu: TÜ Kirjastus 2007.

Kiviorg, M. '§ 40 - 41' (freedom of religion and conscience). In *Eesti Vabariigi põhiseadus. Kommenteeritud väljaanne.* Kolmas, täiendatud väljaanne (Commentaries to Estonian Constitution), edited by Ü. Madise *et al.* Tallinn: Juura, 2012.

Kiviorg, M., Roosma, P. '§ 40 - 41' (freedom of religion and conscience). In *Eesti Vabariigi põhiseadus. Kommenteeritud väljaanne.* Neljas, täiendatud väljaanne (4th edition, Commentaries to Estonian Constitution), edited by Ü. Madise *et al.* Tallinn: Juura, 2017.

Kiviorg, M., Roosma, P. '§ 40 - 41' (freedom of religion and conscience). In *Eesti Vabariigi põhiseadus. Kommenteeritud väljaanne*. Viies, täiendatud väljaanne (Commentaries to Estonian Constitution), edited by Ü. Madise *et al*. Tallinn: Juura, 2020.

Linnas, R. 'Islam Eestis'. In *Mitut usku Eesti II. Valik usundiloolisi uurimusi: kristluse eri*, edited by L. Altnurme. Tartu: TÜ Kirjastus, 2007.

Lõo, J. 'Perekonnaseisu ja abielu seaduse eelnõud'. *igus* 2 (1922): 40–46.

Maddison, E. 'Usuühingute ja nende liitude õiguslik iseloom'. *Eesti Politseileht*, (221) 13, no. 11 märts (1926), 161–162.

Meder, W. 'Ülevaade Eesti kirikuõigusest'. Õigus 1 (1938): 10–26.

Nõmper, A. 'Jehoova tunnistajate lapse arstide kriminaalasjast'. *Juridica* IV (2000): 212–223.

Pukk, A. 'Kunst ja eetika'. *Kristlik kasvatus* 3 (2002): 8–9.

Rohtments, P, Kiviorg, M. 'Usuvabadus – inimõigus või võluvõtmeke', ERR, 23 Dec. 2020

Saard, R. 'Eestlane ja luterlus I'. *Akadeemia* 6 (2007): 1238–1268.

Saard, R. 'Eestlane ja luterlus II'. *Akadeemia* 7 (2007): 1424–1451.

Saard, R. 'The Church at Decisive Periods of National Identity in the 19th and 20th Centuries'. *Estonian Culture* IX (2007).

Index

The numbers here refer to paragraph numbers.

Index

www.ingramcontent.com/pod-product-compliance
Lightning Source LLC
Chambersburg PA
CBHW071340230926
51846CB00002B/401
9789403541228